Remember the Catskills

Remember the Catskills
Tales by a Recovering Hotelkeeper

Esterita "Cissie" Blumberg

PURPLE MOUNTAIN PRESS / FLEISCHMANNS, NEW YORK

Remember the Catskills: Tales by a Recovering Hotelkeeper
First Edition

Published by
PURPLE MOUNTAIN PRESS, LTD.
Main Street, P.O. Box E3
Fleischmanns, New York 12430-0378
914-254-4062, 914-254-4476 (fax)

Library of Congress Cataloging-in-Publication Data

Blumberg, Esterita, date
    Remember the Catskills : tales by a recovering hotelkeeper /
Esterita "Cissie" Blumberg.
        p.   cm.
    Includes index.
    ISBN 0-935796-80-0 (alk. paper)
    1. Blumberg, Esterita, date-   - -Biography.   2. Hotelkeepers- -New
York (State)- -Catskill Mountain Region- -Biogra;phy.   3. Jews- -New
York (State)- -Catskill Mountain Region- -History.   4. Hotels- -New
York (State)- -Catskill Mountain Region- -History.   5. Catskill
Mountains (N.Y.)- -Social life and customs.   I. Title.
TX910.5.B58A3   1996
647.94'092- -dc20   96-9570
[b]   CIP

Manufactured in the United States of America on acid-free paper

1 3 5 7 9 8 6 4 2
Frontispiece and title page photo courtesy of Al Kross.

Contents

Part 4: Turn, Turn, Turn

P_{reface}

I remember the Catskills . . .
I remember Green Acres . . .
I remember your kindness.
But most of all,
I remember your blintzes.
Almost as good as my mother's.
Reading the book, I could taste the sour cream.
I thank God for placing those mountains, so close to
    New York City.
Route 17 was my highway to show business.
It was my training ground; it gave me my career.
I send you a hug for keeping the Catskills alive
    with this fine book.

----Red Buttons

Dedication

Larry Blumberg

My best friend, my husband, my partner,
Whose love and laughter sweetened the living of our story,
Whose encouragement enabled me to record it,
and
To whose memory it is dedicated.

With Thanks

MANY PEOPLE urged me to write this book and helped along the way. I am more than grateful to them.

Stan Raiff and Dr. Howard Coron were kind (and brave!) enough to be severe critics of early manuscripts and then offered advice, care, attention and endless friendship to build my morale for the re-write. Thank-yous are inadequate for the kind of support they provided when I needed it most.

The *Catskill\Hudson Jewish Star*, published by Edith and Jerry Schapiro, has from its inception provided me with the space every month to reminisce and share memories, helping to keep our unique history authentically alive.

Lisa Rosenberg and Ellen Nutters, talented, gentle and effective editors, were of inestimable help. Clemence and Hiram Frank were always ready to read, to offer suggestions and bolster my confidence. Janice and Sherwin Harrison and Benjamin Posner generously added their recollections to my own and provided consistent support.

Special thanks to my children, Paul Blumberg, Amy and Michael Goldbas, and Kristin Ohlson, my brother, Bob Rosenberg (who served as a remarkable memory bank) and Harriet

Rosenberg, my sister-in more than- law. They were all a font of love and strength.

In addition, there were others who offered interest and friendship above and beyond the call of duty: Linda and Dan Berkowicz, Judge Lawrence Cooke, Steve DePass, Anita Garlick, Lila Ginsberg, Sharon Jones, Arlene and Fred Lesny, Deidre McCoy, and Marion and Cyrus West, have my heartfelt gratitude.

For their contributions of memories, memorabilia and mentoring, I want to acknowledge Dr. Harry Galinsky, Leni Binder, Florence Neukrug, Elaine Shapiro, John and Lynn Weiner, Michael Lessac, Dorothy Shapiro, Al Kross, Michael Gold, Ben Kaplan, Bernard Cohen, Doris and Bill Bernstein, Zane Morganstein, Marilyn Gottlieb, Jan Fleischner, Aline Palmer, and Doug Heinle.

Last, but certainly not least, thank you to Wray and Loni Rominger, the publishers of Purple Mountain Press, for their trust and enthusiasm.

Introducing "The Mountains"

*M*YRON COHEN, the celebrated comedian/raconteur, who began his career as a silk salesman in New York City's garment center, had a favorite anecdote. He was forever being accosted by critics with the question, "Why does every story you tell begin with 'Two Jews met' or else, 'Two Jews were in conversation.' Do you always have to start with 'Two Jews'?"

"Very well," replied Cohen, "Two Presbyterians met and one asked, 'Does Pesach come out on the 12th this year?'!"

While in a real sense this is a tale about every person and group that has struggled and achieved, it is particularly the saga of the Jewish immigrants and their progeny, who built hotels and allied industries in a two-county corner of New York State, and lived in its small villages.

My name is Cissie. I am a recovering hotelkeeper. The stories I tell are true. Even the names have not been changed to "protect the innocent"——they were all innocent. This is a personal tale——it is my story and my parents' story. But it might be recounted around a kitchen table by any of my peers, raised in one of the hundreds of small Catskill resorts. Through this anecdotal history, I want to share and preserve the essence of a special time and place, to celebrate a mountain miracle.

Sullivan and Ulster counties, our Catskills, were, for over half a century, the largest resort area in the United States. More than 500 hotels, countless bungalow colonies and *kochalayns* (rooms with shared cooking facilities), and later children's camps, earned the area international renown in the tourist world.

The miracle was that immigrants with no training, no experience, little money, and without even a real grasp of the language, built that resort mecca. And, as if poverty and broken English weren't challenges enough, their new country neighbors greeted the neophyte hotelkeepers with hostility and distrust.

The family owned and operated hotels enriched this territory and affected the lives of countless thousands. Each inn had a singular operation and personality, but all the resort families had to overcome hazards and obstacles unknown to the corporate Marriotts and Hiltons.

This then is a collection of memories about my people, and it is their history that I chronicle. Only those with their backgrounds and experiences could have created so wonderful a chapter in the history of the nation. They stamped the Catskills with all the charm, determination, innovation, and courage, that distinguish them as a people. They were unprepared for the task of creating an industry. But their values, hospitality, generosity, and capacity for labor made them more than equal to the task. They developed an oasis of relaxation and pleasure for which "the mountains" will ever be known.

The texture and truths of our story have been lost among the often repeated cliches, myths, and stereotypes. What started as comedic exaggeration became our history. I seek to rewrite that history, restoring the humanity and the reality.

I know that the myriads who came to the Catskills have indelible memories that this book will surely refresh. And for those who never knew us, I want to bring to life the rich tapestry of a remarkable time, place, and people.

It is my hope that from this compilation of 45 years of memories and *meises* (stories) the hotel owners, the guests and staffs, the vendors and tradespeople, the entertainers and the relatives, friends and neighbors will be preserved with all their color, humor, and individuality intact.

New York's Lower East Side:
Orchard Street (looking south from Hester Street), 1898.

Courtesy Museum of the City of New York. The Byron Collection.

Part 1:
On the way to Green Acres

What I recall most about the Catskills is a small hotel called Avon Lodge and a unique little village called Woodridge. My personal memories of working, fishing and kibitzing at my uncle's hotel are mixed with the impressions of a village where first-generation Jews and fourth-generation Gentiles lived in peace.

----Sid Caesar

This memoir of a family hotel and the resort industry in the Catskills is vivid testimony of strong faith, relentless toil, gracious hospitality and beautiful people.

----Lawrence H. Cooke
Chief Judge New York State Court of Appeals
Retired

Grandparents Theresa and Ignatz Rosenberg and their son Elmer, the author's father.

A Stopover on the Journey

*M*EMORIES OF GRANDPARENTS, whose flights from "the old country" assured my own growing up in Sullivan's green hills, are fragmented. I learned more about them from the stories that their daughters told than from their own narration. Along with my contemporaries, I regret the questions I did not ask. I do know that both sets of grandparents arrived in the United States in the early 1900s, unknown to each other. My father, Elmer Rosenberg, and his parents came from Budapest, Hungary and my mother, Rose Braverman, with her tribe, came from Grudne in Russia/Poland.

Eastern Europe was home to most of our ancestors. Russian-Jewish emigration to America began as early as 1845 when conscription extended to Poland, and increased somewhat after an economic crisis in 1861. During the reign of Alexander the Third, when the infamous anti-Jewish May Laws escalated persecution, that trickle of emigration became a flood. Between 1891 and 1914 one-and-a-half million Jews fled Russia for the United States. Add to those numbers the tens of thousands from Romania and Hungary and you have the largest wave of emigration in Jewish history.

Three-fourths of those immigrants landed in New York City and remained there. The Lower East Side became the most densely populated section of New York, teeming with immigrant life. Life in the overcrowded, run-down tenements overflowed onto the sidewalks. People congregated as peddlers hawked every possible household product from pushcarts and storefronts.

It was to those streets that my family came, leaving behind all that was familiar—the house, the little town, the friends, and most important, the remaining family. It was not a time when one could phone, and poor people didn't travel to Europe for a visit. The life left behind was left forever. But also abandoned in Europe were the restrictive laws and limitations imposed on Jews, the ghetto lives of narrow opportunities, the forced military service, and the physical danger.

According to my maternal grandfather's stories, all of the above applied to his decision to seek a new life. He had another more personal reason for emigration. At the time he left Europe, my *zeyde* (grandfather) had five daughters and to assure decent marriages to men of worth, a *naden* (dowry) was expected. Knowing that limited finances would condemn his children to the lowest rung of the social and economic ladder in Poland, he resolved to move the brood to America.

With money for only two tickets, the *zeyde* and his oldest daughter left with the hopes of earning enough for the family to follow shortly. Like millions before him, my grandfather's first experience with America was at Ellis Island.

History did not always record the extreme difficulties encountered on the road to becoming Americans. The "tired and poor and huddled masses yearning to breathe free" were often scorned, conned, and herded by those who got here first. Hostility and indifference from minor officials at Ellis Island quickly shattered the warm welcome offered by the open arms of the lady in the harbor. The port of entry was vast, crowded, and its systems were largely unintelligible to the newcomers. The bureaucracy of immigration became an unexpected hurdle for our ancestors. Dignity was a precious commodity and difficult to maintain in the face of the "welcoming committee" which was not even patient enough to try to preserve the unfamiliar names.

Knowing that names were to be altered, some of the arrivals tried to pick ones that would be acceptable before facing the official who would register them.

One such fellow, the story goes, arrived at his turn and found he had forgotten the translation that a friend had suggested for his name, Shmeryl Bogdonovitch.

"Name?" said the official. "*Shoyn fergessen*" (I forgot already), he answered in Yiddish. "Sean Fergusson it is," recorded the officer.

My maternal grandfather and his family managed to keep their names in the process of registration, but my father was one for whom a translation was applied. He arrived as Elamare and left Ellis Island as Elmer----the bureaucrat in charge decided that was close enough.

Four years after my grandfather arrived in America, he was able to send for *bubbe* (grandmother) and the four younger children. Major or even slight illnesses were grounds for refusal to admit, but health examinations at the port were waived for those arriving in first or second class accommodations on the ships. My grandmother was not so fortunate, she arrived in steerage. When her youngest daughter was found to have an eye infection, that timid woman somehow found the strength to bribe the examiner. Years later, her voice shook as she told of her terror in facing return to Europe.

A year after the family was reunited in America, yet another daughter was born. My *zeyde* would smile when he recounted the pleasure of naming the newest child in a synagogue where no one knew that this one was a sixth female!

My mother never spoke of Ellis Island, but she recalled vividly her arrival on the Lower East Side. Rivington Street was their first address and the family must have reached it on Halloween. The loud noises and strange costumes that greeted

Parents Elmer Rosenberg and Rose Braverman Rosenberg

them led my mother to believe a pogrom was in progress. She still carried the memory of being hidden in a root cellar as a small child in Poland when rampaging Cossacks swept through the town. My mother disliked Halloween to the end of her days.

Their new home was itself another kind of ghetto by the time the family arrived. The New York ghetto was not created by official decree, but by the new immigrants' poverty and their need to be together. Jews with beards and *peyes* (forelocks), frock coats, and a Saturday Sabbath could not easily blend into existing American culture. This ghetto provided familiarity and comfort in a strange land. Here, foreigners lived among *landsleit* (fellow countrymen). There was joy in their sameness. Here they could practice their religion, conduct their day-to-day lives while speaking a familiar language, and gradually become accustomed to their new homeland.

Still, adjustment was difficult, and life extended beyond the ghetto itself. My mother recalled a distant cousin who had died before I was born. That very pious lady was apparently intol-

Grandparents Sam and Anna Braverman with three daughters.

erant of some of the compromises that family members made in the new world. Particularly odius to her was the common practice of working on the Sabbath. With jobs scarce, a six-day week was often unavoidable if employment was to be secured. Cousin Malke accepted no explanations or excuses from her kin and was vituperative in her condemnation whenever the family met. *"Zul zey brenen"* (let them burn) she would explode; but she was quick to make an addendum, *"Achutz meine kinder"*. . .(except for my children)!

Tenement flats were dingy at best, and the bathrooms were "down the hall," but the living conditions left behind in their *shtetls* (small villages) were hardly palatial. Tenement living was, for most, more of the same kind of discomfort to which they were accustomed.

Not everything was the same. A friend tells of his mother's discovery----a wonderful kitchen closet. She scrubbed it carefully, lined it with paper, and placed the cooked food for dinner on the shelf to await the evening meal. When suppertime arrived, she opened the closet to find the dinner, and the shelf, completely gone. It was, of course, a dumbwaiter used to remove garbage----a unique device of the new world. The dumb-waiter became a conduit for conversation with upstairs and downstairs neighbors, a kind of urban back fence over which to visit.

To help with assimilation, each family had its teacher whom it considered wise to the ways of the new world. That relative or friend, who had arrived perhaps only six months earlier, was already a "Yankee."

Bubbe's Yankee and English *mavin* (expert) was her older sister. On an early shopping expedition, grandmother expressed in her recently acquired English/Yiddish that she wished to purchase "jelly." Her sister replied, "Oh, Chana, in America *zogt mir nisht* (you don't say) jelly, *mir zogt* jim!"

Bubbe was never really able to master her adopted tongue. Most difficult of all for her was current idiom. On one occasion, a son-in-law called and said, "What's cooking, Mom?" *Bubbe* stared into the phone and answered, "You smell something?"

What Rivington Street lacked in luxury, it made up for with conviviality. Food was not always plentiful, but still it was impossible to enter a home without being invited to share whatever there was. My grandmother created a meat loaf that seemed to stretch for as many as came. Her chicken soup filled the apartment with an unforgettable aroma, and the pot was bottomless. For people who had little more than their meager meals, sharing food was sharing all they had. It was a hallmark of their existence and a tenet of their culture. If a fellow human being turned to you for sustenance, you never refused.

When cousins or even acquaintances arrived from Europe, it was a given that they would be welcomed into the already crowded homes of family and friends. Sleeping arrangements were two or three to a bed, and standard equipment for any apartment was a "lunge" (lounge) in a foyer or kitchen to hold one more body.

My family didn't know it then, but life on the Lower East Side was the training ground for their future as hotel owners. My mother never quite accepted the fact, in later years, that our hostelry was a business and not her home. Welcoming paying guests became as natural to her as entertaining the *landsleit*.

It was the mama who created the meals and clothing and cleanliness that supported the family. Without any appliances, our grandmothers waged an endless fight against dirt and grime in dingy old tenement apartments, while raising their large broods. Laundry was boiled on the stove and the kitchen linoleum was worn from constant scrubbing.

My grandfather, like so many others, entered the world of commerce. With a horse and wagon he began a delivery service for seltzer. Five feet three inches tall, asthmatic, and frail, he managed to *shlep* (drag) the heavy cases of blue bottles up the many flights of stairs. *Zeyde's* livelihood revolved around the purchase of bottles and keeping the sway-backed horse alive to do the job. Inevitably, when he had finally paid for the bottles, the horse expired.

Our grandparents and parents scratched out their livings in an overpopulated and relatively small area. Falling victim to tuberculosis and all the diseases of poverty was an ordinary occurrence. Still, their new world opened new vistas.

The Lower East Side was a marketplace for ideas. There were newspapers of every political hue published in every language. There were street corner meetings, and developing trade unions to address working conditions. Artists, writers, and philosophers might be met over a cup of coffee in local cafeterias.

The Jewish immigrants transplanted the roots of their heritage, culture, and religion when they came to New York. It became possible to add to that rich background by attending the available free schools, either by day or night, and using public libraries. Settlement houses offered all kinds of instruction, and there were even Yiddish-language theaters.

But our ancestors' greatest hopes were for the *kinder* (children), who would derive the full benefits of the social and economic mobility available in the new world----their children would be Americans! Indeed, from those teeming streets came tradespeople, judges, physicians, labor leaders, actors, musicians, artists, writers, and captains of industry.

Long after the children left Essex Street and Orchard Street and Grand Street, nostalgia continued for the place of their youth---the gateway to a different life.

As one story tells it: A man was walking along Madison Avenue when he saw a face that he recognized from the old neighborhood. "Goldberg," he shouted, "Goldberg, is it really you?" There was no response, so he ran to catch up, tapped his old chum on the shoulder, and repeated the question. The man turned with obvious recognition and said: "Of course it's me. Sorry for not answering right away---but things were so bad for Jews in the job market when I graduated college that I had to change my name. For 15 years now, I've been C. O. Stanton. No one calls me Goldberg anymore. But it's not like I forgot the old days---Stanton is for the street where we lived." So, what about C.O.?" asked his friend. "Corner Orchard," came the reply!

The rosy glow of nostalgia doesn't change the reality of immigrant lives on the Lower East Side. It was, after all, a ghetto existence. Our forebears worked in sweatshops for pennies a day. They lived in overcrowded, airless, run-down tenements, and poverty has always bred crime.

New York's streets weren't "paved with gold." Life in America did not begin to resemble the immigrants' dreams. It wasn't long before new ones took shape---dreams of fresh air, green fields, and property to call their own.

Like the pioneers before them, our parents moved west--- but just a little bit west---to Orange, Ulster, and Sullivan Counties. With the help of Jewish organizations, with money borrowed or painstakingly saved, they once again headed toward what promised to be a better life. This time, they hoped to find it on farms in "the mountains."

Westward Ho! (Sort Of)

⌒HE NEW AMERICANS arrived in the Catskills and bought the land on which to build their dream. With little or no experience in agriculture, they found themselves owners of acreage that good Yankee farmers had abandoned in disgust. The soil was rocky and overworked, but the farms were theirs.

Most Jews had little history of permanence in whatever corner of the world they called home. They never knew when a new ruler or set of rules would result in banishment. Now they could enjoy real ownership——protected by this nation's laws. Sparkling lakes, green acreage, and majestic mountains could be theirs forever. Here, *only* economics threatened their occupancy.

All too soon, the reality of their inexperience, difficulty in growing crops in the poor soil, and a short growing season led to many farm failures. Those who found no alternatives returned to New York City.

There were others, however, who discovered that they had "commodities" that were indeed saleable. The scenery was magnificent, there were eggs from the chickens and milk from the cows. The fresh air promised a cure for the diseases stem-

25

ming from the pollution that plagued those left behind in the city---a ready-made clientele. The farmers could offer cool breezes to people whose backyard was a fire escape: *landsleit*, fellow workers, kith and kin.

The families moved to their barns for the summers and the farmhouse rooms were rented. They were accustomed to cooking for large families, so adding a few more plates was not difficult. Taking in boarders was a way of augmenting their meager incomes. They could stay on the land---the resort industry was born!

At the same time, the growth of the unions in New York City led to a living wage, and introduced the idea that working people were entitled to vacations. For the first time, the cutter and the buttonhole maker, the secretary and the taxi driver found that they had the time and the where-with-all for a moment in the sun, and they were sought-after guests. Our parents provided reachable, affordable accommodations. Public transportation via inexpensive railroads made the trip possible, and the food, the hospitality, and the ambience were familiar and comfortable. To the city dwellers, coming from cramped, hot tenement apartments and over-crowded neighborhoods, a week in the country was a week in heaven.

One such early patron of the Catskills, now an octogenarian, shared his memories: "I wonder if you have the slightest conception of what it felt like to live in New York City during August," said Bill Santoro. "Not only the heat, but the humidity made you feel as if you were well roasted on both sides. To me the first miracle was that upon arriving in the Catskills, a sweater was necessary during the evening; honest to goodness you needed a sweater and it was August. Up early and to swim before breakfast in vapor-shrouded water. Then to be waited on and to eat as if you had not eaten in days. The odor of the food and the sweet pine scented air made you drunk with a spirit of ecstacy. I have traveled far and wide, but there is nothing that gave me a greater thrill than those priceless days that were spent in the Catskills."

While the Catskills had "gentile resorts" in operation long before our ancestors arrived, they either were posh and expensive, or restricted, or both. Abby Dan, who grew up at Sha-Wan-Ga Lodge (High View), has the original brochure used by the Christian resort owner who sold the property to his grandfather. The Dans used the same brochure with one monumental change: "No Hebrews Accommodated" became "Kosher Cuisine Featured."

The immigrant hotelkeepers created the first vacation possibilities for Jewish working people. When a New York Jew said he was going to "the mountains," there was no question as to his destination—there were no other mountains.

Our ancestors had never heard of a "feasibility study." When the farmhouses could no longer hold the growing guest population, the neophyte hosts added rooms and services to create hotels. They forged ahead and made their operations "feasible" for decades and decades. They would develop a plethora of individually owned hostelries more numerous than any other known in the nation up to that time.

My maternal grandparents were among those early hotel people. They joined a cousin as partners in her already established farm/small hotel (the Hillside) in Lake Huntington, on the western border of Sullivan County. The family relationship did not preclude problems. At the close of their first summer season, they discovered that their cousin had overdrawn on the bank account, and checks were beginning to bounce. The cousin was nowhere to be found. Neighbors advised the family to seek advice from the "assemblyman just down the road." It was a story with a happy ending, because the "assemblyman" would become my mother's husband.

Several years before, my father had fallen in love with the moonlight on Lake Huntington while on a brief vacation in that area not too far from the Pennsylvania border. Doctors had warned him to leave New York City after he suffered a first heart attack. Concerned about the support of his parents, he decided on an "easier" life for them all in the Catskills. The year was 1920.

My father had already attained the First Vice Presidency of the International Ladies Garment Workers Union and had served a term in the New York State Assembly (elected on the Socialist ticket). A popular figure in the 6th Assembly District, he was known for his spectacular oratory, both in the union halls and on the street corner. He had used the slack season, common to his trade as a cutter, to learn English and to spend countless hours in libraries. Completely self-educated, he was distinguished by an Oxford accent, which he acquired inadvertently by choosing phonograph records from London to learn the language of his adopted country.

Lake Huntington had, at the time of my father's arrival, a Ku Klux Klan and a thriving German American Bund. It had as well a Property Owners' Association whose charter included a covenant restricting the sale of property to Jews.

Perhaps it was my father's impeccable speech, or his atypical blue eyes and black hair; or perhaps it was his acceptance without question of the first price proffered on the property, but Elmer Rosenberg bought John Harner's restricted farm/boardinghouse. Harner was the president of the Lake Huntington Property Owners' Association. With no experience in either farming or resort management, my father became the first Jewish hotelman in Lake Huntington and the proud owner of an 87-acre property in Sullivan County.

We were to hear many times the story of our father's arrival at the railroad station in nearby Cochecton. Waiting to be picked up at the local saloon, he found himself in the midst of a group of men. Guessing at once that he was looking at a vigilante committee, and they were waiting for him, he bought "the boys" one drink—then another. He turned on his charm and told a few stories. The "boys" responded with stories of their own.

In about half an hour he asked why they were gathered there. "We're waiting for the Jew," was the answer. "Gentlemen," said my Dad, "I'm here!"

The new-found friends were abashed. "We thought you were one of those bearded Jews," was the explanation. My father did not wait long to grow a beard.

That committee returned with him to Lake Huntington to remove the gasoline-soaked rags from around my father's new home, and became our "good neighbors" for years to come.

While the Rosenberg family was accepted, it didn't mean that the local population had experienced a change of heart. The Klan was very much in operation, and, when a neighboring property was sold to "Kitty" Katz from Brownsville, it was rumored that they intended to burn him out. They were starting with the wrong man. Katz had survived the violence of his urban neighborhood by fighting fire with fire. He called upon friends from New York to come to his aid.

The day after the planned burn out, every member of the KKK was identifiable—by a broken arm, a blackened eye or some other injury delivered by the fighting Brownsville boys. Katz's buildings stood untouched, and the Klan didn't try again.

The small boardinghouse, purchased by my father in mid-season, continued to cater to a summer crowd of firemen and policemen. The lodgers paid their week's room rent on arrival, ate family style when the dinner bell summoned, and spent a good deal of time at the local bars.

My father never really became a farmer. He continued the boarding house business as it had been run, using the cook and the staff (such as it was) who were already there. The name of the establishment remained the same, "Huntington Lakeside." It was soon apparent that every village in the immediate world that boasted a lake had a resort named "something Lakeside." The hotel was eventually renamed "Green Acres" and the family kept that name for all our days in the business.

Little by little the clientele changed from the inherited guest population to members of my father's former union, New York friends and family, and those who were attracted by the small bit of advertising done in city newspapers. New menus reflected my father's Hungarian background, and food was prepared under his mother's watchful eye. When my parents married, the hotel had a new hostess. My mother was the prototype of resort keeping women, who knew by family tradition and instinct how to make people feel at home.

My parents shared with the other fledgling owners a naivete about every aspect of the business. They and their fellow hotel people learned by trial and error and survived by intensive labor. When, many years later, my young groom asked about buying a kitchen scale to weigh incoming merchandise, my parents told him that it wasn't needed, after all, the butcher and the other purveyors had scales. My husband insisted, and the accurate scale paid for itself in its first month of use.

Not only did the mountains have a short growing season, it had a short resort season as well. It was more the rule than the exception that those early hoteliers needed to find other work when the fall arrived. Many returned, temporarily, to jobs in New York City, so that they could maintain their summer world.

The literary and theatrical worlds have always featured characters who cling to, protect, and love their land. Many a plot and scenario are built around the plantation, the ranch, or the farm on which generations leave their mark. For our pioneers the hotels were often the first property they had ever owned. That property, large or small, was cherished, toiled over, and was a source of pride as deep as that in any Tara, Cimmaron, or Walton's Mountain.

Against All Odds

THE ROAD from farmhouse to hotel was an uncharted one, filled with hazards for those who made the journey. The original properties provided only a minimal number of accommodations to house guests, so the first order of business had to include a building program if the resort was to be viable. Financing that initial expansion was not possible on the small profits from the early seasons.

It was the rare hostelry that began with money in the bank. Original down payments came from family or friends or partners taken into the property, so things could get going. Redlining by the banks (excluding whole areas from borrowing privileges) was part of the reality of the times. Anti-Semitism figured heavily in the practice. The new owners sought mortgages, which were sometimes available from the builders who created the actual expansion. The hotel people used bank loans when they could get them, and/or financing from the vendors, in the form of short-term notes. Paying off debt over a realistic period of time was always a serious problem.

It is my guess that interest payments on Catskill boarding-houses/hotels over the years would have funded a small European country!

Originally, any kind of credit was hard to come by. However, once in a while there was a minor miracle. Dave Levinson of Tamarack Lodge (Greenfield Park) tells about his father's search for credit in the spring. The local bank, where he kept his account, thought that after five years of being a farmer and a boardinghouse owner, Levinson shouldn't need a loan. Soon after that refusal, a bank error was made, and Mr. Levinson found $800 in his account, credited to him by mistake. He withdrew the money, used it, and waited to hear from the bank. In about a month they called. "Sorry," said Levinson, "I don't have the money now, but I'll be glad to give you a promissory note." When that note was paid at the season's end, he had established credit.

My maternal grandfather never had the courage to approach a lending institution. When he made the move to Lake Huntington, it was the savings of his daughters and loans from extended family that made the family's new enterprise possible. *Zeyde* did have a few debtors. Among those he had helped was a *landsman*.

My grandmother was much disturbed by the outstanding debt and urged the gentle *zeyde* to ask "Mr. Adelman" for the money at a gathering of friends, which they were to attend. The party was in full swing, and my grandparents, along with their brood, were mingling with the guests. *Bubbe* prodded her husband—"Ask now, we won't see him for another month."

Asking for return of a loan was against my shy grandfather's nature, but his wife was insistent. So stoutly my small grandfather pulled himself up to his full height, summoned up all his courage, and approached his debtor. "Mr. Adelman," said he, "Mr. Adelman . . . goodnight, Mr. Adelman." The whole family of course was then obliged to depart! "Goodnight Mr. Adelman," for all the years to come, became our code for losing your nerve.

While individual boardinghouse operators found their answers to financing in different ways, the newly begun industry, as a whole, faced another problem that was pivotal to its very survival. When mortgages were finally able to be negotiated, the mortgagors insisted upon fire protection. In seeking the insurance policy that should have been merely routine, the pioneering immigrants were once again faced with religious discrimination. The myth that Jews were fire-makers, and therefore uninsurable, threatened their dream of independence in the new world.

Fire was a hazard for all of the multi-story, wooden buildings that had been built in the mountains, long before the arrival of the immigrants. Fires never asked who owned the buildings before burning them to the ground. Dozens of the original gentile-owned hotels succumbed to that peril. Still, the bromide of "Jewish lightning" (arson) was accepted, and insurance for the fledgling hoteliers was virtually unobtainable.

In the few cases when companies willing to write the policies could be found, their rates became the roadblock. Rates charged by companies to insure farm properties were low, but when a farmer took in even one boarder, he was charged hotel rates, which could be as much as five to ten times greater.

The Jewish farmers/boardinghouse owners found an answer by creating their own cooperative insurance company, which was organized in 1913. It was a time of rampant and undisguised anti-Semitism, of cruel caricature and vicious stereotyping. It was the year that Leo Frank was falsely accused of murder in the South and murdered by vigilantes.

Yet in that year, our forebears—determined, self-educated, intrepid leaders—managed to bring into being an insurance company to service farmers, hotelkeepers, traders, and private citizens. While the cooperative was born of Jewish need, it served the whole community, regardless of religious affiliation.

The early innovators negotiated the endless red tape and bureaucracy of the State Insurance Department, traveled over the far-flung territory by horseback and buggy to solicit their neighbors, and learned to write insurance.

The story goes that the chief of the Cooperative Bureau of the Insurance Department greeted our first representatives with, "And what are fellows like you doing in this business?" To fully appreciate the monumental accomplishment of "fellows like those," we must remember their inexperience with "big business," their difficulty with legal terminology, and the barrier presented by a language that was not their own. They eventually accomplished the foundation of five cooperative companies to cover the growing needs of the population and were licensed to write policies on properties in Sullivan, Ulster, and Orange Counties.

The Associated Cooperative Fire Insurance Company served a pragmatic purpose, but it represented far more. It was a triumph of the human spirit and became a forum, a marketplace for ideas and ideals, a lesson in *menchlichkeit* (humanity), and a study in democracy.

The "Official Organ" in Yiddish and English.

The first office was up a rickety flight of stairs, over a drugstore in the hamlet of Woodridge. It was a single room, heated by a potbelly stove, furnished with a table and chairs, and manned by a paid staff of one, Rose Hecht. She was, at once, the office manager, janitor, and interpreter for non-English speaking directors. Her most vital responsibility involved translating the original policies (written in Yiddish) into English so that they could be sent to the insurance department. Mrs. Hecht served for 50 years.

It was in the Woodridge High School auditorium that the membership held its annual meetings. To my knowledge there was no other existing insurance company that issued its "call to meeting" in both English and Yiddish. For the board of directors, those meetings were "the moments of truth." While most commercial companies have annual meetings attended by a handful, the co-op drew hundreds of members every year. Each member was a voter and had the privilege and duty to elect representatives. Everyone had the right to express approval, or lack of it, on the running of the company. The rhetoric was memorable. It was a New England town meeting with a Yiddish accent! The gatherings lasted all day, until the elections of directors and the year's business decisions had been taken care of by the membership. True to their heritage, no meeting was conducted without serving a box lunch, lest someone *cholish* (faint away) from lack of food.

My father ran for and was elected to a directorship on the Cooperative Board when I was a child, and served the company for 20 years. From the time that I was old enough to do so, I attended every one of those annual meetings. Contests were hotly fought and issues were passionately debated. The meetings were full of fervor and color, surely color that the Prudentials and Metropolitans of the insurance world knew nothing about.

One director, a hotelkeeper, had been a Yiddish actor before coming to the country. Louis Rosenblatt rose at every meeting to announce: *"Ich vil redn English"* (I will speak

English)---not an English word was to follow! He was small in stature, bent and gray, although not actually as old as he looked. When he spoke, his voice rang out, he gestured emphatically with his hands, his eyes might even brim over with tears as he made a point. Each speech came alive with excitement. Even I, who did not understand every word, became caught up as I was offered a brief glimpse of Yiddish theater.

The entire community valued Mr. Rosenblatt's gift for speaking. Nowhere was he more eloquent than at a funeral. On one such sad occasion, the deceased was given a royal send-off, but after a long recital on the virtues of the departed, it became obvious that the eulogist was having trouble bringing his address to a close. At last the final words were found: "*Gay gesunte hait*" (Go in good health)!

Directors of the company were elected to serve their own home territories. The title "director" gives the impression of men behind desks, but these men not only made company policy, they wrote the actual insurance policies and settled the losses. They were paid the same pittance (50 cents per policy initially) for a large hotel as for a small home. So it was not the promise of reward that drew men of varied experience to do the endless trekking and to attend the meetings that lasted long into the night. The directors sought to innovate and expand. They succeeded beyond their own wildest dreams.

By its very presence on the insurance scene, the Woodridge Co-op, as it came to be called, forced stock company rates down. By example, it showed that a not-for-profit cooperative company could declare dividends reaching as high as 35 percent of paid premiums. Most important, the same Jews who had been rejected as dangerous risks by major insurance companies had taken control of their own lives, and proved the fallacy of that offensive stereotype, "Jewish lightning."

For us, as children, the cooperative spirit was a guiding force. My father, representing the Lake Huntington territory, often took us along to inspect a property, or to renew a policy. He was always welcomed as a friend by the home or farm

Thirty-fifth anniversary commemorative booklet.

owner, and it was obvious that the service he provided was appreciated. Directors were more than aware that for the policyholders, continued coverage was a must for survival. Without insurance, those who gave the loans would take back the property.

I remember a call from my father to my mother when someone to whom he had issued a policy was unable to meet a premium payment. My father proposed to pay the $260 out of his own pocket. He knew that his payment would probably not be a real solution to the neighbor's problems, but, as he put it, "I don't want to hammer the last nail in the coffin." The premium was paid, but the neighbor lost his property anyway, as predicted. Still, our dad's Don Quixote efforts provided a powerful lesson that no lecture could replace.

The fact and fiction of the early times merge after more than 80 years. Memory tends to embroider and men become larger than life. There is nostalgia for the "good old days" when idealists, tilting at windmills, outnumbered the Philistines, when strong men solved "insurmountable" problems, when dragons were slain. Regardless of where truth ends and fiction begins, we know that the founders transformed a vision of cooperation into reality, and that success was born of self-sacrifice. The co-op became the core around which lifelong friendships were forged. Working for the mutual good was a given, and the example of cooperation was emulated in the community. A farmer's cooperative was formed, and a cooperative bakery, and a cooperative dairy.

Pioneering assumes some glamour when viewed from a distance; living it was another story. Faded minute books reveal that the company's first loss occurred on August 29, 1913. It was a $200 loss—fortunately there were assets of $911.

Those early years were filled with problems, and for the directors, endless work and decisions without precedent. Mortgagors had to be convinced to accept cooperative insurance on their properties. Those who sold insurance for profit resented those who were insuring at cost. Members and directors were in a constant battle against misinformation and slander circulated by the vicious or unknowing.

Before a law was passed permitting cooperatives to set up reserves, the directors faced some agonizing hours. They offered to give personal notes on their own properties if needed, to secure necessary credit from the banks. The already poorly paid directors asked the membership to pay them even less; the company survived.

During the early 1930s, in the depths of a nationwide depression, members of the cooperative desperately needed credit. Local banks and loan companies placed every obstacle in the way of securing a loan. There was endless waiting, restrictive signatures required on everything that wasn't nailed down, and a terrible sense of subservience. It seemed as if the more a loan was needed, the harder it was to obtain. Often those who could not get a legitimate loan were at the mercy of the local usurers. The problem solvers went to work once again.

The hotel operators first considered organizing a bank, but with the passage of the Federal Credit Union Law in 1934, the way was clear for a solution. The Cooperative Federal Credit Union was chartered in 1936, sponsored by the insurance cooperative.

The new lending organization tailored its procedures to the members' needs. Loans were not repayable monthly, but rather during the summer season when the area had a source of income. Interest rates were low, the mechanics for borrowing were kept simple, and the overriding philosophy was: "Grant the loan if it is at all possible!"

For loans of $5,000, two signatures were required. The choreography was wonderful. Cohen signed for Segal and Segal signed for Cohen. They both signed for Schwartz, and so it went, a lesson in applied friendship and trust. Everyone knew there weren't 5,000 cash dollars among the whole assemblage, and yet the system worked. Loans were taken, repaid, and taken again.

Since borrowing was so important a part of life, it inspired a _meise_ (story), which made the rounds: A _melamed_ (teacher) in the old country devised a way to add to his meager income. He had a wife famed for her wonderful gefilte fish, and he planned to sell it in front of the local bank on Friday mornings. His fish stall became an instant hit and the word of the *melamed's* new found "wealth" spread through the community. Hearing of his colleague's success, a fellow teacher approached the *melamed* for a loan. Knowing that repayment would be almost impossible, the fish seller explained his refusal: "You see that bank across the street? We have an unbreakable agreement. I don't make loans, and they don't sell gefilte fish!"

Happily, the Credit Union created by the Cooperative Fire Insurance Company continues to serve the public to this day. They proudly adhere to their original precept: Not for Profit, Not for Charity, but for Service.

The picture would not be complete without other true stories. There were black pages in the history, when opportunists tried to use their positions for selfish purposes. There were directors who sought gain for settling a loss or writing a policy. Some practiced outright blackmail by demanding a cow, or cash, from those who were at their mercy. In every case the offenders were discovered and expelled. It was at the annual meetings that the fireworks took place, when the case was laid out before the membership. The action was swift and decisive. The proceedings were exciting to audit—no Chautauqua stage had better orators.

Because times change and nothing lasts forever, the Cooperative Fire Insurance Company eventually became an anachronism and could no longer survive in the marketplace. It evolved into the Associated Mutual, which provides service, but is not the much-loved original. It was the cooperative directors who created the new mutual company when they recognized that the limited parameters of our co-op could not meet the requirements of a vastly more complicated world. Those directors continued in the Mutual company. Their idealism, devotion to community causes, generosity as employers, and fairness as underwriters, still distinguish them. Without question, the cooperative solved the hotelkeepers' biggest problem, obtainable and affordable insurance—the gateway to funding the industry's growth. Its formation made it possible for Green Acres, where I grew up, to exist, and then to expand. It was just one of many hotels for which both cooperatives, the insurance company, and the credit union, made existence possible.

Woodridge, the town where they were born, would eventually become our family's home for the winter months.

Centerville station on the New York, Ontario & Western Railway. Centerville is now Woodridge.

When We Were Children

*W*HEN BROWN'S HOTEL was the Black Apple, the Raleigh was Ratner's, the Pines was Moneka Lodge; when Avon Lodge was the House of Joy and the Ashram was Gilbert's and the Windsor and the Brickman; when there was no Villa Roma; when old Route 17 was the only access to our side of the mountains and the trip from New York City took four to five hours—I was growing up at my parents' hotel in Lake Huntington.

There were over 500 hotels in Sullivan County and, in spite of the fact that a thriving egg farming industry had developed, it was the resort business that defined our lives. The hundreds and hundreds of rooming houses, bungalow colonies and *kochalayns*, along with the hotels, assured this area of an untold number of tourists every summer.

Both the Erie and the Ontario and Western railroads serviced the towns with a steady stream of vacationers from the New York boroughs. The fare was $4.95 roundtrip.

Air conditioning was unknown to the general public and the Catskills was the place for fresh cool air and room to breathe free. It was a time before indoor pools, night clubs and sports centers were even considered, a time before the comedians and ill-advised publicists had dubbed us the "Borscht Circuit."

My young son, Paul, once asked, "Did they have libraries when you were young, Mom?" I answered that we did, even though the stone tablets were difficult to carry! But indeed, while it was in the same community, the world in which we grew up was light years from the one in which we raised our children.

Our home was the original farmhouse in which my father began his hotel career. By the time we were of school age he had built a new main building on the property, added cottages and "niceties" in the form of tennis and handball courts, and a swimming crib at the lake.

The hotel was open for business from Memorial Day through Labor Day. Because every room was precious during that season, we moved out of our home every spring into smaller quarters so the house could be rented as individual guest rooms.

The winter house was 100 years old and had undergone many renovations. Still, the kitchen of the homestead was dominated by an old-fashioned, black cookstove, fueled by coal and wood. In addition to warming our food, it provided us with heat and hot water. Best of all, on frosty winter mornings, we could fly down the stairs from our frigid bedrooms, and dress in the cozy warmth of the open oven.

I don't have a clear memory of our menus, but do recall one treat that cannot be duplicated. Rye bread, which didn't come sliced, was cut and toasted on top of the stove. The uneven edges burned, and when garlic cloves were scraped over the rough surface, then topped with chicken fat, a gourmet dish was created to rival any *petrave* (succulent morsel) that I have tasted since. Having survived to adulthood, I will assume that the positive value of the garlic canceled out the heavy doses of cholesterol.

The house was heated by a coal stove in the living room. Theoretically the upstairs bedrooms were to receive the rising warm air that came through heat registers in the floors. Our house defied that law of science, and the bedrooms remained frigid. What saved us from hypothermia were the incomparable *perenes* (feather beds) brought from Europe by our grandparents and equal to the icy nights.

The registers served another purpose. While lying on the floor you could look through them to see and hear adults in conversation.

Pinochle was taken very seriously and was the entertainment of choice when neighbors arrived in the evening. My father insisted that there were but two good pinochle players in the county----and that he was both of them! We soon found out that players who made errors not only lost the game, but were reminded of their ineptness for months to come. I decided not to take up the game.

Best of all was the picturesque speech and patter that punctuated the evening when my father and his cronies played: "In jail you should deal . . . you should have one tooth and that should be for a toothache . . . I should come to you for bread and you shouldn't have any to give me . . . !"

We listened, as well, to the inevitable talk of business and plans for the next summer, finances and politics, insurance and the hotel association. It was a liberal education well worth the loss of sleep.

Our home furnishings were taken each fall from the lobby of the hotel. It was to be many years before we had what could be called personal things. The crockery, too, was the same as that used in the hostelry----clumsy and heavy, white with a green stripe, which marked it as "commercial."

Lake Huntington was, and is, a place of real beauty. Built on the shores of a tree-lined natural lake, the small hamlet was one of the early settlements of Sullivan County, probably because of its proximity to the Delaware River.

Our extensive property fronted on the lake, had lawns and forests and endless places to roam and "make believe." We caught perch and sunfish from our own dock, waded the marshy shores in search of frogs, swam, and had our own trees in which to read undisturbed.

I most vividly recall the autumn with its changing leaves reflected in the water, so that the lake looked as if it were afire. It was a pastoral scene to nourish the soul. It should have been an ideal place in which to grow. But, in that day, Lake Huntington was isolated and unsophisticated in the most restrictive sense. Jews were in a tiny minority, and members of the majority in the community were hostile to any thought, philosophy or, indeed, person, who was perceived to be of another culture or religion.

As kids, we couldn't understand why we weren't accepted. We wanted to fit in. Except by a few Jewish youngsters who lived in town all year, we were either ignored or harassed. My brother and I never reported to our parents the incidents of namecalling and assault that we endured. In the movies, the Jewish kid wades in and beats his tormentors into some kind of respect. My brother and I, smaller, weaker, and younger than our attackers, also waded in, but we were forever the losers of the battles.

We knew that our parents suffered slights and insults as well. There was a time when rooms were rented from a neighbor to accommodate our guests on an overflow summer weekend. The neighbor submitted a bill that included an extra charge for "fumigation" after occupancy by our Jewish clientele. All this we heard "through the register" when we were thought to be safely in our beds and asleep. We instinctively knew that repeating our stories would only add to the hurt.

We did have a few victories of our own. When Solly Katzoff, of our faith and considerably stronger than we were, emerged as a protector, things looked up. He was a good fighter and made his own rules. His well-placed kicks and bites succeeded in making our walks to school uneventful.

There were no big incidents, but the succession of small slights and the atmosphere of social separation from the towns-

*Miss Mary Martin (far right) and Miss Lillian Scher (left)
and their pupils in Lake Huntington, circa 1938.*

people left their mark. It was a series of "little murders"
committed against small children.

By all the laws of psychology, my brother and I should have
suffered terribly from sibling rivalry. My parents had a friend
who never failed to comment when she saw us as to "what a
shame that the boy is so handsome and the girl is so plain," or
"the girl is such an extrovert and the boy is so shy." Neither
of us accepted the comparisons of those elders, and we share
today a host of memories that are ours alone. Our isolation in
"the hinterlands," our parents' absorption in a demanding

business, and the hostile environment in which we lived, have given us the plus of a nourishing lifelong friendship.

We shared, too, a remarkable educational experience. My brother and I attended a two-room schoolhouse to which we walked a mile each morning. It boasted two teachers for the eight grades housed, but no indoor plumbing. We were blessed with a dedicated and talented teacher. A normal school graduate, with what may have been two years of training, she controlled and guided, and held her bailiwick together with an iron hand. Miss Mary Martin literally spoke softly and did indeed carry a big stick!

Juggling four classes, each of which came to the front of the room in turn for recitation, she managed to cover the syllabus. She encouraged independent study, introduced us to music and nature, and acted as our physical education coach at recess time.

We shared the delights of discovery and play in that tiny school and rural setting. Though I was a country girl, it was Miss Martin who first introduced me to tree planting on Arbor Day. We were twenty children, of assorted ages and sizes, but somehow the act of planting brought us

Cissie and Bob
Rosenberg

together in a rare moment of sharing. Our teacher dug the hole
and we carefully placed our tiny tree to stand beside the larger
ones planted in earlier years. We learned a ball game, played
over the woodshed roof, called "Hilly-hilly Over," which
found us shrieking in delight when our opponents lost a point.
We played marbles in the schoolhouse yard, returning from
recess with muddy knees and scuffed shoes. Those were the
times when we felt we were accepted by our schoolmates and
differences were forgotten in the excitement of the game. It was
always fun to stop on the way home at a local grocery, where
candy really sold for a penny, and to ride sleds down the hotel
hill, which seemed as large as any Alp to a six-year-old girl. We,
and Sunny and Vivian Vogel, picked hickory nuts in back of
their Viola Hotel. It took whole evenings to take the nuts from
their spiny pods, warm them in the oven, and painstakingly
extract every choice morsel. My brother and I "raced" frogs,
swam in the lake, rode bikes, and spent long hours walking in
the woods on the hotel property. Unencumbered with the
advantages we later provided for our own children, we invented
amusements, and had all the time in the world to do so. Best of
all, our converted farmhouse/hotel always had room for assorted dogs and cats.

For some reason, Jewish people of my grandparents' time
did not keep pets. It was probably because their limited incomes
precluded leftovers with which to feed them. Certainly the
minuscule spaces in which immigrants lived were already more
than crowded with human beings.

When our *bubbe* and *zeyde* visited us in Lake Huntington,
they couldn't get over the presence of animals in the house. My
grandfather particularly developed an antipathy for one
friendly cat who kept cuddling up and providing him with
unwanted attention. "Fluffy" didn't get the message. She
jumped into his lap at every opportunity and rubbed against
his legs wherever he walked.

Zeyde was in the kitchen one day when the inevitable happened; the cat got under his feet and her tail was trod upon by his slippered foot. A series of shrill meows broke the silence. And then my flustered grandfather lectured the wounded animal: *"Nu, avade, dos is vos du krict fun gayn arum borvis"* (Well, certainly, that's what you get for going around barefooted)!

The summer provided my brother and me with new friends and a glimpse of what city children were like. They joined us in endless games of Monopoly, swam with us, and allowed us to lead them on hikes over the property. We had, in addition to all the facilities of the hotel, a good deal of adult attention. Ours were the years before the advent of day camps, so time was unregimented. We relished being "the stars" at Green Acres, with guests and staff providing yet another dimension. We looked forward to the arrival of the "regulars" each season and still remember the Greens, who never missed a July 4th, the Cohens, who always reserved a room with "samuel-private"

Vogel's Viola Hotel in Lake Huntington.

bath, and the Staubs, who danced the Chardash! In addition we had the excitement of entertainment that was provided for the patrons. Permitted by our parents to attend the shows on a limited basis, we were totally uncritical, and hopelessly starstruck.

The change of seasons triggers sharp memories of hotel life. Early September was a period of transition. We greeted the end of the summer season with bittersweet feelings. From a bustling, populated property, the hotel became a ghostly, deserted one. The lobby was inhospitable and lifeless; the loudspeaker, which had summoned everyone to meals, was silent; the playground looked forlorn without its summer children. There is nothing quite as empty as an empty hotel.

Family, and the few remaining staff members, took their meals together in the cavernous kitchen. There, footsteps echoed with a hollow sound, and the chill forced us to keep bundled up in coats and sweaters. It was often warmer outside than in. There was a pervading odor of cleaning materials, still air, and the remaining scents of a thousand meals.

My brother and I were, of course, looking forward to returning to a more normal family existence, without the guests and staff who kept our parents constantly involved. Still, the many goodbyes we had spoken, the separation from familiar faces, and the sudden emptiness, are gray memories for me.

Once the chef had left, my mother took up her chores as cook. There she was, behind the huge, black Garland range, apron over her sweaters, using the oversize pots and utensils common to hotel kitchens. A few of those tools my mother took with her to use when we moved to smaller quarters. For some reason, it is the industrial strength potato masher that I most recall, and how incongruous it looked with the normal-sized pots and four-burner stove we had at home.

Waste was deemed the largest of sins, and because economy was always practiced, our meals in early September depended largely on what was left over from the season. There was one year when we had half a 40-quart container of sour cream remaining in the cooler. We had sour cream pancakes, sour cream and cheese, sour cream and fruit, and just plain sour cream.

With the departure of the last guest, my brother and I engaged in our annual hunt. We ran expectantly from room to room, looking for "treasures"----a forgotten book, a used bathing cap, and sometimes even an abandoned toy.

Difficult as the farewells were, the other side of the coin involved the conversion of our property back to a family habitat, with no sharing strangers. Our parents, distracted and involved for the summer, were now totally ours, and we had their full attention. The guests were gone, we moved back, and that 100-year-old house was once again ours. It was good to be at the familiar round table in the winter kitchen, with uninterrupted conversation at mealtime. The past season was to talk about, and the next one was months away. The hotel became home once again.

Behind our house, there was an apple orchard that was a good example of "survival of the fittest." We never attended to those trees, or sprayed or fed or did anything to insure their growth. Yet every fall there was a wonderful crop of misshapen, tart apples to pick. The deer came nightly to take care of those that fell, and my brother Bob and I picked as many as we could to take to a nearby press for making cider. Unwashed and unculled, those apples produced a nectar not to be duplicated in the sanitized juices available today. The apple "harvest" and pressing at Pop Schmidt's, just up the road, were a pure bonus of country living. My mother took advantage of the elderberries and wild grapes that grew on our property, and as soon as we moved to our house each fall, she began making wine. The pungent smell of fermenting fruit and our mother's hands stained purple from the process are still vivid memories to me a half century later.

Back then, the Catskill hotels were only open in the warm months and had to be prepared for the country winters. Pipes were above ground and needed to be drained, blankets were camphored and stored, curtains and drapes taken down, kitchen areas scrubbed, and sporting equipment and outdoor furniture brought indoors. Once our hotel was "put to bed" for those cold months, old bedspreads were draped over the lobby furniture and we moved yet again.

The year that I entered school, my father was appointed executive secretary of the Mountain Hotelmen's Federation, with offices in Liberty. We moved there for the months that the hotel was closed, until the Federation moved its offices permanently to Woodridge.

School usually began on the day after Labor Day. For the fall at least, we attended, in the elementary grades, that two-room schoolhouse. Until entering high school, we were never in one place for a whole school year.

Transferring from one school to another was not unusual for the children of hotel people or for others whose business was seasonal. Somehow, while moving back and forth between schools, I missed out entirely on the study of grammar. I picked it up a "few" years later, as a graduate student.

Moving between two very different communities was never easy. When I look back, I have strong, but different, memories of Lake Huntington and Woodridge.

A Tale of Two Shtetls

MANY PEOPLE talk about the Catskills and think Jewish. While there is no question that almost all of the resorts, bungalow colonies and camps in Sullivan County were built by Jewish immigrants, the truth is that they were never more than a 15 percent minority of the resident population. The outside world viewed us as an enclave of *landsleit*, secure in our homogeneity. We were but a small minority, and it took decades to win the battle for acceptance.

The majority of Sullivan County resorts were clustered in its eastern part, while the hometown of my youth, Lake Huntington, and its environs on the western border, boasted only some 40 small inns in its heyday. Each resort averaged fewer than 50 rooms and only a few survived to grow and modernize; among them was our own.

I grew up on both ends of the county. My father had the idea that it built character to live in conflict. Certainly his own life reflected battles for a great many causes. So I suspect that he didn't give a lot of thought to what it was like for his children to grow in the chilly atmosphere of a town steeped in anti-Semitism and reaction, which Lake Huntington was in those days.

Our move (for the winter) to Woodridge was not occasioned by my father's concern for the isolation which my brother and I endured in western Sullivan. Rather we moved because the Mountain Hotelmen's Federation decided to locate its office in the new building built there by the Cooperative Fire Insurance Company.

It was almost a schizophrenic experience to shuttle between the two villages. They were as different from each other as Manhattan's Yorkville and the Lower East Side. In the one we were perennially the outsiders and in the other, part of the mainstream.

The difference in the towns was not only in the religious makeup of the populations. They were philosophically, politically, and socially light years apart.

In one dwelt a third and fourth generation of German Americans, and in the other East European immigrant Jews who came to the Catskills via New York City.

The Woodridge residents included trade unionists, socialists, and avid supporters of cooperatives----dreamers who survived persecution and deprivation in Europe and believed that

Horse-and-buggy days----Railroad Avenue in Woodridge.

they could thrive in, and contribute to, a world of equal opportunity for themselves and their children.

In the Lake Huntington of my youth, the local farmers recoiled from new ideas and suspected anything or anyone who was different. It was a time that antedated television, when travel was limited, and when there was no forum for the exploration of current concepts, or opportunity to meet those who espoused them. The provincialism of our fellow towns-people was probably par for the course in any upstate New York community, and certainly in the Catskill villages. The population feared and distrusted, for instance, Franklin Roosevelt and his New Deal. The people in Woodridge, Moun-taindale, and Fallsburg, conversely, with a New York City experience in liberalism, embraced both the man and his vision.

It was in those three hamlets that Jewish culture predomi-nated, and in them alone. Because nothing is black and white, I must add that there were individual demonstrations of friend-ship in Lake Huntington that could be treasured. For instance, when our hotel was afire in the icy winter of 1941, it was our neighbors in the volunteer fire department who risked their lives, vowing to keep Elmer Rosenberg's main building from being consumed.

During World War II, the butcher's son, Izzy Moses, was rescued at sea. He had been serving on a ship that was torpe-doed, and he was reported "missing in action." When he was found after 30 days on a raft in the Pacific, the news arrived by telegraph. The operator was so excited that he forgot the phone and bicycled to the Moses' home to deliver the telegram! The entire town turned out to celebrate. Church bells rang. We spanned our separate lives to touch each other in a rare moment of fellowship.

Unfortunately, there are other things to remember. When, as a teen-ager, I attended the funeral of our next door neighbor whom we knew as "Aunt" Lily for all of childhood, I was shocked to find a huge floral spray on her coffin which bore the message: "To the Secretary of the German American

Sign, circa 1910, at the entrance to Woodridge.

Photo by Michael Gold.

Bund." In truth, I can recall no overt act or propaganda that the Bund put forth, but the knowledge of its existence was in itself chilling.

Arriving in Woodridge, for me, was a little like entering heaven. That town, where I attended school from fifth grade through high school, provided memories of friendship and nurturing. It boasted none of the beauty of Lake Huntington, but I was almost an adult before I realized that a railroad ran through its main street, that the store buildings were old and shabby, and that our living quarters were crowded and undecorated. As a child, I was so happy in Woodridge that it even *looked* wonderful to me. I have had a love affair with the place for all of my years.

The population of the town was a mix of first-generation Jewish immigrants and third- and fourth-generation gentiles, who were able to live peaceably together. Numbering only about one thousand people, the town provided a mini-lesson on what was possible for populations at large.

Still visible on an empty building that stands at the entrance to the town is a faded sign with the legend: "Stapleton and Penchansky." A partnership between an Irish Catholic and an orthodox Jew was remarkable in the early 1900s. The partnership flourished and in the years to come added another partner, James Elliot (a Protestant). The villagers referred to the triumvirate as the League of Nations.

Long before it became common to speak a second language, Woodridge had one. It was Yiddish, and it was not only the Jewish population who used that tongue. John Stapleton, the Christian partner in the produce firm, spoke Yiddish to his customers. His son, Robert, became fluent in that speech by attending *shul* (synagogue) with the children of his dad's associate. A good part of the population became bilingual.

A story is told of Bob Stapleton, a tall, handsome Irishman, who left his native Woodridge to attend St. Johns University: On the day before a heralded prom night, the only Jewish tailor in the neighborhood was besieged with students who needed pressing or alteration of their tuxedos. Finding himself at the end of a long line, Stapleton called out to the shop owner, "*Luz de goyem vartin*" (Let the Gentiles wait)! He was moved to first place and never again waited for tailoring services.

Woodridge had character. And it had characters. Around those characters there developed *meises* told with warmth and love, and repeated until the threads of remembrance were woven into an oral odyssey. Those stories represented the heart and soul of the village.

Woodridge, nee Centerville, had its tales of horse thievery and even arson in the days before it was renamed. But when I knew it, crime was practically unknown. Our police "chief"

Klein was a one-man constabulary who doubled as a truant officer. My sister-in-law, Harriet Rosenberg, remembers him as a comforting presence who walked her to school each day when she was an unwilling first grader. Like many of his fellow townsmen, the peace officer could not read or write English. When apprehended for speeding, stranger or resident was handed the book in which to write his own ticket. Needless to say, Donald Duck and Albert Schweitzer, among other names, never showed up to pay the fines.

For many years it was Chief Klein who was a character witness for those aspiring to citizenship. After swearing for hundreds of people over the years, he queried the town attorney, "You think maybe I should get my citizenship papers too?"

Trust was a part of the atmosphere. Hymie Balbirer was the local milkman. He entered the houses, even in the absence of the owners, delivered the order he thought was wanted and rotated the dairy products in the ice box. It may be that the passage of time has blocked out the memory, but I have no recollection of any crime in the village. Strange as it may seem in this world of deadbolts and security systems, most of the people we knew never locked their doors in either of the towns in which we lived. Indeed, my dad was fond of saying, "Don't worry, no one will put anything in."

In a day when department stores existed only in big cities, we did have a mini all-purpose emporium. The General Store in Lake Huntington sold everything from newspapers and provisions to shoes and overalls. In addition to providing a complete source of supplies, life was easier because credit was offered to the patrons. The proprietors sometimes had a way of adding interest to the prices. The store was operated by the Wolen family and their in-laws, the Helfands. They all lived in an apartment over the place of business. On one occasion, the father in law was alone when a customer requested a box of corn flakes. The elderly gentleman, never able to memorize prices, called upstairs: "Albert, how much is corn flakes?" Came the answer, "Who is it for?"

Today, when push-button phones allow national and international access without a human voice along the way, I am reminded of the olden service in the small towns. Our number in Lake Huntington was 3 and in the metropolis of Woodridge, 182! To place a call, one cranked a lever, and a warm, familiar voice answered: "Number please." "Marie, will you ring the General Store?" could have been my words, "I'm trying to find my mother." "She's at the Post Office," may have been her reply.

Our telephone offices, manned by neighbors, were a life line and a comfort. All these years later, from the two towns in which we lived, I remember the supervising operators—Marie Wormouth in Lake Huntington, and Vera Cauthers in Woodridge.

Very often it was the ingenuity of these operators that made it possible for some of our townspeople to negotiate the long-distance call. Nate Ruderman of Woodridge, had moved to California, and his mother wanted to reach him. She carefully repeated all the information he had given her to span the continent: "Please be so kind and give me Los Angeles ----PONCHAK 6-4512." Vera was stumped. She could find no Ponchak in that area.

"We can't seem to find that exchange ----are you sure of it?" "Listen, dear, do you have maybe a car?" the Mama asked. "The first part of the number sounds like the name of a car." After some consultation at the telephone office, the problem was solved. "Ponchak" was _Pontiac_----the call was put through. From then on it was only necessary for his mother to pick up her phone and say, "Get me Natie."

In the towns of my youth, people were identified by what they did for a living. Among others there were Fox the barber (in both towns), Babcock the plumber, and Moses the butcher.

It was to Mr. Moses' butcher shop that I once went with my father to pick up something for dinner. "Moses," asked my dad, "do you have brains?" "If I had brains, would I be a kosher butcher in Lake Huntington?"

In those years, it wasn't just the butcher or baker that we knew by name and called a friend, our physicians were also an integral part of our lives. The doctors carried with them a virtual pharmacy of pills and nostrums, but it was the balm, relief, and comfort of their presence that was unforgettable. Physicians didn't become corporations in those days, no P.C. followed their names, and dunning letters for overdue bills were hardly ever sent. Many was the time that our country doctors accepted home baked goods or fresh eggs in lieu of payment. It took our modern society to produce the phenomenon of a physician who sends a summons, or, conversely, a patient who brings suit against his doctor.

To our joy, we still have among us some of the family doctors who reach out and practice the compassionate medicine of yesteryear. Somewhere along the line, however, the days of perfect trust have disappeared with our youth. The godlike MD, so revered, emerged as merely human, and our humor reflected the new disillusionment: A gentleman passed away, arrived in heaven, and was met by Saint Peter. He offered his name and asked to be admitted. "Sorry, Mr. Jones, I'm looking at my list for today and you are not on it. You must be expected down below."

There too, they were unable to find his name on the roster. "What's going on here?" said Jones. "I was up, now down, and no one seems to have heard of me." "We'll get the Big Boss," was the answer. God arrived with a huge register and searched thoroughly. "Jones . . . Jones, ah, here you are. You weren't expected for another ten years. Tell me, who's your doctor?"!

I wouldn't want to turn back the clock to the days before penicillin, CAT scans and MRIs, or to forego the extended years that advanced science has given us. But even in small towns today, with specialization, technique, and technocracy, the pleasure of the personal touch has been lost.

All but obsolete are house calls made by the family doctor. Yesterday's smalltown residents took them for granted. Dr. Gains in western Sullivan would come by sled when the roads were bad. Dr. Immerman from Woodridge once arrived at a patient's home in the bucket of the town's frontend loader when the roads were considered impassable. Doctors in both small villages knew the patient and the family. They were in attendance from birthing on and were specialists in the whole person.

Woodridge provided for us the happiest of growing up years. It was certainly not the grandeur of our three-room apartment which made that so. Nor could it have been the physical appearance of the village, which had little to recommend it architecturally.

What was not visible on the surface was the interest, enthusiasm, and intellect of our first-generation neighbors, who were the majority of the citizenry. If I have one lasting recollection of them, it is their almost palpable yearning for a better world and their aspirations to give the children "culture," missed by so many of them in the consuming struggle to make a living. Many small apartments, like our own, found room for an upright piano, and the parents managed to spend the $2 per week for lessons. They respected the written word, attended any and all lectures available, and were devoted to the exchange of ideas.

One didn't have to go far in Woodridge to hear a debate. The arena could be the post office, the barbershop, or the corner candy store. Good talk came as naturally as the rivers ran, and information was treasured. A library was established and a hall to bring in the world of ideas. It was called the Labor Lyceum, served as a real movie house, but also was much more than that. It was a place to attend concerts, and to enjoy, along with the cultural events, lecturers of every political hue who were imported to expound their theories. I need not mention that it was a time before McCarthyism silenced any view that the majority might deem heretical. It wasn't so much that there was unanimity of thought, but rather the free expression of opinion, which was so remarkable. And there it didn't matter if the presenter spoke with or without an accent.

Pesach Shabus was the town blacksmith. He was a giant of a man with hands as large as paddles. I remember him towering over us, and as a gentle, beautiful person with a white mustache and a warm smile. Only in Woodridge could he have been the *mavin* on pianos! When the Lyceum needed a new instrument, it was to Shabus that the committee came. The theory was simple. Any piano that could withstand a real *chmallyeh* (smack) from their blacksmith, was a piano that would stand the test of time!

The extended family, in New York City, provided the cultural experiences that we were denied by small town existence. Aunts and uncles were the overseers of expeditions to the planetarium, the museums, zoos and theaters when summer was over and we had school holidays or weekends to spend with the family. Those trips added a wonderful dimension to our lives. It wasn't only the broadened perspective that was so enjoyable, but the attention and approval that awaited us when we stayed with the *bubbe* and *zeyde* and our mother's sisters. We were thrilled with everything —the subway ride, the confection called a Charlotte Russe, the automat, and the sights and sounds of the metropolis.

Like so many of the first generation, desire to enrich intellectual life extended to the elders as well. It was from that endeavor that a *meise* was born: An Americanized daughter, seeking to add culture to her mother's life, persuaded mama to visit the Metropolitan Museum of Art. The trip was not the elderly lady's first priority, but one tries to please one's children, and so she had agreed. They entered first the museum section housing early religious paintings and the daughter was pleased with her mother's close attention. To add to the experience, the daughter then explained in detail the background for the Nativity scenes being viewed. Always the pragmatist, the mother commented: "Married she isn't. The baby is wrapped in rags. They're both sleeping in a stable—but for *pictures* she has money!"

The immigrants who populated Woodridge were, for the most part, self-taught. Lacking formal education themselves, they fiercely sought it for their offspring. Without the benefit of statistics, I venture to say that the numbers of the second generation who attended college and became teachers and doctors and lawyers were high for the times.

A friend, Max Alpert, went to school in Woodridge a generation before I arrived there. Back then, the Jews were just beginning to arrive in the village where members of the Ku Klux Klan still lived. Max shared with me his experience of culture clash in the community. Frequent fights broke out, the atmosphere was tense, and at school an all-Christian faculty had difficulty accepting the immigrants' children, with whose accents, customs and backgrounds they were unfamiliar.

I was more fortunate. By the time I arrived in the town, the population balance had changed. During the Depression in the early 1930s, the board of education hired many of its own graduates, and the teaching staff reflected the composition of the population at large. When I was enrolled in the Woodridge school, I met my first Jewish teacher, Miss Ruth Kronenberg, who became Mrs. Arthur Weisbord.

The school was the town's most impressive building and certainly the heart of the community. What it lacked in extensive equipment and diverse courses of study was more than made up for by small class sizes, intense teacher interest in each student, and the opportunity to participate in every extra-curricular activity that was offered. Coming as we did from Lake Huntington's two-room schoolhouse, everything from the three-story structure, to the "expanded" student body, to what seemed like wondrous facilities, was both exciting and a bit intimidating.

The local board of education was made up of men (it would be a while before women were included), willing to give their time and thought to the coming generation. The townspeople supported every event that involved children. There was no trouble getting huge turnouts for plays, oratorical contests, debates, concerts, and so forth, not to mention the enthusiastic attendance of fans for every sporting meet. The town was child oriented, providing wintertime safety with a flooded school yard for ice skating and hill roads closed to traffic for sledding.

Vitally concerned though they were with school life, it was their offsprings' preoccupation with team sports that confounded the parents. Most of the European elders had never gone to high school, much less participated in anything so frivolous as basketball.

My father never did come to terms with my decision to give up piano lessons for cheerleading! His friend, William Horowitz, who served on the school board, attended the games out of a sense of duty. His considered opinion, after his first basketball game experience was: "Why should they fight? Give each one a ball!"

As youngsters, we took for granted the dedication of our teachers which went well beyond the prescribed courses of study. They all added to their workdays by coaching teams, advising the newspaper staff, directing plays, sponsoring clubs, and tutoring anyone who needed extra help. In those days, all that after-school work brought no additional remuneration to the teaching staff.

In the absence of guidance counselors, our principal, Louis Blumberg, drove hundreds of miles to take applicants to the colleges of their choice and launched many a career. I don't think I ever said thank you to Elizabeth Kronenberg Budin, Rebecca Levy Hechtman, Ann Rosner, or Louis Blumberg, to name just a few of the Woodridge faculty.

From 1950 on, small towns consolidated their schools, instituted busing for those in more distant locations, and discontinued the tiny institutions in which we had studied. There were many advantages to the consolidation, but there were losses as well. A student at Woodridge High School didn't have much chance of not being included, if he so wished, in any and all of the teams and clubs.

The school barely had enough "men" to try out for the "first-fives" of the junior varsity and varsity teams and to cover the necessary substitutes. As for the cheerleading squad, it consisted of three, and I was one of them! My mother made our outfits, we practiced assiduously, wept when the team lost a game, and made basketball the centerpiece of our lives. No one ever forgot the night that Sevilan forgot her underpants that matched the miniskirts we wore. She was the only one of the cheer leaders who could do a decent cartwheel and was without question the hit of that game and possibly of the season!

Truthfully, when I remember those school days, it is not the academics that most move me. I remember the prom and the "to whom it may concern" fur stole that every girl borrowed (at one time or another) from Betty Horowitz. I remember the oratorical contests, the bus trips to "away" games, hot chocolate and egg creams at Levine's drug store, and dancing to the music of records in the gym. I remember putting out the mimeographed paper we called "The Tattler," movies every Friday night for 20 cents and a G.O. card (student identification), the friendships that lasted "forever," and the mountain laurel bedecked stage in the auditorium where my class of 17 graduated.

For all my growing up years in Woodridge, I can remember no incident of religious slur or conflict—not in that enclave. But we were known as a "Jewish town" and would experience insults when we ventured forth to other villages, particularly during sports events. "Jakie" Kiriluck, a Catholic member of the basketball team, was called a dirty Jew during the heat of one game. He didn't explain or deny that he was Jewish. He merely punched out the offender!

Jack was called "Jakie" because nicknames, essentially Jewish nicknames, came with the territory in Woodridge. They were, to say the least, picturesque, and for those dubbed, impossible to shed. The residents spent lifetimes as Kishke and Pimple, Bubby and Pussy, Sticky and Pitty. I never did find out the origins of those appellations, but there were others that came from *mama-loshen* (mother tongue) translations of American names. So I knew my schoolmates as Muttle and Heshy, Beryl and Shim, Shmerel and Dudie . . . and those were the Methodists! Our Christian neighbors, who were not exempted from the nickname phenomenon, learned our language, knew our customs, and observed our holidays.

The now defunct newspaper, *PM*, once did a feature story on the town I considered my own. They called it "Utopia in the Catskills." The article dealt with the inordinate number of cooperatives that were organized, and with the remarkable achievement of a community where Jew and gentile lived together in harmony. They were taken too, I think, with Jews of the time in unexpected positions. When the article was being written, there was a Woodridgeite running in the election for the position of county sheriff. He never failed to answer the phone in his wholesale grocery with "Hello, Two-Gun Sam Katzowitz here!"

The way back to those "days that were" is studded with small memory signposts that illuminate the spirit of the *shtetl* and always reflect the humor of its population.

The dream for all the immigrants who migrated to this land was to become part of their adopted nation. The first step along the way was attaining citizenship.

"Aunt" Fanny Felixson had raised her family and spent a good part of her life in the hamlet, when, during World War II, she decided that it was time for her to attain that precious status. Not very comfortable with the English language, and without any formal schooling on which to rely, she asked for and received the help of a friend, attorney Frances Cosor. Many lessons on the laws of the land, the names of elected legislators, and other pertinent subjects, were carefully taught and painstakingly learned.

The big day arrived when Mrs. Cosor deemed Fanny ready, so mentor and student journeyed to Kingston to appear before the court. "Can you tell me who your state senator is?" asked the judge. Fanny answered, "No." "Who was our first President?" Again the answer was, "I don't know." The questioning continued, and in the face of the unfamiliar and formal courtroom and robed official, our lady lost every bit of the information that had been memorized. At long last she looked up at the judge, and said, "To tell you the truth, your honor, I don't mix in." Noting his petitioner's obvious distress, the understanding magistrate then asked another question. "Do you have a son?" "Yes." "Is he in the armed forces?" "Yes." She received her citizenship papers!

To the immigrant, largely disenfranchised in the old country, the law and judicial process had special meaning. So it was not surprising when Pincus Kagan responded with pride when called to jury duty. The case involved a drunken driver, and the Woodridge juror-to-be was questioned about his use of alcohol. His answer was: "I am drinking, but I am not drunking." That was apparently a satisfactory response and Pincus took his seat on the panel.

When the trial was over, he came to report to his friend, attorney Benjamin Cosor, who told us the story. "Ban," said Kagan, "it was an interesting case. On the first voot we were split 6 to 6. But Ban, I got up and explained them what was what. I explained upside down and inside out. We took another voot ----- 11 to 1!"

Because Woodridge had no Catholic church, the folks of that faith journeyed to nearby Woodbourne to attend services. The story goes that the son of an elderly Jewish couple was visiting them, along with his Catholic wife and their children.

The son was about to drive his family to mass in the next town one Sunday morning, when one of the youngsters approached her grandfather: "*Zeyde, zeyde,* aren't you coming to church with us?" Unwilling to hurt a grandchild for any reason, the grandfather replied: "No, darling—I vas already!"

In the late 1930s, during the Spanish Civil War, the village of Woodridge donated an ambulance to the beleaguered Abraham Lincoln Brigade which was made up of volunteers from the United States fighting for Loyalist Spain. It would take Pearl Harbor for Lake Huntington to respond to the menace of dictatorships abroad.

As different as the two communities of my youth really were, they had *kleyn shtetldik* (small townish) qualities in common. Both the hamlets in which we lived during the 1930s and 1940s, were populated mostly by have-nots. While deprivation was not a state to which we aspired, neither was there any pressure to keep up with the Joneses. Mostly the Joneses didn't have any more than we did. We never felt poor. I think it was because our world did not include any *alrightniks* (well to dos) and what one didn't see, one didn't miss. We were short on conveniences, but long on company and friendship. Best of all, children were always part of everything. There were no finished basements to which they could be banished.

Ann Landers had not yet decreed that one must "phone for an appointment," so drop-by company was more the rule than the exception for small town dwellers. If no one was at home, the visitor came right in and waited. If the family was at the dinner table, the visitor joined them. Social life in my parents' set relied heavily on cards and conversation—and food. They served bowls of fruit, homemade cake (honey and sponge, rugelach and strudel), and always coffee or a *glessilah tay* (small glass of tea) accompanied by the customary lump sugar which was dipped into the drink and bitten off.

Television is blamed for a great deal of our modern-day isolation. Actually, while radio may not have been as compelling, we certainly had our routine of programs on a "not-to-be-missed" basis. *The Lone Ranger, The Fat Man, Lux Radio Theater, The Green Hornet, Jack Benny, Fred Allen,* and *The Shadow,* were just a few of our favorites. Lowell Thomas, Gabriel Heater, H. V. Kaltenborn, and Walter Winchell had a slavishly devoted news audience, and every Saturday afternoon Milton Cross took us to the Metropolitan Opera; our imaginations supplied the pictures.

When my maternal grandmother came to visit, she enjoyed the English-Yiddish WEVD, but her all-time favorite was "Arthur Gottlieb." We could never bring ourselves to tell her that it was Arthur Godfrey with whom she was so charmed.

There seemed, in those days, to be a greater concern for one's neighbors. Marilyn Cauthers from Woodridge told the story of her grandmother's church quilting bee. The event was a social one, complete with covered-dish lunches and good talk. One lady who attended did terrible sewing, but there was no thought of excluding her or of commenting on her lack of skill with a needle. When the session was over, someone quietly undid her work and repaired the damage.

Coming home one night, I found a ladies' canasta game in progress . As I stopped to watch, one player declared her hand as "10." I saw plainly that she had about 60 points remaining and started to speak when my mother's glare stopped me. It seemed that everyone playing knew the woman cheated at cards----the friend was more important than the game.

There is an old Yiddish song whose lyrics proclaim, "*Vus iz geveyn is geveyn, und nisht do.*" (What was, was, and is no longer here.) While the logic of the truism is unassailable, it does not take into account the very real existence of memory and its influence on everything we are. Interestingly, the view is sometimes clearer in retrospect than it was when we lived it, and the past is very much a part of the present. It is obvious that much has changed, but then, there are things that never change: Laura Kaplan was visiting her mother-in-law. On preparing to leave, she was urged to take along some homemade

Aerial view of Lake Huntington and Green Acres.

schav (sour grass soup). Laura demurred, "Mom, the kids don't eat it, and I don't particularly like it either." The mother-in-law continued to insist until finally, the daughter-in-law accepted: "Ok, you win----I'll take some home for Shammy." "Oh," was the instant response ----"for my son I have *fresh schav*!"

Our urban guests were often incredulous that we hotelkeeping families actually spent the entire year in the country. They found it difficult to believe that it was possible to survive without large places to shop, multi-movie theaters and the excitement of life in the city or the suburbs, surrounded by near neighbors. In truth, we did look a bit enviously at them for those very experiences, and worried about the things that we were missing.

Still, looking backwards once again, I believe that the pluses more than outweighed the minuses. With all the "things missing," the compensating factor was that small-town life provided a safe haven that was at once nurturing and challenging. Even now, there is something terribly comfortable about living where "everybody knows your name."

Woodridge was our stamping ground for winters only. Spring, summer, and fall found the family back in Lake Huntington and at the hotel. Crucial to every hotelkeeper's life was a period of time we called "The Season."

The original Green Acres in Lake Huntington, circa 1940. It was completely modernized in 1963 and destroyed by lightning in 1966.

Part 2
Reasons for the Seasons

I think it was a magnificent experience to live through the special world of the old days in the Catskill Mountains----everything it represented and the character and quality of what that era encompassed.

----Jackie Mason

Those were wonderful fun times. The stories Cissie tells are true. They bring back delightful memories. And let me add that:

The pure essence of any revelation can be obtained not only in the core of the examination but in the rigourous application of these principles that we do so cherish even though we go our separate ways.

---- "Professor" Irwin Corey (The World's Foremost Authority)
Former bus boy at Green Acres

SULLIVAN COUNTY'S POPULAR SUMMER RESORT

FALLSBURG NEW·YORK

·A·
GLORIOUS HAVEN
FOR FUN·FOR REST·FOR HEALTH
EVERY INDOOR and OUTDOOR SPORT

·GOLF·
BEAUTIFUL LAKES·HORSES
HANDBALL·TENNIS·DANCING·BASEBALL
SOCIAL ACTIVITIES·ENTERTAINMENT

TELEPHONE 41 F 12

The Butler Hill House

PINCUS COHEN, PROP,

LUZON STATION, SULLIVAN COUNTY, N. Y.

POST OFFICE, HURLEYVILLE, N. Y., BOX 9

FIRST CLASS
STRICTLY כשר KOSHER
TABLE
In Every Respect

Bathing, Boating and Fishing
Near the Premises

DIRECTIONS: Take O. & W. Railroad at 42nd or Cortlandt Street Ferries and get off at Luzon Station.

DECORATION DAY--MAY 30th, 1947
Rate Schedule

THREE DAY SPECIAL -- DAILY RATES PER PERSON

Number of persons in room	Bath nearby	Adjoining bath	Private bath
2	$ 11.00	$12.00	$13.00
3 or 4	$10.00	$ 11.00	$12.00
Single	$13.00	$14.00	

If stay is 2 days - add $1.00 per day to above rates.
Deposit of $15.00 per person, required with reservation.

HOTEL AMBASSADOR · Fallsburg, N.Y. · Tel. 80

74

Twelve Short Weeks

A STORY went the rounds years ago, about two hotelkeepers who met during the season. "How's business?" one asked. "Terrible," replied the other, "I have an empty room." "So what's terrible about one empty room?"

"It's the dining room!"

Individuals, professions, and businesses tell time by periods of the year. Student lives are proscribed by semesters, accountants by tax season, and department stores by holidays. For Sullivan/Ulster hotels, "The Season" was spring/summertime, particularly July and August, when business was in full swing.

Life in the Catskills, when I was growing up and, indeed, grown up, revolved around that season. We prepared for it, worked night and day while it was on, and discussed it for the balance of the year. It was a time when our quiet countryside came alive. The village streets were vibrant with a steady stream of humanity. The county's population, so small in winter, swelled a thousandfold—and most of the local people concentrated on the business of tourism.

The stretch of highway leading west from Old Falls to Fallsburgh remains memorable as the symbol of the resort industry when it thrived. That road, less than two miles long, was home to the Ambassador Hotel, the Flagler, Hoenig's Nassau (later called the Saxony), Hotel Levit, Pollack's Fallsburgh Country Club, the Irvington, the Elmshade, the Riverview Hotel, and a host of bungalow colonies and rooming houses as well. Cars inched their way through strolling summer people on both sides of the highway. The hours after dinner, and before the evening shows, were the most hazardous for an automobile to navigate. Custom dictated that time as the one when guests took a walk and every road had wall-to-wall pedestrians. The hotels were brightly lit, the throngs of vacationers were part of the scenery, and there was a sense of excitement and activity. It was a scene repeated in all Catskill resort villages.

Before the advent of indoor complexes, connected buildings, and ski hills, the hotels, camps, and bungalow colonies, as well as the many businesses that depended on them, all made their living (or didn't) in the time between Memorial Day and Labor Day or the Jewish holidays.

It meant, for the owners and their families, that the summer months had only one theme, and that was the operation of the hotel. The entire family, once they were old enough to contribute in some way, was expected to be a part of the work force. And the business affected all aspects of family life.

Marriages rarely took place during the season. We were all too busy making a living, and no one could expect to book a wedding party when the hotels were filled with guests. The business provided married couples with a new form of birth control----the 18-hour workdays of July and August! Checking the local birth records reveals an unofficial rule . . . no babies born during the season. "Normal life" took place during the off-season.

I married my high school sweetheart in my eighteenth year (preseason of course), and we attended college together when he was discharged from the army after World War II. During our years at Syracuse University, we traveled home to the hotel on spring weekends to help get ready for the season, spent summers at "hard labor," and came home from school once again on fall weekends to close the property for the winter.

It was a given that we would spend every summer at the hotel, and that any personal plan would be altered to accommodate the format of the business. We adjusted to living in a hotel "fishbowl," where privacy was almost impossible. With impending motherhood, I was bound and determined that my personal announcement would not be "hotel news." One evening, with a full lobby of people waiting for the dining room doors to open, I started to move a chair. From across the room came my mother's frantic voice . . . "DON'T LIFT!"

We worked so hard to make our guests feel as if they were part of the family that I think we succeeded a little too well, and they felt entitled to any and all news that concerned us.

During all my years "behind the front desk," I had two recurring nightmares. In one, I saw streams of cars driving up to the hotel's entrance on the first of July----but nothing was ready and the place was dismantled and disheveled. In the other, we were spruced up, shined and primed to receive our guests---and no one came!

My family's hotel, Green Acres, was well off the beaten track (17 miles from Monticello, the hub). We were without heat, and rarely filled before the July 4th weekend. Memorial Day could be disastrous when the weather did not cooperate. My father once told his good friend about saving a few thousand dollars by remaining closed for that unpredictable holiday. "I have a wonderful idea," replied his fellow innkeeper, "stay closed for the season and make a fortune!" In the bantering of my elders, I came to know what it was to laugh with *yaschikes* (tears in your eyes).

We were always bedeviled by the weather. I can recall a succession of cold and soggy Memorial Day weekends, and frigid Augusts, when the biggest prize to be garnered was an electric heater, and every dry-goods establishment in our area

Paul's, Swan Lake, 1960s.

Evans, Loch Sheldrake.
Original main building, 1930s.

was out of blankets. Those days were part of the Lake Huntington story. On that property, buildings were unheated, were not connected, and there were no indoor facilities. When Green Acres moved to Loch Sheldrake and became a 12-month resort, it was our thought that at least the weather hurdle was behind us. The "second Green Acres" (which I will talk of later) had heat, air-conditioning, connected buildings and an indoor pool. No more weather problems? Wrong.

Late fall and winter brought other hazards. Thanksgiving was never much of a hotel holiday, so one year we created a special "Singles Only" event. Imagine our delight with a full house of bookings well in advance of the weekend itself. What could go wrong?

On Wednesday the snows began, and continued and continued. By Thursday (check-in day) the state police were turning cars back at the Quickway, the main means of access. Of the 400 guests reserved, 60 got through. To add insult to injury, the band arrived and then the acts for the evening show. They knew the side roads to take. It was one time, knowing the holiday was a total loss, that we just decided to relax and enjoy it with our minuscule guest population. If nothing else, it was an artistic success----more men than women on a singles weekend!

From that time on our "winter prayers" were for snow during the week to cover the ski slopes, stopping promptly on Friday, early enough to allow for clearing the roads and safe passage for the arrivals.

Once small hotels opened, the staff and the owners were at their jobs every day until the season ended. Economics did not allow for the relief workers who would have made possible the luxury of days off. Like our farming neighbors, we dealt in a "live" product, and were responsible for the guest population on a 24-hour basis. During my working life in the hotel, I can recall only one occasion when I permitted myself to stay in bed with an illness. If someone died, with prevailing black humor,

An early Esther Manor, Monticello.

the question was always: "In the middle of the season?" Besides providing the nuts and bolts of the operation, we felt absolutely responsible for every facet of the guests' experience. That even included the weather. When, on one occasion, I was told accusingly by a patron that "it's raining at your hotel," it took me a few moments to overcome my guilt and assure him that Grossinger's was experiencing the same downpour.

An American Plan hotel in the Catskills was made up of many businesses: restaurant, inn, children's camp, nightclub, bar and, of course, recreation.

It goes without saying that we were the hosts, overseers, engineers, talent scouts, reservationists, housekeepers, decorators, stewards, landscape artists, advertising executives, and general factotum(s). For most of the hotel people I knew, expertise in their many roles was learned by trial and error. Our resorts gave a new meaning to "a man for all seasons." Small wonder that we looked enviously at those who earned a living doing only one job and who had time off to boot.

Hotel Brickman, South Fallsburg, before modernization.

We learned, and later our children learned, to have a healthy respect for labor. A talented handyman was worth his weight in gold and a sober dishwasher was a joy forever. It was possible to substitute for a missing maitre d' or master of ceremonies, but the loss of a chambermaid was devastating. Our source for emergency help, the employment agency, was eighteen miles away, and once the season was launched, there were precious few applicants available even there.

We were also aware that the agencies in our area were not above "improvising" on staff experience. "I need a gardener," they would call out to assembled job seekers. We once asked the "gardener" delivered to us from Monticello where he had learned his work. "Mrs. Meadoff (the agency owner) taught me on the way here," was the honest answer.

At my brother Bob's hotel (the Olympic in Fallsburg), a dishwasher who had a glass eye was sent by Elkin's Employment Agency (Woodridge). The new employee terrified the waitresses by removing his visual prosthesis as they went by. "The dishwasher you sent is so ugly that I'm losing the dining room staff," my brother complained to his supplier. "Well," responded Mr. Elkin, "please excuse me, but Clark Gable wasn't available today."

"The Season" was a taskmaster not only for the hotel owners, but for the myriad of industries that sprang up to serve the resorts. In addition to the employment agencies, there were the vendors: meat sellers, wholesale grocers, oil and gas purveyors, printers, vegetable and dairy suppliers, bakers, florists, and stationers. Then there were those who provided services: laundries (there were, at one time, twelve steam laundries in Sullivan County), plumbers, electricians, air-conditioning experts, garage mechanics, and insurance companies.

The community tradespeople responded with instant service when the need arose. They came by day, by night, and on weekends when they were called. An extended arm of the resort business, they adjusted schedules and lifestyles to the main industry.

So it was not surprising when my brother, a social studies teacher at Fallsburg High School, used the area resort names as a tool of association for his students who were studying definitions. It didn't always work. In response to his test question, "A nation's representative to another nation is called ----------," he got the answer, "a Flagler." Well, it was a good try, for the Ambassador Hotel was just down the road from the Flagler resort.

Even our physicians were very much a part of the hotel scene. They did yeoman service during July and August when their patient load swelled as our resorts and the bungalow colonies and camps filled to capacity. Given the condescension of our city cousins toward rural society, nowhere was there greater surprise than when a New Yorker discovered a skilled doctor in the country.

Dr. J. Arthur Riesenberg was the choice of the Grossinger management (in Liberty) when they required medical service for their guests. Among those he treated one summer was an elderly Manhattanite who was more than thrilled with his skill, manner, and dedication. As the doctor visited his patient daily in the local hospital, she was lavish with her praise. "Such a wonderful doctor," she enthused, "I am more than lucky. I can't believe that you don't have an office in New York. You belong on Park Avenue." Archie Riesenberg was, of course, pleased with her ebullient endorsement of his skill. Each day, as he visited her in the hospital, she repeated, "Such a perfect physician---such concern." The gratitude came to an end when the patient was ready for discharge and received her bill. "How dare you charge me like this," the lady exploded. "Where do you think you are---Park Avenue?"

Like many other businesses, ours had a slow season, even in such a short period of time. From Memorial Day until July 1st, there was a reduced market of possible guests. We catered to families, and for them vacations didn't begin until school closed at the end of June. In addition, whole industries in New York shut down for weeks of vacation, but only during July and August.

For many hotels, the springtime found a minuscule guest population in residence. It was then that we added other responsibilities to our "job description." Economics dictated that we fill in for staff who would not be hired to arrive before the full complement of crowds appeared.

We substituted for maitre d's, and took extra shifts in the office, but most challenging of all was the role of "entertainment committee." We organized game nights, built campfires, arranged round-table discussions . . . even sang! There were no televisions on which to fall back, and with the constant fear that our patrons might be bored, we gave catering a new meaning. I used to feel apologetic for the small numbers, but as I rethink the matter now, I'm sure that the quiet of early June was the lure that brought those guests. Our springtime clientele enjoyed all the facilities of an estate. The countryside was most beautiful then, there was no wait for a tennis court, and the management danced in attendance.

Hotel Levitt, South Fallsbrug.

That slow season gave rise to a favored "in" story for hotel owners: A heavenly messenger was escorting his recently deceased charge into the empyrean elevator that would carry him to his reward. They moved downward a bit and the doors opened. Outside, the passenger glimpsed a gala scene. A huge crowd danced to the music of a rhumba band while cocktails and canapes beckoned on a long table. The dearly departed began to exit the elevator when he was pulled back by his guide. "No," said the heavenly messenger, "This is hell—you are bound for heaven." The elevator door closed and the cab continued its journey . . . up, up, and up. When the door finally opened once again, they looked out at a group of 15 people sitting quietly on overstuffed chairs. "My goodness," was the passenger's concerned comment, "how can this be heaven? Down below there were drinks and hors d'oeuvres, plus a rhumba band!" And the reply: "For 15 people we should have a rhumba band?!"

The business wasn't exactly heaven for friendships. Once summer arrived, our friends understood that we were absolved from all social obligations. It was a strain on relationships when weddings, bar mitzvahs, and anniversaries found us missing, but we were forgiven. My godchild, Jamie Nishman, decided on an August wedding date, and worst of all, chose a Sunday afternoon. Needless to say, we could not attend the festivities on what was, for us, a check-in day. Generally we felt terrible about missing so much. But confinement was accepted as part of the season; it was a way of life for everyone in the industry.

Personal visitors received as much time and attention as we were able to offer, but we were at best distracted company. My brother had a small niece who questioned, "How can you tell when Uncle Bob is listening?" It was a strain to concentrate on a visitor when your mind was whirling with some thousand-and-one details.

If we were to select a name for our present home, it could realistically be called "Blumberg's Last Resort." There are small delights, which the rest of the world takes for granted, that we only came to know after leaving Green Acres. The house in which we now live is our first residence that doesn't share grounds with a hotel. There is something wonderful about living on a street instead of Route 52, of having mail and

The lounge at Chester's, Woodbourne.

a daily newspaper delivered, and of enjoying the pleasure of privacy. Blessed is the peace and quiet in the absence of a relentless public address system calling guests to meals or phone calls, and the staff to countless emergencies. "John, the handyman, call the office," still echoes in my dreams.

Retired innkeepers doubly enjoy the experience of a sunny summer day. It is still an unexpected pleasure to do the Sunday *Times* crossword puzzle on Sunday or accept an invitation to a summer Saturday night event.

And yet, in spite of all the years that we have been "civilians," the hotel routine created automatic reactions that do not readily change. I still shudder when it rains on a July day. I compulsively check out the parking lots of the existing resorts, and worry if the crowd looks thin. I am unable to have dinner in a hotel dining room without inspecting the service. And when the leaves return to the trees, and the crocuses show their heads, I miss the anticipation of another season.

Heiden Hotel, Fallsburg, used as a set for the movie Sweet Lorraine.

With Open Arms

SECOND-GENERATION HOTELKEEPERS were born into the business. I went to college and studied to be a teacher. Running a resort and living in the country was certainly not my dream. Still, in 1948, at ages 23 and 20, my husband and I found ourselves managing a hotel with my parents. My father, never healthy, was anxious for his children to stay "for a while" to maintain the business. Three years later, when my father died, our responsibilities increased, and "a while" in 1951 turned into forever.

Around that same time, many members of the second generation were either taking over, or joining in the management of the area hotels. The reasons for the changing of the guard are as many as the numbers of hotels. In many families, the grown children combined their chosen professions with hotel work, with one career in the winter and a return to the resort for the summer months. There were others who found the operation of a resort to be their "cup of tea" and became hotelkeepers full-time and year-round.

The difference between being a "working child" and being in full charge was monumental. It wasn't fun and games anymore. My dad left us with an unpaid mortgage and a place badly in need of updating.

Sullivan *Gibernia* (county) and life in a resort, provided those of us who grew up and lived here with the unusual "Catskill experience" that has no counterpart in the rest of the nation. I am reminded of the family slogan which my mother inadvertently coined: Our family was staying with an aunt in Manhattan when an inordinate number of visitors arrived. My mother was in a tizzy when she realized that there was just not enough food to invite them all to dinner. Not feeding guests, in her view, was tantamount to sin—adultery or maybe felony murder. What to do?

She phoned her brother-in-law, Arthur, still at his place of work, to share the problem. When he arrived home an hour later, he brought with him roasted chickens, potato salad, and all the fixings — enough for the army who waited. My mother was overcome with joy. "Oh, Arthur," was her enthusiastic exclamation, "you and I are just like me!" Mother's words remain the family slogan for our shared experiences.

What is truly remarkable are the parallel lives that we hotel families lived. Our experiences, our practices, our philosophies of operation, our problems, and even our economies were similar. We of the second generation, reacted in essentially the same manner, made many of the same mistakes, and share similar memories. Reminiscing finds us in helpless laughter over events which, when they occurred, were disasters. Some of them involved bad seasons, or impossible employees, or difficult guests. But one, which I recently recalled at a gathering of retired innkeepers, surprised me by being so familiar to them all.

Rooms with a bath on floor were just that. They were listed on every small-to-medium-sized hotel rate schedule as the least expensive accommodation available. The only plumbing they boasted were sinks. Showers and toilets were "down the hall." Our descriptions read: "bath and shower convenient."

I was in the office late one night when I heard the chilling sound of running water. Investigation revealed the source. The steps leading down to the lobby from the bedrooms had become a small Niagara Falls! To the sound of the flowing stream was added the wail of a guest who explained that "for no reason at all" her sink had separated from its mooring on the wall, breaking the pipes and creating the flood. It didn't take a genius to conclude that the occupant had decided her sink was more convenient than the "convenient" bathroom on the floor!

Hi and Clem Frank from North Branch (Woodland House) had the same experience with an oversized lady who threatened to sue them for injuries caused by their "faulty plumbing." Florence Neukrug (Avon Lodge, Woodridge) remembered the very same incident, as did Ben Posner (Brickman, Fallsburgh). I am repeatedly struck by how the worst of times become good stories with the safety of distance. But maybe the reason we hotel folks survived is that we learned early on to find some humor in all of the events that plagued us.

The owners' deep identification with their businesses was reflected in the names they gave the various properties. Of course, there were simple ones like Paul's (Swan Lake), Brickman's and the Nemerson (Fallsburg), Klein's Hillside (Parksville), Brown's and Evans (Loch Sheldrake), Chester's (Woodbourne), and Stier's and Grossinger's (Liberty). There were also the more fanciful ones, which were equally personal: SalHara (for Sally and Harry in Woodbourne) or the Kanco (for Kanter and Cohen in Ferndale), plus the Hotel Flomel (for Florence and Melvin) in Loch Sheldrake.

Billboards on the road that led to our mountains proclaimed their owners' aspiration to grandeur. Where but here could you find Hotel Rosenblatt and Country Club (Glen Wild) with a subtitle that featured the latest and most expensive addition—copper plumbing! What other area would have a Finkelstein's Foibles, a Didinsky's Villa or a Gesunte Heights?

Charles and Lillian Brown in the 1940s.

If there is one word that can be applied to the hotel people of my day, it is "largesse," and that spirit of giving was not confined to paying guests. I cannot recall a salesman or delivery person who was not ushered into the dining room or kitchen "for a bite" before he went on his way. Interviews were conducted over coffee and cake, and many are the tradespeople or servicemen who went home with a "care package." One such recipient collected wherever she went. A telephone company representative, she came each year to teach the new switchboard operators proper procedure. She didn't drive, so each hotel provided transportation to the next. Somehow, without consultation, we all had the impression that the lady was needy, and saw to it that a package of goodies was ready for her when the instruction was over. It was many years later that she became Sullivan County's most generous philanthropist and wrote a will leaving three million dollars to the local hospital! Some of us decided that it was our gefilte fish, fresh rolls, and roast chickens that made her generosity possible, although we're willing to admit that her telephone company stock may have helped.

It was a time when "business is business" was not the slogan of choice. Perhaps it was because people who spent every waking hour at their hotels understood that there was too much of their lives involved in the enterprises to consider them merely businesses. I'm not sure whether they verbalized that concept, or even if it was clearly thought out. It seemed reflexive, and more the rule than the exception for the people we knew.

Most of the owners were up to their eyeballs in debt. Still, they were givers and good members of the community. There is not a church, synagogue, fire department, service group, or charity that did not seek hotel contributions and receive them. From sheet cakes to whole dinners and the use of facilities, hotel owners were asked and rarely refused. Although busy and involved, innkeepers found the time to serve on school boards,

Brown's Hotel and Country Club, Loch Sheldrake, early on.

hospital boards, PTAs, credit unions, and to work for charitable organizations.

Friendship was a high priority. We were told by our parents that you must accept your friends with all their shortcomings. When the philosophy extended to business, it didn't always make sense to us. One friend was the local creamery operator. My mother discovered that he was skimming cream from the large pails of milk delivered to the hotel. When confronted with the fact, the gentleman protested, "If you can't take a little from your friends, who can you take from?" That story was repeated for years as humor----the friend continued as our supplier.

No one realized that our family and most of the hotel owners were, at best, living in the middle class. There we were, on acres and acres of land, owners of large buildings, and overseers of all we surveyed. Neighbors perceived us to be the privileged few. During July and August every meal was a banquet. And then, with the arrival of fall and the end of the season, very often the waiter went home with more cash than the owner!

Personal comfort during the summer months was the last of our concerns. Abandoning the winter quarters, we moved into crowded lodgings to make space for guests. It was just not conceivable to us that we occupy the eight or so rooms of the farmhouse when they could produce some income. So move we did ---- lock, stock, and refrigerator, *every* spring. On occasion, we even moved again when there was a sudden rush of check-ins. Only the birth of our children stopped that idiotic process. Elizabeth Gibber Berman (Gibber's, Kiamesha) remembers similar moves. We both look back with surprise at our easy acceptance of the lifestyle.

Those who joined the hotel families with expectations of resort life were in for a shock. When Clemence Eskenazi married Hiram Frank, she arrived from Seattle with her golf clubs and tennis racket. She was instantly drafted as a chambermaid/kitchen assistant, despite her two college degrees. There went her dreams of glamorous hotel living. In-laws took the jobs assigned----few resisted.

Manny Halbert (Raleigh, Fallsburg) married into what he thought was a large and successful enterprise. When his first season ended, he found himself in the basement painting the lawn furniture. Manny is sure that Nicky Hilton didn't spend winters that way.

Hotelkeepers tried to be the consummate hosts. There was not a property, from small inn to large hotel, where at least one member of the family was not forever visible to the guests. While most places had maitre d's who walked the dining room floor, those professionals were never alone in their labors. At mealtime, owners visited with their guests but kept a sharp eye on the food service. They stopped at each table to chat, sat down for a cup of coffee, and if there was a special request, thought nothing of going into the kitchen to fill it.

We were always there, at the desk, in the dining room, at every show, and even in the coffee shop for a late night visit.

Fallsview, Ellenville, 1920.

Our day did not end until the band in the nightclub played its last note. That meant that guests could come to us, at any time of the day or night, with a small or large complaint, and expect (and receive) our personal attention.

Part of the vacation mystique was an absence of real-world problems. We sought to give our patrons an idyll of fun and games, to refresh their spirits and suspend them in a rarified atmosphere. So whatever our own troubles were, business or personal, as hosts we were expected to internalize them, smile at the guests, and seek swift solutions.

All of the innkeepers could greet each patron by name. It was an attribute that most distinguished the Catskill resorts, and made being in our mountains a truly warm and memorable experience. We knew which rooms guests occupied, how many children they had, and what their lines of work were. There are countless thousands of people who visited this vacation land who will remember the man or woman who welcomed them, made them feel special and at home, and greeted them by name on their next trip.

In my case, that knowledge was less than remarkable. I spoke with prospective clients when they made inquiry, took the reservation when it was placed, assigned their rooms, checked them in, and selected their dining room seats. There was ample opportunity to know them.

I must admit that I was a bit of a *nudge* (nag) in urging the office staff to learn the guest names. They were delighted when I finally got tripped up. On one fall weekend, we checked in a polka dance group of 300 Polish Americans. Their names seemed to contain no vowels and I went down to defeat!

Particularly, in the early years, all hotelkeepers had to be salespeople par excellence, and every establishment had at least a portion of its rooms that required special skill to rent. We were "blessed" with varied accommodations, including rooms with private baths, rooms that shared one bath between two rooms, and rooms with a bath on the floor, which have all but disappeared in today's modern resorts. At Green Acres, it was not merely bath facilities but location that made rental so difficult. We had 50 rooms at the bottom of the hill, and 18 rooms on the third floor of the main building. There was no elevator. There was no air-conditioning either, so it was always a boon to rent those accommodations early in the spring. The renters, at that time, were people who drove up to see the place and pick the room they would occupy for several summer weeks. When asked whether those top-floor rooms would be hot I could reply, on a chilly day in April, with a technically true but less than honest answer, "Does it feel hot?"

For third floor rooms, the big trick was to distract a prospective guest from the climb he was taking. We always paused on the second floor to point out the view and chat a bit before resuming the upward trek. For the rooms at the bottom of the hill, the rule was to conclude your sale right there so the guest never climbed up again to the main building until he arrived for his vacation. But, of course, the guests understood and our "sales technique" was one to laugh about with them.

Many of us ran resorts that catered to families long before we built additional rooms really large enough to hold a couple with two or three children. In order to house those numbers, we used double-decker bunks. One of our customers put it this way: "Isn't it bad enough that our kids are in our room . . . do we have to have one in the balcony and another in the loge?"

On spring weekends, when people came to look, we all took many tours of the property. The potential guests who journeyed to see the place were planning a four-to-eight-week stay, and were vital to the operation. Each member of the family acted as a guide.

On one such weekend, both my mother and I were showing rooms. We had one two-room bungalow that was particularly desirable. It was our only two-room bungalow! We both showed it; both our customers liked it. I pulled my mom aside to tell her of the dilemma. We didn't want to lose either party. Mother approached "her" family. "You're going to love this cottage," she said, "and I want to assure you that the noise of the pump behind it will hardly bother you at all." They took another accommodation!

For guests who wanted extended vacations, less desirable rooms were cheaper and could mean additional time in the country. Since they almost always came up to see the hotel, and selected the actual accommodation, those guests lifted the responsibility from us as salespeople. We were most concerned about the clients who reserved cheaper rooms over the phone, sight unseen.

My own solution was to undersell. I was careful to let the inquirer know that some of our rooms were at best simple. Very often the calling guest ended up convincing *me* that the room would be okay. Our business involved not only the marketing of a product, but then spending time with the purchaser. There was no point in presenting a "pitch" that was unrealistic. I was completely secure in our services and never comfortable with our older sleeping quarters. So I used the bromide that my colleagues used: "With all the activities we

The uniquely styled Commodore, Swan Lake, 1938.

The Flagler, Fallsburg, a premier hotel in its era.

offer, how much time will you spend in your room?" In planning for our own family vacations, when a reservationist asks me that question, I always reserve a more expensive accommodation.

With hindsight, I recognize that we hotelkeepers created some of our own problems by using high-flown adjectives in our rate schedules. Our "Pine Lodge" was formerly a chicken coop, "deluxe" described nothing at our hotel in those days, and we had a penchant for calling any two spaces "a suite."

We told the prospective guest that our rates were so reasonable we weren't charging for the room at all. The funny thing is that we were right. We were giving wonderful value at affordable prices—the rooms were the least of it. Summer in the Catskills became a way of life, with a population that returned year after year, even to the third floor and the rooms at the foot of the hill.

Years later, after the vast modernization programs were undertaken, and when the luxurious adjectives more readily applied to our resorts, anyone could show and sell a room. But ask any of us old-timers and we'll have a story about the days when there were rooms that really needed selling.

Without consultation, all the innkeepers practiced the same types of economies, some of which now seem inexplicable. Anyone who ever worked in a hotel dining room, for instance, will remember the "saving of the bread." Carefully retrieved from the tables, the slices were lined up and covered with a damp cloth. Whether or not the savings from the stale and soggy results were worth the effort, it was a universal practice.

There were other gimmicks that we all used. Guests seemed to love a full house, I suppose because it was a confirmation of their own correct choice. A full dining room was the sign of success, and we discovered early on that success breeds success. So if the population dipped a bit and there were empty tables, it was our practice to remove them, and create more space between those that remained. Then our guests could state, with satisfaction: "There isn't a vacant seat in the dining room!"

Similarly, we made sure that the parking lot visible from the highway was kept as full as possible. When things were slow, all house and staff cars were moved from the rear and more convenient parking area to the front where they could indicate to the passing world that "business was brisk." Sometimes, we may have been confused as to where our enterprise left off and we began. A bad season hit our pocketbooks. It was just as devastating to our egos.

The pleasures of this verdant area were virtually unknown to the members of the entire industry. We missed picnics and boating, trips and barbeques, tennis, and just sunbathing or sitting under a tree. We missed summer.

Since life during the season was never lived in our homes, it was only at the hotel that we could see our friends. The easiest way to entertain was at dinner, and then we didn't get to see too much of personal guests because of a million-and-one

Schenck's Paramount, Fallsburg, reflected an assortment of styles.
Photo by Michael Gold.

interruptions. Every dining room had a "family table." Its occupants were the family itself (or at least the family that wasn't working in the kitchen), plus the bookkeeper, assorted working relatives and visitors. It was generally located in the least comfortable part of the dining room and was the first approached when lead items on the menu were getting short. If the "headliner" of the day (that is, steak or lobster) was in short supply, my mother, or in later years my husband, came running out of the kitchen to warn us to order something else.

As a group, hotel people were remarkable in their daily exercise of tact. My mother was a master of that art:

One organization that chose our hotel included the installation of their officers as part of the festivities. The acceptance speech of the newly elected president revealed him to be a mean spirited and limited human being. As the group was leaving the room in which the ceremonies had taken place, one of the members confided to my mom: "*Ich denk de naya president iz a groys nahr.*" (I think the new president is a big idiot). Spotting the gentleman in question right behind them, my mother recovered with: "I agree—but do you think Harry Truman will ever be reelected?"

From the time that the resorts offered only the very simple "room and board and fresh air," to the latter days of elaborate facilities and programs, hotel owners kept their eyes on the needs of the prospective clients and made every attempt to meet them.

The "menu" for vacationers was laid out every Sunday in the resort section of the *New York Times* and on Tuesday in the *New York Post*. It was on those pages that the breadth of availability was visible. At one time a dozen or more pages were reserved for our Catskill hotels.

While many establishments had similar offerings (pools, tennis, lake, day camp, gala entertainment), each had a style, a feature, and a personality all its own. Pauls, an all-adult resort, ran a tag line that read: "Honeymooners treated with studied neglect." It was also known for its owner's hobby of raising flowers and for its "accent on tennis."

Leibowitz' Pine View (Fallsburg) and The Pioneer Country Club (Greenfield Park) touted Glatt Kosher cuisine and religious services on the premises. A friend of mine was lunching at the former, and found sinks outside the dining room door for ritual washing. She of course rinsed her hands, and as she did so was addressed by a distinguished, bearded patriarch who was next on line: "*Madele, madele, mach schnell ----ich doff gain tsum* golf course!" (Young lady, hurry up, I'm due at the links.)

Early on, White Roe and the Waldemere (Livingston Manor), Sha-Wan-Ga Lodge and Tamarack Lodge courted "singles only" clienteles, well before all the hotels created special weekends for the unattached.

Beginning in the early 1920s, Fannie Schaeffer Konviser's Vegetarian Hotel (Woodridge) was just that—nutritionally and ecologically concerned, decades before those disciplines gained credence, it provided for the early disciples of a different food regimen.

Either by design or serendipity, there were hotels that developed reputations that attracted people with particular interests. The Windsor (South Fallsburg) was a magnet for card players, while Sunny Oaks (Woodridge) was, and still is, a haven for folk dancers.

There were properties where the personalities of the owners were often more important than the physical plant and all the accouterments in attracting and keeping guests. A host such as Meyer Arkin, the ebullient innkeeper of Avon Lodge; was an actor and a force. He was ever-present in the operation, from singing the menu on the loudspeaker as an invitation to dinner, to individual attention to all who came.

Louis (Lepke the Farmer) Rosenblatt, in the hotel that bore his name, attracted more attention than his "paid for" entertainment when he read Sholem Alechem in the lobby.

Chester's Zumbarg advertised itself as an "adult hideaway" and was proud of serving "the nicest people anywhere." They, along with Maud's Summer-Ray (North Branch), Harmony Country Club (Monticello), South Wind (Woodbourne), The Eager Rose Garden (Bushkill), and Skliar's (Monticello), were noted for the intellectual climate that they fostered. In those resorts, one could find chamber music festivals, artists in residence, literary lectures and avant garde entertainment.

Family resorts abounded. Fieldston, Vacationland (Swan Lake), The Morningside (Hurleyville), The Olympic, and Gilbert's (Fallsburg) were among the early ones, and eventually almost every hotel provided care for children. It would be a concept which would be copied by other resort areas in years to come. Along with many vacation destinations, the well-known Club Med organization now offers its own version of the day camp service which we began.

Our place, Green Acres (Lake Huntington/Loch Sheldrake), catered to young families. Children, from babies to teens, were handled by a huge staff of counselors; we observed strict division of the age groups, and provided all the activities of a sleep-away camp. We featured a physician in residence, separate children's dining rooms and swimming pools. We headed our advertisement with the boast: "Parents' Delight . . . America's Finest Parent-Child Resort."

Rosenblatt's, Glen Wild.

Self-serving adjectives have a way of coming back to haunt you. I will never forget the mother whose child just couldn't adjust to separation, cried day and night, and generally was miserable. The poor woman, with her vacation days disappearing, accosted me in the office: "Parents Delight? This place is a parent's nightmare!"

No matter what we provided, there were endless things beyond our control. If a marriage was on the rocks, no amount of leisure could create a honeymoon. If the kids were out of control, a vacation couldn't straighten them out.

Our resorts, in season, were worlds, or at least villages, in microcosm. With 100 to 150 in staff, and 300 to 500 guests, all living and/or working in a confined area, even the numbers justify the definition.

Like any place where the population spends from four to nine weeks together, "people watching" was the indoor sport of choice. The summer romances of fiction were real—both licit and illicit!

Gloria Weiner Paul spent her formative years at the Stevensville Lake Hotel (Swan Lake) where her parents were part owners. She attended the children's day camp while her older brother worked on the athletic staff. Gloria told the story about lining up for lunch in the lobby one day, when the athletic director walked by. "There goes the athletic director," little Gloria announced, "he rooms with my brother." A small guest companion piped up in disagreement. "No way," said she, "he sleeps with my mommy!"

Cash to open the hotels in the spring was in short supply, so many owners took "season partners." Those moveable hotel people, many of whom worked in other areas such as Lakewood, New Jersey, in the winter, supplied a few thousand dollars in advance rent, and added their own clientele who followed them from place to place over the years. They all had their own styles of catering, usually exclusively to the people they brought to the hotel. They are a phenomenon now long gone.

More common than the seasonal partners were the permanent partnerships that developed in the industry. In many cases the properties were jointly owned by family, and in others by friends. It is a tribute to the values of their day that those "weddings" continued for years. I can remember almost no clashes that led to breakups.

The partner names became forever linked: Horowitz and Bernstein (The Olympic), Leshner and Regalson (Harmony Country Club), Dan and Atlas (Sha-Wan-ga Lodge), the brothers Posner (Brickman Hotel), Gartenberg and Shechter (The Pioneer Country Club), Leshnick and Podolnick (The President Hotel), Dinnerstein and Weiner (Stevensville Lake Hotel), and Kantor and Cohen (Hotel Kanco). In spite of the tension, worry, fear, and exhaustion to which hotel owners were heir, through seasons good and disastrous, almost every relationship survived.

From the largest to the smallest operation, it is my contention that the hotelkeepers' most serious error was their failure to charge sufficient rates. In the farmhouse days they didn't take into account the cost of goods produced on their own property. From the early days until the present time, they never valued their own labor. The "good buys" that existed in our area were more than that, the hosts consistently shortchanged themselves. Fiercely competitive at all times, undercutting of one another's rates was commonplace. The hotelkeepers never came to understand that they were preventing themselves and the entire industry from increasing income to meet the rising costs of doing business. Despite the existence of a trade organization, self-destructive aspects of competition continued.

Spring found each resort writing to every other resort. The ploy was to receive the competitor's rate schedule by using a city relative's address. Once that information was in hand, hotels could charge rates lower than their competitors'. My father once handed out a sheaf of rate schedules at a hotelmen's meeting . . . "Save me postage," he said, "here's the rate!"

A glance at some of the "specials" for weekends and the discounts offered is ample evidence that the rates were too low for any era.

During the 1940s and 1950s, middle-sized hotels, such as our own, charged rates as low as $45 per person for a full week (including three meals a day).

As if the low rates were not enough, hotels continued to add facilities and services without a compensating charge. Early resorts added a late evening snack after the entertainment. The owners created a spot where coffee, tea, and an assortment of pastries were laid out for the guests. They called it a tearoom. Ours was manned by an unwilling busboy whose compensation was to be the tips the patrons would leave. A saucer containing change was conspicuously placed to remind the people that they were being served. Very often even the change disappeared!

I remember the Hotelmen's Federation meetings that went on into the night. When opinions differed, voices were raised and passions expressed. I remember how my father argued vehemently until he finally convinced his peers to eliminate the tearooms; how he unsuccessfully urged cooperative buying and a central office for hiring staff and booking entertainers. He didn't win a lot of the battles. Each hotelman felt he might lose in the ventures that were joint.

I also have memories of the individual interest and personal support from some of those hotelkeepers. I remember acts of kindness and generosity. The year my father died, Emanuel Paul arrived daily at Green Acres on his motor scooter to see if anything needed fixing. Harry Grossinger sent a full set of dishes when our kitchen was decimated by fire in 1941 and supplies were not available. Milton Kutsher guided my husband and me, when we were young in the business, to getting a mortgage that made it possible to build a long overdue outdoor pool. The Posner brothers (Brickman) were a storehouse of advice and material when we moved to Loch Sheldrake.

I remember integrity. William Horowitz (The Olympic) and his season partner, George Bernstein, were having a serious dispute. It boiled down to who paid what for a renovation. They had arrived at $300 as the base of contention. Unable to settle the matter, they called on my father to arbitrate. Now Willy was my dad's best friend, so he leaned back in comfort. Not only did my father decide in favor of Willy's partner, but he raised the figure to $600! Dad thereby earned the title of "the hanging judge," but never for a moment the resentment of his friend who knew that my father had acted in conscience.

Lest the readers think that I am an incurable Pollyanna, be assured that I remember the other side of the coin as well. We considered, at one time, advertising in the *Catholic World* to reach a new market. Upon examination of its resort section, I came upon an ad, in the early 1970s when discrimination was no longer legal, promoting a neighboring hotel which will remain nameless. Included in the ad's copy was the line: "Busses to churches." I called the neighbor, "I'd like a favor. When your busses to the church pass our property, could you please stop to pick up some of our people?" "What are you talking about?" responded our fellow hotel man, "I don't have a bus going to church." It was clear that "Busses to churches" was simple code for "Jews not welcome."

If hotelkeepers gained nothing else from their years of labor, each one of them has a hundred and one stories that they are happy to trade with colleagues who will more than understand. A favorite of mine was told about Leshnick and Podolnick's President Hotel in Swan Lake:

An infamous member of a Lower East Side crime family, Bugsy Siegel, had been their frequent guest . . . much to the discomfort of that management. Siegel was hardly the kind of "star" to do their reputation any good, and he travelled with an unsavory entourage. The partners finally determined to refuse the gangster's next reservation. When the request for a room came in, Mr. Siegel was told that the hotel was fully booked and he could not be accommodated. Several hours after the phone call, a large black hearse pulled up to the front entrance of the President. "What's this?" asked the worried door man. "Very simple," replied the driver of the hearse. "Either Mr. Siegel checks in, or Leshnick and Podolnick check out!"

Fellow hotelkeepers were part of our lives and were important to us; so was the Federation to which almost all of the resorts belonged. We certainly developed an affection for the staffs who were in our employ. There was no question, however, that what moved the industry was our common concern, attention to and planning for the centerpiece of the whole picture . . . our guests!

The Guests, God Bless Them

"WHAT DO YOU WANT TO BE when you grow up?" Every child faces that question about her dreams and aspirations. It has been part of adult conversation with youngsters for as long as anyone can remember. I'm sure that I responded with the desire to be in every one of the professions at some point. I had in addition, another unspoken wish. "When I grow up, I want to be a hotel summer guest!"

Resort owners and their children never took summer vacations for obvious reasons. So as a child and adult, I looked with envy at the magical world of leisure and fun that we provided, and longed for the experience.

Fortunately for us, so did the untold numbers of others whose summer pilgrimages to the mountains paid our bills and sent our children to college. They came by the thousands when recreation and time away were recognized as life's necessities.

If the world knows the Catskills for anything, it is for being the training ground of now famous comedians. The mountain stories told by those masters of mirth became, at the same time, a boon and a burden. Comedy is by nature exaggeration, so the comedians naturally stereotyped and exaggerated any foibles of the largely Jewish clientele and all aspects of life at the resorts. It didn't take long for their comic take to be accepted as accurate depiction. Over time, the jokes were forgotten and the distorted images remained. Thus, the multiple thousands who vacationed here and the area's hotels were tarred with the same brush, and what emerged as their description is as misleading as it is demeaning.

I wonder, after all the propaganda to the contrary, if the world will take my word for the fact that there is nothing ludicrous about Jews on vacation. I cite my own 30 years behind a resort desk as reason enough for being a *mavin*.

We have known thousands of Catskill vacationers. For the most part they were decent, appreciative, and as fun loving as their counterparts in the Berkshires and Poconos. For every fat lady looking for an eligible son-in-law, there were myriads of people looking for a breath of fresh air and some time in the sun. For every porch sitter and pinochle player waiting for the next meal, there was a host of hikers, swimmers, baseball players, berry pickers, and dancers who were wonderful to watch and exciting to know.

Our guests weren't any more or less overeaters than clients at American plan (three meals provided) resorts in any part of the world. When presented with varied menus featuring a sumptuous array of goodies, served by waiters who anticipated large tips for ignoring "choice of" on those menus, people went overboard. In a comedy routine, wining and dining can become gorging and gluttony. Real life is not a comedy routine, nor were the majority of our guests funny. They would never make the repertoire of a Henny Youngman or Jackie Mason. For the comedians, the exceptions became the rule and the exaggerated descriptions became accepted as fact.

Among the many guests at any hotel, some were certainly characters, and there *was* humor to be found. But it was the individuals who were funny, and the situations that magnified idiosyncracies. There was no typical guest, but there were lots and lots of people. Being human, we remember those who were the most ridiculous.

For instance, there was the lady who kept sending her breakfast eggs back to the kitchen, expressing her dissatisfaction. The distraught waiter finally asked my husband to come out of the kitchen and deal with her. "What seems to be the problem?" he asked. "I can't describe it exactly," she replied, "they seem to taste too eggy."

As the hotel's reservationist, I once sold a long stay to a family who was anxious to vacation at an atypical Catskill resort. Since we weren't kosher, we figured that could describe our place. The wife was intent on establishing "difference," and posed a test question: "Do you serve borscht?" I wasn't thrilled with the examination, and answered with what I thought was a bit of cleverness. "We serve Pink Velvet, Mrs. Goldstein," said I, assuming she understood. Weeks later, she arrived in time for lunch, found that "Pink Velvet" was indeed on the menu, and then charged out of the dining room with obvious anger. I stood at the desk with my mother as the irate lady shouted, "This place is pure borscht!" My mother's quick retort was, "And what are you . . . consommé?" We all loved the story, so from that day forward, borscht was officially rechristened!

In many resort areas of the world, one seldom meets an owner. Here in the Catskills, our business was intensely personal and as owner/managers we were constantly visible. That made us targets for any and all complaints.

On one Memorial Day weekend, I met the woman who was to become an entire department of complaints. With 300 people in the house, one was ever present, and nothing pleased her. Mrs. Abraham found the room too small, the food uninteresting, the show boring, and on and on. She shared her discontent with me at every opportunity. So, when the weekend ended and she departed, I was relieved. One week later she phoned, "Do you have a room for July 4?" was her question. I couldn't resist, "Mrs. Abraham," I answered, "you didn't like the food or the room or the entertainment---are you a glutton for punishment?" "Well," was the response, "all in all I had a good time."

I try, as I get older, not to confuse experience with wisdom. Still, we hotelkeepers were in a unique position to observe people. From behind the desk and on the reservation telephone line, we had a wonderful opportunity to see a great deal---to observe our fellow man with all his virtues and warts. And I think we all have a compelling desire to share our observations.

It is remarkable how forthcoming people can be in the comfort of their homes and in conversation with a total stranger. Talk that began with questions about a vacation, often strayed far afield. It was an opportunity to get to know a great many men and women. They could be warm, funny, ridiculous, vulnerable, and almost always interesting. By the time they arrived at the hotel, I had no trouble putting groups together for tables in the dining room; and that creation of compatible company, I still believe, is where the vacation can be made memorable. So we never used the usual clues on dining room vouchers that related to "young, middle-aged, or old". . . most of our guests were in a similar age category anyway. The best plan was for me to do the arranging on a chart after every check-in, and the maitre d's to do the actual seating. It was probably what I did best.

The most memorable story of seating people in the dining room was a result of circumstance and coincidence, not great skill. The drama of people and events played on the "stages" of all the hotels. During a summer in the 1970s, at Green Acres, the "set" was our dining room.

We often had three or four families who vacationed together. When they did, arranging seating in the dining room was a pleasure. A member of one such group came to the maitre d' with a problem. Her widowed mother, Mrs. Schwartz, planned to join them, and she felt that the other young couples might object to sitting with an older person who would also be at the hotel for a long stay. Initially, when the mother checked in, she requested seating at her daughter's dining room table, and we had no choice but to accede. After a few days, the daughter requested again that we find another table for her mother. It was a real conundrum since there wasn't anyone in that age group at the hotel. The maitre d' promised to be on the lookout when the weekend brought new arrivals. Luck was with us since an older couple, as well as a single gentleman and lady arrived. Mrs. Schwartz, however, was not ready to move. One morning she came to breakfast before any of the daughter's table mates had yet appeared. We prevailed upon her to join the older table "just for one meal," and to see how things went. When she agreed, we were delighted to find that it was a happy arrangement, and that she would remain with her new companions. In the middle of the lunch meal that day, we were startled by screams coming from Mrs. Schwartz table. Both the maitre d' and I rushed over to find two people, standing together. They were holding on to each other, crying and kissing and everyone present was speaking at the same time.

Mrs. Schwartz was a Holocaust survivor who at age 21 had been separated from her family in the concentration camps of Nazi Germany. Brought to this country after the war by distant cousins, her attempts to find surviving relatives were fruitless. Mother, father, and her younger brother were gone. On a July afternoon, in our hotel dining room, she discovered the "single man" at her table was that brother!

For everyone who witnessed it, the reunion was like being present at a miracle. Locked in each other's arms, the sister and brother alternately laughed and wept, periodically pulling away from each other to gaze into the new found face, and then embracing once again. The waiters and busboys, the guests and all of our family stood around them, feeling as if we were part of that miracle, too. We all found ourselves laughing, and we hugged whoever stood next to us. There wasn't a dry eye in the house.

Even as I lived it, I was aware that a decided perk of the "inn world" was the garnering of great stories, all of them reflecting and revealing a bit of the human condition. Our guests would have shuddered, I'm sure, had they known with what scrutiny they were regarded by the denizens of the desk. We were all amateur psychologists and developed a sixth sense, which was helpful in handling the crowds. The late-night postmortems of client behavior certainly added to our education, our interest, and yes, to our entertainment!

It is good to be able to report that the "people experience" was a positive one, that in a sadly deteriorating world of victims and villains, I can look back at a host of patrons with a great deal of affection. Even in the touchy realm of finances, we had a surprisingly good track record with the people who stayed with us. We were very vulnerable to cheats, if there were any, since we operated in the days before credit cards became the payment of choice. We accepted checks at the end of guests' stays, and had a good number of people who sent their room and board charges after they had returned home. We never took license plate numbers or checked addresses, since there just wasn't sufficient time or staff to do so. And of course, it just isn't possible to "take back" a vacation. Yet, in all the years, we suffered only minuscule losses.

While they were mercifully very few, I do indeed remember the people who left the premises without the formality of paying their bills. One such incident was reported to my mother. The couple left very early in the morning, but the housekeeper brought to the office an upper denture, in a glass of water, which had been left behind. The law precludes innkeepers from holding any body part such as artificial limbs, or even eyeglasses, and certainly false teeth, to guarantee payment. When we received a call from the "skips," asking about their property, my mother suggested that they return, pay the bill, and that she would then "look for" their lost item.

There was one annoying trait that too many guests had in common. It was their absolute certainty that they understood our business. Not only did every accountant, teacher, and manufacturer feel qualified in the hotel industry, but they were more than willing to share their suggestions with us, with or without invitation to do so.

At the hotel of a friend, one persistent gentleman followed his host all day, constantly voicing his unsolicited thoughts on the possibility of a golf course, the advisability of additional rooms, a change in the menu, or extra entertainment. The hotel man, Willy Horowitz of the Olympic, tired of the lecture, so he found a way out. "Look, my friend," he said, "you are making all these valuable contributions of your ideas, and I may forget them. Please write down everything you want to tell me so that I can consider your suggestions in a quiet time." When he checked out a few days later, the critic/guest left an entire notebook, closely written, with his commentary on every facet of the hotel!

Known for his droll humor, Willy was prone to a straight-faced gag for his own amusement: Springtime brought "shoppers" (prospective guests) to our mountains who booked family accommodations for long stays. As in many businesses, rates were quoted, and in some cases, negotiated.

One warm May day found the area inundated with "lookers," many of whom flitted from hotel to hotel seeking the best deal. There were those who barely glanced at the property, concerned only with the cost. Even a seasoned hotelkeeper grows weary, eventually, of too much *handlen* (bargaining). So after being questioned by a rather pushy woman, Mr. Horowitz made the following offer: "The room will cost $1,000 for your entire family for an 8-week season, but——you must make your decision *right now*." The potential guest answered that she would just run to her car to consult her husband who was waiting there. Since the legitimate price for the accommodation would have been over $2,500, the husband replied enthusiastically to "grab it." When the hapless wife returned to Mr. Horowitz with an affirmative answer, she was told, "Too late! I told you that you had to decide *right now*!"

Perhaps our most distinguished guest was Benjamin Cohen, the great advisor to Franklin Roosevelt and a U.N. representative from Chile in later years. That world-renowned diplomat checked in late for his first night in residence at the hotel. His wife and children had arrived earlier, but when he got to Lake Huntington it was too late to exchange the double bed in the rooms for twin beds. We did our usual thing—we set up a cot. As luck would have it, the cot collapsed in the early morning hours. I was telling my mother about the catastrophe as she stood with her back to the staircase, from which Mr. Cohen was descending. "My goodness," she said, "you mean the United Nations fell at Green Acres?" Hearing her, Ben Cohen couldn't stop laughing.

I was at my desk one evening, tired and talked out from a hundred conversations. A woman called, after a dozen previous phone meetings, to make final reservations. I started to repeat her vital hotel statistics and began with: "We are holding a room with bath for Mr. and Mrs. Charles Gerber" when she interrupted, "Please," her voice was angry, "the reservation is for *Doctor* and Mrs. Gerber." "Well," said I of the loose lip and questionable humor, "it has been my experience that anyone who insists on the title is a chiropodist." Dead silence on the other end of the phone, and then, "Who is this?" "You'll never know," said I, "we just fired me!"

For every story, there is the opposite side of the coin: I heard a page on the loudspeaker one day, "Telephone for Dr. Ted Newman." The Newmans had been with us for several vacations, and I had never before heard the title, so I asked about it. "Well, you see," said Ted, "my mother was afraid that you and the rest of the hotel didn't know I have a Ph.D.—it was she who had me paged as Doctor."

Our mountain hostelries generated an unusual amount of loyalty, and each property had a remarkable number of guests who returned yearly. Customers did, however, exercise their right to compare. What Green Acres guests rarely knew, was that one of the competition, the Olympic, was owned by my brother and his family. They were not aware, either, that I very often spoke of my guests to them by name.

One family's name was in itself a repeatable item. The Obenzinger family, season guests for several summers, took our least expensive two-room setup in a renovated building. Each of the rooms would have made a reasonable closet, and the bath was down the hall. One spring, they went to the Olympic to compare. The description, to my brother Bob, of the accommodations at their previous spot was one of a "charming two-room suite." They never mentioned the name of our hotel. Imagine their surprise when my brother said, "Oh, sure—I know the hotel and the building—it was once a chicken coop!" As Bob intended, Green Acres did not lose the account.

Guests were sensitive to our ups and downs. One of our observant customers once noted that the size of pets accommodated was a sure sign of a good or bad economic scene. He was absolutely right. We always answered the request to bring along an animal with "yes, if it is small and well behaved." The definition of "small" varied with my degree of nervousness regarding advance reservations. One slowish summer found us with two sheepdogs in residence.

The strangest addition to the hotel family came to us from a guest who reserved for a six-week stay. He took two rooms for his family of five, and then informed us that he traveled nowhere without his pet snakes. The size of the account overcame my overwhelming terror of anything coldblooded that crawls or slithers. To further complicate life, the gentleman had a compulsion to convince the unwilling that they could accept and hopefully come to love the "beautiful" reptiles. He visited the Day Camp to present them to the children, and we thought that was certainly an educational plus. It was when he invaded the office once a week with his serpents in an athletic bag, and offered to let us hold them that I wished I was in another line of work. I've always felt that my surface calm during those encounters merited at least an Academy Award.

The final insult came to us at Labor Day when the snake lover announced sadly that one of his boa constrictors had escaped! He was returning to Brooklyn and leaving us with the hope that the monster would be found. Strangely enough, the snake did show up once again. My husband was crawling under a building to disconnect some plumbing, when he looked up into the malevolent face of the boa. The pet met its end under the wrench Larry was carrying. It was a swift demise for the ophidian reptile. Larry took a while to recover.

If our population thought that any of their activities went unnoticed, they were wrong. Our young bellhops, office staff, counselors, and others were veritable Hedda Hoppers and knew every bit of gossip.

The hotel world was ripe for small "affairs." Husbands were at work in the city all week, the children were cared for in camps all day and by a counselor hall patrol in the evenings. The male staff was ready, willing, able, and young. It occurred to me at the time that I had a great (albeit unusable) line for an ad: "Green Acres : where children enjoy their childhood and adults their adultery!"

Public exposure was rare, but we did have a few hair-raisers. Our Adonis tennis pro was "carrying on" (my mother's description) with a season guest. The affair was discreet but nonetheless had not escaped the office gossip. Night patrols left the corridors at midnight. When the guest's child woke and cried at 1 A.M., friends in neighboring rooms were unable to get into her locked quarters and called the front desk. We entered the bedroom to find the children alone and mama missing. By this time all the children were awake and howling—other parents came to help comfort them—the whole floor was awake, and imaginations ran riot.

Green Acres' day camp, 1960s.

"She wouldn't willingly have left the children alone . . . she's been kidnapped," was one observation. "Maybe we should call the police."

Within a short time the missing lady arrived (in spotless white slacks). Seeing the gathered group she was visibly shaken, and came up with a creative explanation: "I was attacked near the laundry room," she wept. "The new porter came after me in the parking lot and threw me to the ground." Her hysteria increased as she received the sympathy of the assemblage. It didn't take a Sherlock Holmes to perceive that her white outfit had never hit the red shale of our parking area. I pulled her aside and cautioned her: "Change your story, I know where you were." Her peccadillo was an expensive one----for us! We lost the season guest family and were forced to fire the tennis pro. The hotel buzzed for days.

It is my hope that the reader knows these few stories are gleaned from my years and years of contact with thousands of guests. The myriad families who passed through our lives who were wholesome, faithful, and loving, just didn't make for good storytelling around the kitchen table or as tidbits for our friends at season's end. Memory is selective, and it is the unusual guest's tale that stays with us. As for the vast majority of the others, we liked them, we enjoyed knowing them, we even remember them . . . but we have no stories about them.

My brother Bob remembers one wonderful "re-tellable" from his hotel days. A patron was engaged in a season-long "alliance" with a waiter. The "spies" reported that she was rewarding the young man with gifts of her jewelry. When the summer drew to a close, the lady apparently realized that she would need an explanation for the missing gems when she returned home to hearth and husband. She announced to everyone that she had been robbed. "Maybe the chambermaid, or the bellhops are guilty . . . after all they have access to keys," she suggested. There was no hard evidence with which to challenge her, and the talk was not doing the hotel any good.

My brother told the story to one of the acts who was appearing at the Olympic. Mac Murray was a "mentalist," a self-styled mind reader who did a one-man evening of entertainment. Mac was a great showman, but only the most unsophisticated could take him seriously.

Bob asked him to talk with the troublesome lady and try to convince her that he had "read her mind" and knew the truth. It was the entertainer's finest hour—his quintessential performance, delivered, of course, offstage. The woman actually believed that her mind had been read. She checked out quietly the next day.

August was the month (and probably still is) during which New York psychiatrists take their vacations. Our guest list was filled with members of that profession, along with their families. By and large they were a most satisfactory clientele. They were bright, appreciative, a knowledgeable audience for our shows, and the entire family stayed for the whole month! So don't expect any "crazy shrink" stories from me.

There was one set of doctors, however, who did add to our repertoire. Since 30 years have gone by, the "little one" of this story is now an adult, and I have always wondered if she became the creative person whom her professional mother and father were so anxious to produce.

In order not to "stifle" their offspring, they were providing the three-year-old with a world without rules. If she wished to dine on the lawn that was where she was fed. Since brushing upset the child, her hair went uncombed. Long after all the children were asleep, she was in evidence in the halls and in the lobby, followed by the doting mother and father. Counselors were admonished not to frustrate the darling, who carried an oversized stuffed animal to all activities. Our camp director complained that he had a surveillance team in constant attendance behind the trees of the camp area, so we knew the parents never took a break.

Woodland House day campers, North Branch, 1940s.

Actually, we should have expected what we got. In the much reread letter of reservation from the psychiatrist couple, there was an inclusion describing the "type of counselor" we were to provide for their child: "She should be gentle and yet firm, loving, intelligent, and mirthful . . . A free spirit with a sense of responsibility . . . and she should enjoy gamboling on the green with her young charge." As you can see, I never forgot that letter. They were describing the girl I wanted my son to marry.

Hotel income is calculated in rooms and days. An empty room represented a loss of income, the season was limited, and each day was crucial. It follows, therefore, that it was vital that we who did the reservations fill every space when bookings were available.

We knew that even if a room chart was completely filled on Saturday night, there would be a percentage of fallout by Sunday check-in, and on Monday rooms could be vacant. The majority of reservations ran from Sunday to Sunday, so that filling in during the week was rare. That verity led eventually to gambling on the odds and to over-booking. It was a nerve-racking game which I never managed to handle without terror. Mostly, things did work out. Sometimes they didn't.

For one summer week, I had booked a Marcantonio family. They wanted our best accommodation, which was a divided room with private bath and shower in a newly constructed building. The check-in went smoothly on Sunday, but no one dropped out and no one canceled. By late afternoon the only space remaining at the hotel was a room with bath and shower "convenient" on the third floor of the main building. It was that accommodation in which the luckless Marcantonios landed. My apologies were profuse, but they didn't get anything remotely like what they had reserved. It was a great surprise then when an early booking during the following summer came from Richard Marcantonio. I told him honestly that I had never expected to hear from him again. "Well," was the response, "I figure that every hotel follows the same practices. It could happen again somewhere else, but at your hotel it would never again happen to me." He was absolutely right.

A typical lake crib for early resorts.

An experienced psychologist could write a tract on what guests left behind at our hotels. Every establishment had a "lost and found," usually located somewhere behind the front desk. Groundsmen brought us items they found at the pool or on the lawn, and maids returned overlooked items in the rooms. The bathing suits, sweaters, scarves, and the like, were par for the course, but there were, in addition, the more unusual items for our collection. Valuable items were almost always missed and brought a frantic phone call. On Mondays, we wrapped and shipped packages.

Swimming pool at The Olympic, Fallsburg.

Lobby at Kutsher's, Monticello, 1990s.

One Sunday night I got a call at midnight. "Please," said an obviously distraught woman's voice, "Please look in the medicine cabinet!" That was one package which I shipped personally; I wasn't sure my young bellhops would want to handle a diaphragm.

Perhaps the most bizarre forgotten item was never claimed. A prosthetic leg, complete with shoe and sock, was turned in after a disabled veterans convention weekend. We dutifully put it into the lost-and-found box where it got lots of attention from anyone who was sent to look through that container for his or her own lost item. After several months without a call for it, we instructed the bellhops to throw the leg into the dump truck. Within minutes, three worried kitchen workers came to the office to report "a body" in the garbage.

We always understood that checking in was as traumatic for the guests arriving as it was for us. That touted Sunday "day of rest" for many others was our check-in, check-out, furniture-moving, table-seating day. It had all the elements for one of the levels of Dante's inferno.

Managements actually hoped for a cloudy day, so that those leaving would not be tempted to stay for a few more hours and we could have time to prepare for the new arrivals. But there were always those folks who read our prominently displayed "check-out time" as the moment to begin to pack. In a parent-child resort, readying an accommodation for the next occupants involved a great deal of furniture moving. Where there was a single bed in a room, a crib might be needed, or where there was a crib, it might have to be replaced with a double-decker bunk. Until the room was untenanted we could not begin the process. No matter how much we planned, the day was hectic.

When Sunday was finally over, we would have "turned over" half our rooms; welcomed, calmed, and cajoled at least 100 adults; and introduced a like number of reluctant children to our day camp. The "separate but equal" vacation for parents and children could begin.

For our patrons, a two- to-four-hour car trip with little ones had all the charms of root canal work. Rarely was the room ready when they arrived, and the kids were doubtful that camp would be the heaven we promised. When the room was finally ready, the bellhops were busy, the halls were filled with furniture to be moved, parents were tired, and the baby was wet. It wasn't easy to start the vacation that had been so eagerly anticipated.

I am sure that there were many vacationers who would have considered leaving, if they had the strength. The miracle was that it all worked out. The kids went off to camp and the baby was taken by a mother's helper. The room became available and the bellhops checked them in. By the next day they would all love us; well, maybe not all, but most!

Meeting and settling such numbers of people became a fine art, for us and our colleagues. When the last family was housed, and the dining room seating was arranged (with as much concern as for a wedding party); when the lobby was finally empty and we could leave to dress for dinner, then there came a lovely and satisfying feeling of accomplishment and creativity. Maybe not the great American novel, but creativity just the same.

Hotel owners were always of interest to their clients. I think they saw us as a kind of aristocracy, regardless of the size of the establishment. We, in turn, regarded them as king and queen for a week.

One of my brother's favorite stories illustrates how guests made up their own pictures, not only of us hotelkeepers but of our properties as well. During ski season, Bob's favorite spot for meeting the clientele was in his coffee shop. At the Olympic Hotel it was a place from which one could see arrivals and departures and keep an eye on what was happening. On an afternoon during a freezing January, one of his guests arrived in the coffee shop soaking wet, shivering, and with teeth chattering audibly. Clad in a snowmobile outfit, the gentleman was more excited than dismayed at what he would soon describe as an unforgettable adventure. In response to my brother's concern, the frozen guest said, "Don't worry . . . I'm really thrilled. It was my first ride on a snowmobile . . . I took a chance and drove past the sign that said 'lagoon.' But I landed in shallow water and survived the plunge. I guess I'll always remember the day the ice broke when I rode on your lake!" He didn't know, and nobody told him, that there was no lake on the property. "Lagoon," in hotel parlance, is the name for a sewage system!

Perhaps the icing on the cake, and certainly the justification for endless hours of labor, is the appreciation of the guests for whom all our efforts were expended. Jim and Sheila Weinraub and their small David were typical of the young families who stayed with us. You can imagine that, when it arrived, their letter more than made our day:

> Dear Cissie,
> To repeat what I said at the desk before leaving, I feel like someone who has just finished a magnificent novel. I am jealous of the person who is about to pick it up because I know what he has to look forward to. We spent a wonderful vacation with you and left most reluctantly. The Green Acres rest cure was just what the doctor ordered for Sheila, David, and me and it really did the trick. We feel relaxed and at ease. We are deeply grateful to you.

The letter included special thanks to their waiter, counselor, and for the pleasure of the new friends they had found seated with them.

I never did get to be a hotel summer guest in the Catskills, but when all is said and done, I had a good time at the party—even if it was on the other side of the desk!

After meals the staff often engaged in sports with the guests.

Photo by Arthur David Studios.

The Unforgettable Staffs

$\mathcal{T}$HE FIRST SMALL BOARDINGHOUSES relied on family labor to take care of guest populations. The usual pattern was for a mother to do the cooking, and a father to take charge of outside work; assorted children waited on tables or made beds. If there was a staff at all, it consisted of just a few people—a handyman, dishwasher, or kitchen helper, for example. The change in numbers of paid employees, in time, was as dramatic as the growth of the hotels. When it began, our Green Acres resort employed only three or four. The number of staff, when we expanded over the years, grew to as many as 175. They served 300 to 400 adults plus 100 to 150 children, when we reached full capacity. There were times, during a slow week, when staff outnumbered guests! A large proportion of our employees were students who worked in the dining room and the camp. Although there was a small salary, they depended upon tips for the bulk of their income.

A favorite mountain story concerns a middle-aged man who was rushed to the hospital. He needed immediate surgery and was understandably frightened at the thought of an operation. What made the situation even worse was the fact that time made it impossible for him to select the doctor. So when the surgeon approached and looked familiar, the patient began to breathe a small sigh of relief. "I think we know each other," said he hopefully to the specialist. "Of course we do, Mr. Brown," was the reply, "I was the waiter you stiffed at Green Acres hotel!" In reality, the "stiffs" were few and far between, and tips were very generous.

Added to the legions of guests who were refreshed and renewed at our resorts were the vast number of young people who were a large part of our summer staff. There are countless numbers of doctors, professors, lawyers, executives, and teachers who were able to finance their educations because hotel jobs made it possible. For decades, unskilled students had a rare opportunity. They learned on the job, were provided with room and board and a small wage, and with tips, took home enough to cover a year's schooling. There were literally no other industries that could provide what we did here, and every hotel has a long list of grateful graduates. When, for one reason or another, our family had the occasion to visit a New York City hospital, we felt right at home because so many of our staff were "on the floor," looking not too different since they exchanged their waiters' jackets for doctors' coats.

The work was not easy, and the smaller the hotel the harder the labor and the more extra chores expected. Dining room personnel polished the cutlery, prepared vegetables for the salad man, washed glassware, and swept the dining room. They worked a seven-day week and living conditions were at best primitive.

The dining room positions brought in the largest incomes, but jobs as bellhops were also highly lucrative, particularly in an establishment that had an active card room. There, enterprising youngsters literally went into business for themselves. They "serviced" the card games, provided playing cards, beverages, and simple refreshments, and reaped a share of the winnings. The hotel patrons, knowing that they were instrumental in creating careers (many were themselves "graduates" of the hotels) were more than sympathetic to the financial needs of those who served them.

Additionally, guests viewed the young brain trust who provided services as valued opponents on the baseball diamond or handball court, socialized with them and, for the most part, treated the staff with care and concern.

As in every other form of endeavor, it didn't hurt to be bright and innovative. Staff members knew their guests by name and anticipated their requests. We could almost predict what their lives would be like in chosen areas of work by watching them adapt and improvise on the job.

Maitre d' Sam Beytin and the Brickman dining room staff, 1958.

My mother's opening speech to the assembled diningroom staff at the season's start included the admonition: "A good waiter will steal for his guest." There were those who took her literally! Every waiter had a station that included a service stand. It was meant to hold condiments, extra silverware and dishes, and other necessities so that the waiter could save time and avoid running into the kitchen during a meal. There were always some waiters who used that server as an extra larder, and as insurance for the "seconds" that guests might request. They knew which items on the menu would be in great demand, and stockpiled them so that the people at their station would never be refused. We were not unaware of the practice, and knew just which servers to "search" if there was not enough to go around for first servings.

When Labor Day rolled around, $3,000 to $5,000 in earnings for waiters, was not unusual. It was a veritable fortune in those days, particularly since college tuition was nowhere near what it is today.

There were other distinct advantages to summer resort employment, not the least of which was the vibrant social life that came with the territory. The staff were all young, all on the way to or enrolled in college, and they were very much on their own. The hotel's facilities were a wonderful playground with every facility available to be enjoyed "between meals" and after work. Romance was certainly a part of the scene. My favorite aunt, Birdie, met her husband when he was a waiter at Green Acres, and many a counselor and bellhop remember us as the place where they found each other. *Marjorie Morningstar* aside, we certainly had our share of "happily ever after."

Life in the Catskill resorts of yesterday was seen from many perspectives. Owners, struggling to run a business, lived the experience from "behind the desk." Guests knew their vacations as repeated rituals of pleasure. For the youngest staff members, summers at hotels were very often rites of passage. They had heard exciting tales from older friends who had already "worked the mountains." Those sagas, promising adventures of the flesh, were a mighty lure. "Experience" beckoned from the green hills, was eagerly awaited, and made great re-telling for a lifetime.

A former musician shared a forty-year-old memory: At 17, Abe was to be the drummer in a four piece combo playing at a small, very kosher hotel in Woodridge. He couldn't get over his good fortune in landing the job. An older brother, with several seasons of hotel work behind him, had placed Abe in what was called a "pick up" band (musicians put together for the first time for an engagement). The sibling was also the source of many salty stories about amorous adventures with women who were hotel guests.

And so the neophyte Abe was filled with the excitement of his first job, his first time away from home, and the anticipation of . . . his "first time." After all the years that had passed, he remembered vividly the day of arrival in the country. Mostly he was anxious to present himself as an adult, sophisticated member of the entertainment world. A pack of cigarettes, purchased for the occasion, seemed just the right touch. Abe lit up as he stood in the lobby waiting for a room assignment.

It was Friday afternoon of the July 4th weekend. Staff and guests milled around the small front desk. There were laughter and greetings, and a tangible holiday atmosphere. The teenager could almost hear the trumpets sound, announcing the adventures to come. What he didn't expect was how soon they would start!

An "older" woman, maybe 25, approached him within minutes of entering the hotel. "Hi . . . I'm the owner's daughter. Meet me at 6 o'clock behind the kitchen." Abe had all he could do to keep from crowing out loud. His first hour in the mountains . . .and he was bound for glory!

Six o'clock found him scrubbed, shaved, polished, and waiting in the appointed spot. True to her word, "the daughter" arrived and wordlessly beckoned him to follow. Off she went, with Abe in full pursuit, past the kitchen, outbuildings, and baseball field, and finally into a grove of trees behind the handball court.

The young musician's heart beat a furious rhythm. His palms were damp and even the winds of early evening did nothing to cool a fevered frame. He felt a bit nauseous and regretted using the borrowed cologne, which seemed to fill the night with its strong scent.

At last the object of Abe's lust turned to face him. "We're safe here." she said. His feet, unbidden, moved him in her direction. She smiled.

"It's Friday. No smoking at the hotel after sundown. This is where the staff comes for a cigarette."

Each hotel person has a story of an employee who made it all the way to the top and achieved national fame. For us it was a young man who worked his way through college and medical school in our dining room. When he was discharged from the army after World War II, he came back as our first resident M.D. Our family felt as if we were part of the process when Dr. Saul Krugman distinguished himself as the pediatrician who developed the measles vaccine.

The busboy we remember with laughter, however, was not a college boy at all, but an aspiring comedian. At that time, he booked himself into neighboring small hotels for late shows. "Professor" Irwin Corey (the World's Foremost Authority) was to become a sought-after entertainer at the country's smart supper clubs, on television, and on Broadway.

"Professor" Corey was an irrepressible wit, which was fine for the stage, but a source of embarrassment in the dining room. He caricatured the guests, stuck his finger in the soup to see if it was indeed "not hot enough," and clowned wherever he happened to be. My mother would fire him almost daily and my father would drive him to the bus in Monticello. By five o'clock they were both back, my dad convulsed with laughter, and Irwin ready to serve the evening meal.

New York City teachers and administrators, who had summers free, found our mountains a wonderful place for the opportunity to augment their incomes. For the hotelkeepers, those professionals provided a prime source of talent in a variety of positions. Every one of our camp directors over the years came from the city school systems, but so did maitre d's, athletic and social directors, bookkeepers, tennis pros, and musicians. Our summer operations fitted in perfectly with their schedules. Very often the position included a summer vacation for their families, which made the hotel jobs even more attractive.

Dr. Harry Galinsky is a distinguished educator. He is the recently retired superintendent of schools from Paramus, New Jersey, as well as a member of national panels on education, by presidential appointment. Dr. Galinsky credits his success to the "people skills" honed to perfection by half a lifetime as a maitre d' for White Roe (Livingston Manor), Morningside (Loch Sheldrake), and Olympic hotels. In all of them he dealt with the trifecta of staff, guests and owners—a formidable job. We were pleased to hear that he applied the precepts learned in the Catskills to his work in public schools.

"Hotelmen taught us," said Dr. Galinsky, "that the whole operation is customer centered. The owners insisted that it was the job of every staff member to give the guests what they wanted. They insisted that we send vacationers home happy and fulfilled, insuring their return the following year. I sought to inspire the same concept for my school staff. The 'customers' are the student body. When we give students what they want and need and ensure their success, it is the equivalent of the guests coming back."

When Mac Weiner (White Roe) heard of Harry Galinsky's great achievements in education, and his considerable salary as an administrator, he wrote to his former employee: "What good is it," said Mac, ". . . no room and board!"

Anyone who has been in our business will testify that, come spring, the phone was alive with calls from distant cousins, ex-guests, and assorted acquaintances. It was then that we began our hiring for the coming season, and there was a good deal of competition for the summer jobs. People with the slightest connection to a hotel owner did not hesitate to use the "in" they had or thought they had.

After the obligatory "how-are-the-family" questions, the real purpose of the calls became clear. "I have a son/daughter, nephew/neighbor who needs to work." We did our best to accommodate them. Our employment policy (created by my mother) of "family first" was not to be trifled with, and her broad definition of "family" brought us a host of young folks whose relationships were never quite clear. To this day I wonder how some of those "cousins" became cousins! In most cases, things turned out fine; in some, we lost the employee and the relative.

One young man was a disaster as a counselor. Our camp director fired him. While we, as owners, took the privilege of hiring, we never countermanded a department head when he found an employee to be unsatisfactory. In this particular case, the firing was certainly merited since the relative decided to swim in the nude in the children's pool during camp hours! It was our thought that he may have been sampling drugs, and even my mother didn't suggest placing him in some other department. We sent the young man home and haven't heard from his parents since.

Interviews for the summer staff were conducted at the hotel. It seemed as if every 18-year-old applicant claimed a work history of 10 years. For the dining room there was an acid test for familiarity with the serving process. "What's a monkey-dish?" we asked. For the uninitiated, a monkey-dish is a small saucer for dessert or fruit, and the terminology is used by everyone in this resort area. When the applicant failed to know the answer, we knew he had never served in any Catskill hotel.

In the departments where college students predominated (dining room, camp, front office), all hotels suffered from late August departures without notice. Even now I remember the frantic feeling, when, despite my pleas, there were those who wanted to take a break before returning to school.

The first port of call for replacements was nearby camps whose season was at least one week shorter than ours . . . the pickings were slim. Then we resorted to drafting remote relations and the children of our friends. The staff got younger and younger as we became more desperate for warm bodies to carry us through Labor Day. It was during one of those late August periods that an applicant, staying nearby with grandparents in a bungalow colony, was hired as a busboy. Kenny had applied (to our maitre d') a dozen times during the preceding weeks and been refused. This time, though he was underage and without experience, there was no choice. The boy was ecstatic; it was the moment for which he had waited, a rare opportunity to work and be considered for the next season as well. Day one on the job found him enthusiastic and excited. His station included the family table.

I was finishing lunch with a friend, when our brand new employee began to clear the dishes. A half-empty bowl of borscht slipped from his hand. It seemed half *full* to me, since the red liquid landed squarely on my head and dripped from my hair onto the white jacket I was wearing. What remained of the beets ended up in my lap! The terrified busboy fled into the kitchen to tell the maitre d', Arnold Wagner, that he had "spilled borscht on a guest." Arnold rushed into the dining room to see what had happened, and then returned to the youngster waiting in the kitchen. "It wasn't a guest you got," said he. The busboy breathed a sigh of relief. Arnie laughed, "You got the boss!"

Operating our business only for the warm weather days created the necessity of "opening" and "closing." Those are small words that stood for endless toil, hard wear and tear on the buildings, and considerable expense. That reality also provided labor for an itinerant group of people who were the staffs who accomplished the miracle of a renaissance for the ailing structures in which we did business. Initially, they were recruited from the employment agencies in our area and in New

York City. After a while, each hotel developed its own crew that arrived without fail as the snows began to melt. They were, for the most part, alcoholics, separated by hard living, idiosyncracies, and bad luck from the families they once knew.

The spring staff became part of our lives, a kind of extended family, and we were to them the closest thing to a real family that their lifestyles permitted. We knew that winter was over when Blackie and Jimmy, Gordon and Joe, and a host of others, showed up at our doorstep with their "matched luggage"—two cornflake boxes.

Had I had the occasion to meet any one of them on a dark street in the city, I probably would have run screaming in another direction. Blackie, for example, who was typical of the genre, was missing most of his teeth, scarred, and weatherbeaten. His scent was of the cheapest wine available, and his one set of clothing had never seen a laundromat. To us, he was somehow not fearsome. We ate together in the winter kitchen where my mother cooked the meals and was "Mom" to the entire entourage. We thought nothing of giving him the keys to everything, and welcomed his stories of travel and adventure.

On one occasion, during the winter, my mother was on a New York subway when one of the spring crew entered the car. He was in the getup to which she was accustomed: a torn jacket, battered hat, fly held closed with a safety pin, and carrying the inevitable bottle in a brown paper bag. We will never know what the rest of the travelers thought as he barreled his way toward her shouting "Mom, mom!"

Everything I remember of those lost men was gentleness and friendship, and while there were many times that they fought each other, I cannot recall any incident when they were threatening to any member of the family. Either my husband or I could separate two hulking drunkards, disarm them if they were holding weapons, and consider the incident "par for the course." That group lived their lives on the lowest rung of the ladder but practiced a unique code of honor toward us. When our children came along they were treated with a great deal of love, protected and entertained, and gave back to "the men" an affection that was sorely missing in their lives.

The motley crew that readied us for summer was inordinately talented. They were painters and plumbers, carpenters and gardeners, and those who were not specialized, were cleaners extraordinaire. The job was difficult. Buildings in which they worked were cold after the long winter and the weather had caused untold damage. All of our pipes were above ground, so the first order of business was connecting the plumbing that had been drained in the fall. It was not an unusual sight to see water spouting from the windows of a cottage, where one connection had been missed! Year after year our itinerants accomplished "the opening" and were an integral part of the operation. Few made it to summer. Payday found them at the local saloons where they drank up their wages or were cheated out of them. As surely as the winter gave way to spring, however, we knew they would be back.

Not all of the maintenance staff was imported. There were numbers of local people who worked with us for all the years we ran Green Acres in Lake Huntington. Among them was a giant of a man, a Polish Catholic who had lived with Jewish families long enough to learn a good colloquial Yiddish. His appearance was almost stereotypical of how city folks imagine a farmer. He wore denim overalls, plaid shirts, and completed the outfit with a pair of some guest's discarded sneakers. He made them fit by cutting out the toes. During the season Jake was in charge of the tennis courts, which were clay and required daily rolling.

He was hard at work one blistering day when two guests strolled by the courts. One of them remarked: "*Dus is arbet for a meshuggener*" (That's work for a madman). Jake, the unexpected linguist, replied at once, "*Ver geharget!*" (Get killed!)

Such a bucolic-character was the natural recipient of questions on anything pertaining to nature. It was assumed that he knew a great deal about the weather. Jake was consulted on all occasions by the director of the children's camp when planning for picnics or other outings, and he always obliged with what proved to be accurate weather predictions. The notable exception took place when the whole camp left for a day at the Delaware River and was rained out. "Jake," the director chided him on their return, "what happened?" "I don't know," replied Jake, "my radio said fair and sunny!"

If the guest list provided us with a host of memorable characters, the staff more than matched them. "Big John" was our handyman of long tenure. For years he was our only 12-month employee, lived on the grounds, and became part of the family. If anything, he proved to be overprotective of our interests. One summer found him obsessed with the notion that the waiters and busboys were stealing food from the dining room. In reality, most of the young people did take something "for later" and it didn't upset us.

John took to guarding the rear exit of the dining room, playing sleuth. The staff, knowing his pattern, took to wrapping empty boxes to carry out. They delighted to let him "catch" them only to unwrap loot that wasn't there.

Grady was our lobby porter who heard me complaining about the number of blankets that went home with our guests. He took it upon himself to help me. On Sunday afternoon, while the departing guests were having a final lunch, Grady assiduously went through their cars, removing anything that could pass for a bedcover. I returned to my office to find a huge supply of throws, coverlets, baby wraps, and blankets. Some actually did belong to us, but I had no way of returning the rest.

The aristocracy of the hotel staff, and the ones treated with "kid gloves" was the kitchen crew. It always seemed to me that hotel people who handled those prima donna chefs, bakers, and salad men developed the skills to qualify themselves for the United Nations. To be fair, work in the kitchen was grueling—hot, pressured, and relentless; but, in addition, the "stars" of the hotel firmament understood just how vital they were to the operation, and permitted themselves some "acting out."

Joey Keesler, Rose Rosenberg and the head chefs at Green Acres.

Shawanga Lodge, Bloomingburg.

There was one salad man who threw tuna fish when he was upset. We had to be grateful that he took it out of the can! Chefs routinely "punished" waiters by sending them to the back of the serving line so that their guests were forced to wait. If challenged, those chefs were not above throwing a knife or two. Our own son, when he was a children's waiter, said that he began to answer to "little bastard," which was the only name that the salad man had for an employee! Tempers flared and fights were not unusual in the kitchen, but the meals always went out. Just on the other side of the swinging doors, the guests had no clue of upset or delay, and dined serenely.

Most of the chefs at seasonal resorts in the Catskills journeyed south for the winter and worked in Miami Beach. Because we could not offer year-round employment, each season found the hotels in competition for those professionals. Their skills were an integral part of our reputation. While competition for services made salaries high, once satisfied with the work of chef, baker, or salad man, the owners made every attempt to keep him. In many hotels the relationships lasted for years.

My brother Bob's chef, Mr. Brown, was an African-American, skilled in creating the cuisine of a Jewish-American resort. Brown spent the summers at the Olympic and the winter season in Florida, where he was employed at Miami's Lord Tarleton Hotel. The owner of a Cadillac, the chef's trips from north to south and back again were never uneventful. Time after time, in the southern towns through which he traveled, he was pulled over and ticketed, for no reason other than his color. The answer was found for a safer passage. He donned a chauffeur's cap and was no longer a target.

The syndrome of complete immersion in the business went beyond the immediate family to include the employees with whom we worked. Nowhere was this more true than with the office personnel. We spent endless hours together and either directly or indirectly owners "telegraphed" their constant worries and concerns. Bookkeepers, for instance, were privy to the calendar of notes coming due, mortgage payments on tap and taxes looming. One such office worker, Lila Ginsberg, told me that she would wake in the night, filled with apprehension about "the payables."

Life in the office had many frantic moments. The phones rang constantly and the front desk was never without guests who had requests or complaints that had to be addressed. The volume of mail to go out was always monumental; brochures had to be sent as soon as an inquiry arrived. The menus for the main dining room needed to be mimeographed, and it was imperative that the chart of room reservations was kept current. It was a time before computers eased the load, and everything was done manually. Check-in day, on Sunday, found all hands on deck and there were never enough hands. We asked guest arrivals to come at 3 P.M., when there was a chance that their rooms would be cleaned and ready. They began to arrive from 10 A.M. on. The lobby was full of impatient people, and the front desk workers had to deal with them. They all became skilled in calming, welcoming, and solving problems on the spot. The hotel wisdom was that if someone called down for a roll of toilet paper, "Don't go through channels—grab one and run up to the guest's room with it!" The guest who phoned to say "If I don't get more hangers, I'm checking out," just needed a quiet voice to assure him. If all else failed, we knew that "this too shall pass."

At Green Acres, the office staff, was generally very young. Our accountant once asked me how I could trust "children" to handle such an important segment of the operation. In truth, they lightened my day with their humor, were for the most part remarkably efficient, and provided the empathy that helped ease the stressful times. The bookkeepers, cashiers, front desk workers, night clerks, secretaries and switchboard operators, along with bellhops who shared the office space, forged friendships with each other and with me. I look back with pleasure at the time we spent together and treasure the friendships that continue still. My secretary, Josephine Ruderman, will remember that she was not only in charge of all the correspondence, but served as my in-house psychiatrist as well. When I reached "the end of my rope," her answer was a cup of coffee and something fattening, to provide a peaceful moment. It worked, although I had a hard time fitting into clothes after a hectic week.

A sense of humor was almost a prerequisite for office work in a hotel. The young people in ours, led by my daughter Amy, coined names for everyone as one of the ways to break the tension. One inept typist was known always as "Sheila Stupid"; a guest couple were "Mr. and Mrs. Applesauce" (they called with messages for the dining room every day to make sure that fruit accompanied their meal); and still another client couple was dubbed "Dr. and Mrs. Concord" because they told us over and over that they preferred the premier resort, but came to Green Acres for the children's program.

One young man eventually became our "superintendent of service," which at Green Acres meant that he did practically everything. The job included supervising bellhops' schedules, manning the front desk, filling special guest requests, and driving to town for mail and any other supplies we needed. But there were always the extra emergencies that found him fixing a lamp when the handyman was not available, changing a bed, showing rooms to a prospective guest, and answering the phones. He really functioned as my right arm. Starting with us when he was 15 (we thought he was 18), he worked at Green Acres through all his college years and until he received a master's degree. Dr. Mark Meyerhoff is today a distinguished professor and consultant to industry. I tried to talk him into staying in the hotel business!

Perhaps the greatest pleasure that a retired innkeeper has is reunion with the "help" (and that is what they were aptly called) who come back to visit. It is great to be told of the positive impact we made on their lives. It is more than gratifying to hear of the doors they feel we opened, and their lasting warm memories of us and of our hotels.

A letter from a former waiter at the Brickman Hotel, shared with me by Ben Posner, speaks to that "big plus" of hotel keeping. Lawrence K. Feitell, now a New York attorney, says, in part: "My mind is still an album of sharp and wonderful images of the Posners and their staffs, as we went through the summers of 1951, 1952, and 1953. Murray and Ben impacted deeply upon all of us. They were loving caretakers of a place, the things of that place, and a rich treasury of human beings whom they recognized as such. (They) brought many good things into the lives of a staggering number of people who worked at the Brickman. For this they are entitled to lasting admiration and deep respect."

It is impossible to remember every one of the staff members who shared our lives in the hotels, but whenever someone looks familiar to me on a busy street, I feel sure that they once held a tray, carried luggage, or manned the swimming pool at Green Acres. I'm not always right, and can create an embarrassing moment for myself. A good number of years ago I was entering Singer's restaurant in Liberty, when I spotted a tall, imposing dark gentleman. Certain that he had been a former employee, I greeted him warmly, and he smiled a greeting in return. It was not until we were both inside the cafe, and his presence created a stir, that I realized I was looking at Joe Louis who was training at nearby Grossinger's!

Staff members who returned season after season were, of course, unforgettable. Our in-depth sharing of the hotel work in a compressed time frame created special relationships. They weren't related by blood, but they were certainly another kind of family.

A very young Billy Crystal as part of a trio----Green Acres, 1970s.

Part 3
Our House is Your House

There is a "union" of hotel women who alone know of the headaches, the heartaches, the bunions and, yes, the benefits of the resort world. They are a special breed unto themselves, even though labor is non-sexist and the whole family is overworked. Rarely are guests privy to life behind the scenes. Hotel families commit themselves to providing guests with a perfect world.

On reflection, it doesn't seem a bad way to spend a lifetime.

----Helen Kutsher
Kutsher's Country Club

From my first job as a social director at the Biltmore Hotel in Woodridge, to my first booking as a "comedian" at Jebaltowsky's Mountain View Hotel in Summitville (for $15) and through the ensuing 32 years and thousands of "mountain" jobs later, it is love pride and warmth that I still feel for the Catskills.

----Freddy Roman
Producer of Catskills on Broadway

Elmer, Rose, Robert and Esteria "Cissie" Rosenberg.

Cissie and Larry Blumberg, 1946.

A Family Affair

OUR CORPORATE NAME was The Elmer Rosenberg Family. Although we did not incorporate until after my father's death, the spirit of the name existed from the first days that we remember on the hotel property. While certainly it referred initially to the nuclear group of my mother, father, brother and myself, it was to increase easily when I added a husband, and later as the children arrived.

There were, in addition, the extended family . . . those who shared our premises and our lives in the business. I think that every resort became a gathering place for kith and kin. My dad was an only child, but my mother had four sisters, all of whom, with their families, spent varying amounts of time at our "house in the country." My father described the situation: "You can't throw a stone without hitting a sister-in-law!"

So my little cousins grew up with us, my aunts and uncles joined the stretchable "family table," everyone had some job, and we all had an in-depth lesson in togetherness. The aunts worked the front desk or managed a camp dining room, uncles were social directors or solicited business in their home towns and visited on weekends. There were seasons when one or another family member ran the coffee shop or the bar, and as the cousins got older they joined the office or dining room staffs.

Most of the experience was a joy, but where is the family without one maiden aunt who contributes an opinion on every facet of your life and business, without being invited to do so? We had an aunt Sarah who filled that role. It was my mother's concern for making her sister feel needed that found Sarah as the assistant to the hotel's housekeeper. Our overzealous relative doled out linen to staff as if the survival of the hotel depended upon her economy. For years the waiters, busboys, and counselors were tortured over their use of sheets and towels by the J. Edgar Hoover of the linen room. Arguments on the subject fell on deaf ears. Mother's sister remained autonomous in "her department."

It wasn't easy for our parents, their peers, or for us, to raise a family while running a hotel. In order to operate, we were forced to make the business central to our existence, and right or wrong, it absorbed us completely. I realize now that any and all of the families involved in our kind of innkeeping were in danger of becoming dysfunctional. Having ourselves been raised in the hotel, we were more conscious of keeping our priorities straight. The business was inexorable, however, and for all of the years that our children were small, we were conscious of being pulled in two directions.

My mother, when I was an infant, reported that she actually forgot to nurse me often enough and found, at the end of my first summer, that I was bordering on rickets! Hearing that story filled me with sorrow for her. She was the most devoted of parents, and to have in any way neglected me was an aberration and a symptom of a relentless job.

On one spring weekend, my own first born, Paul, fell and injured his leg. He was 18 months old and refused to leave the shelter of my arms for the babysitter whom we employed. It was one of those times in the off-season when I was standing in for a maitre d' and attending to my duties in the office. I checked in the house and seated the dining room——holding my child in my arms.

Those were the days when we employed no office managers or superintendents of service, when there literally was no one who could take over. Indeed, the small- to mid-size hotels never were able to afford layers of management.

The guest list was made up of young families like our own. Most of them were empathetic to our position. There were notable exceptions. During a packed August week, our baby daughter, Amy, awoke one morning with a large lump under her chin. She had a dangerous staph infection that needed to be treated in a hospital and I was there with her throughout a Saturday night. On Sunday we checked in the house. Leaving her nurse-maid with the baby in the hospital, I came home to register the guests. By that time I was exhausted and unnerved and managed to really confuse the check in. I apologized to those I had discomfited and promised to remedy any mistakes by the next day. Everyone seemed to understand except one lady who complained, "This is my vacation and I don't really want to hear your problems." That was enough to bring me to tears for the first time in the grueling experience. Much as we needed every client, and as little as we could afford to be "independent," I took that woman's name off the mailing list.

When we originally took over the management as young-sters, Larry and I were not professionally trained for the jobs that we assumed. Our early procedures were either those used by our parents, or were created as needed.

Accountants tore their hair over the chaos of spring record keeping before bookkeepers arrived in May. Business practices defied Wharton School standards. Particularly difficult for my mother was the concept of keeping staff records for the crew who came and went in the early spring. Our CPAs had to deal with small pieces of paper, labeled "Jake the drunkard" or "Blackie the painter," and guess as to where they lived or what their deductibles were. It was certainly creative book-keeping, and to this day I wonder how the records were ever straightened out. I was too timid to chance the errors. When I became a manager, we hired bookkeepers to start much earlier. My mother wondered why.

For years, no family member was on the payroll. We had one checkbook that took care of the hotel and our personal lives. It read like a family tree—father, mother, brother, husband, and I all appeared on the printed checks. It was my dad who suggested that we just say "to whom it may concern." Of course, the actual signing of that bank instrument took a family conference to determine if there was something to withdraw.

My mother's reservation "system" was carried in her head, and it worked for her, after a fashion. My improvement was using charts drawn on the back of menus or file folders. When I first viewed our friends the Pauls' "store-bought," color-coded, wall-hung reservation charts that cost several thousand dollars even in those days, I was inspired to use **colored** menus and file folders! Through those early years we developed prodigious memories backing up all the systems that, in time, would evolve.

To be sure, there were mistakes made. On one occasion it almost cost my marriage. One season we employed a baker who lived just a few miles from the hotel. Although he was a temperamental misanthrope, the gentleman created diners' delights with dough. My husband gave him a small, seldom-used guest room to sleep in when he was too tired to return to his home. On one very busy weekend I goofed and rented it. Sandor, the baker, found me at the desk at midnight and handed over the keys to the bake shop. An outbreak of cholera would have been less devastating! I think that Larry promised Sandor that I would be swiftly punished, or perhaps banished. At any rate, the baker's services were retrieved and I was saved. Still, we didn't laugh about the incident until the season was over. So absorbed were we with the details of the business that larger events around us went unnoticed. All of our consciousness was directed toward the operation of the hotel.

No matter what our occupancy happened to be, resort overhead was relatively constant. Taxes, insurance, debt reduction, electric service, advertising and the like were the same. So the one area where economy could be practiced at all lay in labor. If it was humanly possible, the family did the jobs.

There were literally not enough hours in the day and certainly there was no time for the community service and political action that were our wintertime pursuits. No wonder that my teen-age son described me as "an activist—in the off-season"!

It is difficult to chronicle the effect of stress on one's priorities. So compressed and pressured was our season that what might have been day-to-day problems in any other endeavor were traumas for us. Larry and I tried to "run away" for small bits of time, if even for a cup of coffee off the grounds, so that we could touch base with each other and regain our perspective. Unfortunately, those times were few and far between, and it was difficult to maintain a marriage. Looking backward now, I wonder that there were few if any "break-ups" among the hotel couples whom we knew.

The family had the advantage of a seasonal operation for a good number of years. While it was an economic liability to operate a business for such a short period, the months of being closed afforded us time to be a normal family. We were fortunate, too, that Green Acres catered to families. Our children attended the elaborate day camp for which we were known, giving them creative summers when we were at our busiest. Most young hotel families employed a childcare worker to augment whatever camp facility they had, and to see to the "off hours" when parents were not available for bathing, times of illness, and dressing.

Maybe a saving grace of the occupation was the fact that, when they became teenagers, we put our children to work. If there were hazards to growing up in a hotel, there were also decided advantages. Spared from parental over attention, the children developed independence, a work ethic, and the ability to "meet the public."

Not too long ago, I had the opportunity to speak with a contemporary of mine, raised as I was, in a seasonal hotel. It surprised me that she expressed a deep hostility to the life that I looked back on with satisfaction. She retained none of the pleasant memories that I could muster, nor was she interested in any way in the "remembering" in which I was engaged. I would guess that parent-child relationships, in whatever mileau they take place, are as diverse as the personalities involved. Regardless of a parent's occupation, the difficulties of communication and empathy with one's offspring are legion. Raising a family in a hotel world only made them more so.

Opening time, April and May, was a particularly difficult period for me. In the early days, all of our reservations were garnered through a New York office. When ads were placed, prospective clients called back to a local New York number. Originally, the phone was in an aunt's Manhattan apartment, and later, in the space provided by our advertising company. That meant spending at least part of the week away from home to follow up the inquiries and sell the rooms. When our first child arrived, I hated leaving him for the weekly trek to New York. The little one was left with his grandmother, his father, and a nanny, but he cried when I left and I wept all the way to the city.

In the mid-1950s, the phone company developed a wonderful new tool that allowed the metropolitan world to reach us at the hotel for the cost of a local call. It made a Manhattan office obsolete and enhanced bookings, but most of all it allowed me to work at home in the spring so that I could be with my children.

Because it was a new service, there was a large time lag between ordering the line and its installation. We placed ourselves on the list as soon as we knew that a New York line was obtainable; it was the year that a second child was expected—

and then we waited and waited. When our daughter was born at the end of December, I called frantically about the probable date for the phone installation, hoping that it would coincide with the placements of our first ads in April. At one time, speaking with a phone company executive, I pleaded, "I would never have had this child if there was any question of a delay on getting the N. Y. line!" "Lady," was his answer, "that's one thing you can't blame on AT&T."

The line did arrive on time, I was able to work at home, and a new taskmaster entered my life in the form of a ringing phone with a potential customer as the caller. From April until June, at which time the staff came up for the season, that reservation line was mine alone. Potential guests, reading our ads in the *Post* and *New York Times* during the spring, had no idea that they were not calling a formal office. They called, of course, at their convenience. Six o'clock was the witching hour. My children shriveled in the tub and my dinner burned while I tried to sound blithe and convincing to the inquirers.

Children see things differently. When our son was about four years old, someone asked him what his parents did at the hotel. He answered that his Dad worked very hard keeping everything fixed, and that his Mom had fun talking on the telephone!

Particularly in small resorts, husbands and wives split the responsibilities. The hotel was more or less divided into "front of the house" (reservations, advertising, entertainment, hosting), and "back of the house" (kitchen, purchasing, maintenance). Since I grew up in the business and was aware of the hazards, I carefully distanced myself from "the back," sentencing my husband, Larry, to that area. It was he who mastered the intricacies of food delivery, and the skill of managing the crews, as well as the mind-boggling technology of air-conditioning, heat, water supply, pools, and construction. He earned the respect of his crews by working with them. One day I found Larry, with a few men, in a muddy ditch, trying to reach a clogged pipe. He looked up and asked, "Are you sure this is in the job description for the president of the corporation?"

Larry loved a good story. These days we tell stories about him.

Our lobby porter, Grady, who had been with us for years, appeared to have gone beyond alcohol to drugs. I discovered him, on one occasion, wielding a hammer and destroying his prized automobile. Having some small knowledge of psychology, I told my husband that the decimation of a favorite possession was tantamount to suicide, and that we should get Grady to the mental health clinic at once.

Larry reassured me, "Don't worry, what he is breaking up is still our car — I loaned him the money to buy it!" The family teased Larry, calling him the "Bank of England," but he only smiled and continued to fund the staff. Our daughter remembers the times that the doorbell would ring and a vaguely familiar person would hand her some cash, with instructions to "give it to your Dad, with thanks" from Marty, John, or Jack, depending on the year.

As with most of the hotel owners we knew, my husband was self-taught in all aspects of management and in technical know-how as well. He soon became a master of all the trades that kept our buildings useable. Always indefatigable, he put in endless hours and energy. We begged him to get a worthy assistant to provide some relief from the slavery, particularly when the summer crew was gone. Finally he set off for the employment agency to hire the carpenter/handyman/plumber who would make his life easier. Larry was back in a few hours. With him was the gentleman of choice, whose left sleeve hung empty at his side. "My God, Larry," I whispered, "how could you have hired a one-armed handyman?" "I had to," was the answer, "no one else would give him a job."

Larry had a profound respect for labor, and for those who labored. In all our years we never heard him issue a direct order. The preface was always, "Would you do me a favor," or "When you have time."

There is a bromide which promises that if you save but one life, you save the whole world. Larry was a lifesaver. He did it by offering his real respect, by taking a chance, and by practicing empathy without condescension or pretension.

Larry Blumberg.

"Papo" was a young Puerto Rican from a New York barrio, who came to us in Lake Huntington as a dishwasher. He was virtually untaught and had a history of gang membership and scrapes with the law. He had as well a brilliant smile and a wonderful gentleness. Larry became the father figure he never before knew. In the years that he was at Green Acres, Papo became a trusted right hand, was given the keys to the kitchen, ate at our table in the spring and fall, and was a friend to our children.

Tom was a wintertime busboy, a low man on the employment totem pole, when we operated in Loch Sheldrake. Emaciated and virtually toothless, he was given to periodic episodes of blind drunkenness. We never knew his story but noted that, in the quiet times, he read the *New York Times* and did the Sunday crossword puzzle in ink! Larry became his friend. The drinking times became less frequent.

"I can teach him to be a steward," said my husband. Tom had no trouble learning. Larry arranged for him to have dental care. With a dramatically improved appearance, his whole demeanor changed. He was a good steward and stayed sober. Eventually Tom attended a local college, became a social worker, and is today married, has a child, a good job and a real life.

In a crazy business of overwork and uncertainty, with emergencies a daily happening, Larry sometime lost his sense of proportion (being a perfectionist and a workaholic), he occasionally lost his temper. He never for a moment lost his humanity.

I always understood that my "front-of-the-house" work was at once easier and more enjoyable than the other end of the business. It was I who had the opportunity to spend time with people I enjoyed and to handle the areas that were gratifying. A hotel front manager gets to be the star of the small resort world . . . who can resist being a star? However, I didn't always come off as the lady executive. There was one time in particular, when I was showing a former college professor of mine around "the estate" and frankly trying to impress him with the creativity of my owner/manager position. A guest rushed up to speak with me. It seemed like the perfect opportunity to show my teacher the importance of the work in which I was engaged, and that my mercantile life was both interesting and rewarding. No such luck. "You've got to do something about my toilet . . . it's still stuffed up!" was the guest's message. So much for my pretensions.

Clogged plumbing and complaints aside, the work I did was, to a great degree, both satisfying and challenging. I got to enjoy booking the rooms, selecting the entertainment, writing the promotional material, emceeing on occasion, and certainly dealing with the public. It was the economics of the career that became the worm in the apple. When I became active in not-for-profit community organizations such as the hospital, my husband noted that they weren't too different from the hotel business. "We're nonprofit too," said he, "only it wasn't planned that way!"

The outstanding negative of the hotel industry was the extreme lack of dependability of income. Perhaps every business is subject to ups and downs, but ours was particularly vulnerable. It depended on too many uncontrollable intangibles as well as unchangeable realities. Our industry provided vacations, which represented luxury, not necessity. We were the first victims of any economic dent or recession. Resorts were always affected by the vagaries of the weather, not to mention gas shortages and even illnesses. The hotel owners carried a heavy debt load, and payments loomed inexorably. That responsibility was always in mind, and I never found a way to live with it comfortably.

With all due modesty, our family members were good operators. We projected, we planned, we innovated, we were conservative in hiring expensive staff, and we were on the job from morning to night. The business offered no more security than a lottery. We could never count on our expertise, our repeat clientele, or the formulas developed over the large span of our tenure.

The offspring will remember that Larry took them each year into the hotel kitchen to meet everyone on that staff. Their visit was always accompanied by his brief lecture. "Of course the chef is important, but you can't run the hotel without the dishwashers." Both of our children developed their father's concern and appreciation for every staff member.

When our son, Paul, was only nine, he brought to our attention a situation that we had completely missed. "How come," said he one winter evening at the kitchen table, "how come you believe that all people are the same, but the black people have all the rotten jobs at the hotel?"

We were shocked. He was absolutely right. Our place reflected the times in staff composition----not because we planned it that way, but because African-Americans of that day did not apply for our dining room and front desk jobs. Employment agencies sent people "of color" for jobs in dishwashing or housekeeping. Our guest list was not complete enough to give us applicants who were children of the black clientele, and the population of colleges did not yet include any great numbers of the African-American community. Shamefully, our absorption with our own problems kept us from examining the work force for ethnic equality, and from practicing at the hotel what we fervently believed.

Once called to task "out of the mouths of babes," we were able to begin to integrate our operation. For the upcoming season we contacted every African-American friend we had, and were able to hire an athletic director, as assistant camp director, as well as assorted busboys, waiters, bellhops and counselors. Those who worked that summer recommended their friends in the following years, and Green Acres was never again "lily white" in the good job department.

It was our policy not to employ youngsters under 18 years of age. We made an exception for our children! Our son, starting at age 15, accumulated his college tuition as waiter and "general manager" of the upper-camp dining room. We didn't exactly plan for him to be general manager. . . it just worked out that way! He decided that the department would have no busboys. . . that the staff would be small and split tips equally, and that he would fight for that status quo! I must admit that he was always able to convince us of the merits of any case he proposed. If his doting grandmother wanted to serve him a steak, Paul allowed her to do so, that is if the rest of the crew with whom he worked got the same meal. If he ate steak, they all ate steak.

It was our daughter Amy's great regret that she could not lift the heavy trays that would have qualified her to become part of the dining room staff where her older brother made his "fortune." She did, however, become an A-number-one, front-desk person, mastering every skill demanded in that department.

Our friend, Ben Posner (Brickman Hotel), called one day when Amy was on switchboard duty. He told me later how impressed he was with the bright, warm reception his call received.

"Green Acres, good afternoon, how may I help you?" Ben asked for Mrs. Blumberg and was reflecting on how well I trained my staff, when he heard a resounding, "It's for you, MA-A-A-A!"

Being "the bosses' daughter" could not have been easy for our youngster, but she managed never to take advantage of that position, to be a friend to those with whom she worked, to bring her warm sense of humor to the office, and to be a past-master in dealing with the guest population. Amy developed her own ethic regarding the staff, and it was only after we had sold the hotel that I heard some wild stories about employee antics, which she did not share when we were still in business. Among other things, we discovered that the office had a "salesman" (still unnamed) who did a brisk business in illegal smokes!

My father, early on, was pretty much in charge of planning and oversight in our business, but he was never well enough for specific, day-to-day jobs. He held court in the card room, pursuing his favorite game of pinochle with the guests. One of the guest players was an attorney. That gentleman eventually ran into some trouble in his profession. If I remember correctly, it concerned the sale of some nonexistent property to a client! At any rate, he served a prison term for his indiscretion, and shortly after being released, brought his family to the country for a vacation. Immediately after checking in, the lawyer joined my father for a game. Now, invective had always been part and parcel of pinochle and was accepted as such. Still, I worried about my Dad when I heard his booming baritone intone a favorite epithet as the playing began . . . "In jail you should deal!"

My mother, until the age of 80, was aware of and active in all phases of the hotel. We summed her up by saying truthfully that "what she has forgotten we will probably never learn." Always innovative and interested, she may have been the most progressive member of our firm. It was she who began our program for babies under two, which included supplying individual nursemaids and a special infant dining room. That specialty gave us complete coverage for children, regardless of age. She was always ready to add, to build, and to change things. Her suggestion for serving a complete Italian dinner once a week, complete with Chianti, was a big hit with our diners. When her sight was diminishing, a young maitre d' once questioned me as to how a blind old lady could spot an empty bread basket across the dining room! Her forte was in dealing with the clientele. By instinct and conviction she was able to make everyone feel at home. I am sure that there are guests of ours who still remember her ministrations to them that were well above and beyond the call of duty. Mother felt personally obliged to fatten up anyone she deemed underweight, so it was her practice to call them to the kitchen in the afternoon for nourishing malteds. As for those leaving the hotel, it was her conviction that the ride home was too long to go without food. Honey cakes and sandwiches were proffered to "nosh" on the way.

For most of our years of innkeeping, the management consisted of my husband and me, and my mother. I can't count the number of decisions that we made together, or the emergencies, hard times, and difficulties we faced. It goes without saying that we had differences of opinion, but never, in all the years of working together, did the business threaten our relationship; we just didn't fight about it. Teasing was another story. Larry once bought surplus army rafts for our waterfront, in the pre-pool days when we used the lake for swimming. They were ugly and unwieldy, and my mother and I both hated them. But fortunately they eventually provided an irresistible target for sharp instruments and were sunk by person or persons unknown. From the day of their purchase the rafts were referred to as "Larry's folly," and he never lived them down.

There is a common misconception that hotel keeping is a rather glamorous career and that those who owned resorts were worldly and cosmopolitan. Perhaps it was so for the owners of the large units, but "worldly" didn't describe our family. We ran bars and nightclubs but didn't drink, for instance. Liquor in the homes of my grandparents and my parents was used principally for medicinal purposes. My mother prepared a potion consisting of hot milk, an egg, vanilla, and a shot of whiskey. She called it a guggle-muggle and was firmly convinced that it had curative powers. I do remember, of course, the wine that was served at Passover and for other holidays, but drinks were not ordinarily a part of the hospitality ritual. Our home, on all occasions, was filled with visitors, but I can't recall that any guest was offered liquid refreshments that contained alcohol. Coffee, fruit, and food were de rigeur, but never an intoxicating beverage. So even as adults, the modern custom of a cocktail hour never became part of our routine.

During one summer, when things at Green Acres were hectic as usual, the house physician prescribed a daily drink before dinner for my mother's tension headaches. I'm sure that his purpose was to provide a time when she would sit down quietly, at least for a little while, before entering the kitchen to supervise the evening meal. Mother figured that if it was good for her, it wouldn't be a bad idea for Larry and me to join in the cure. Dutifully, at 5:30, we three bon vivants went to the bar to follow the doctor's orders. It was a great idea for relaxation, but definitely not a plus for our business. By the time the dining room doors opened at seven, my mother was asleep, Larry was reeling, and I was unable to get out of my bathtub which had turned into a whirlpool! Our son heard about the incident, and from then on he described it as his unsophisticated family's "Days of Wine and Moses!"

My brother, Bob Rosenberg, was with us for only a short time after we all left college. He married into another hotel family, and since they did not have a son, left Green Acres for the Olympic. Having rather similar operations, we were at once competitors. That could have created a problem in our relationship, but it never did. For all the years that we "competed," Bob and his wife were our trusted and able advisors, staunch supporters, and of inestimable help. It was they who steered us into a contract with the college when we needed a winter business, secured our first contract with a ski tour operation, helped with the decoration of the hotel, and prepared rate packages for groups when the math confounded me. They even took over our nemesis, Aunt Sarah, when we moved to Loch Sheldrake! We couldn't see much of each other during seasons, but we talked a number of times a day, constantly compared notes, and knew each other's guests by name. Of course, both Bob and his wife, Harriet, could not resist gags using the New York wire. Whenever there was a quiet afternoon, I could count on one of them placing a call to me. In disguised voices, they presented an impossible-to-figure-out (for me) request for a rate quote. On ski weekends when they knew we were overbooked, there was always a call saying: "This is the driver for Greyhound Tours. You have our reservations. We're only a half hour away and need directions!"

As I mentioned earlier, a good portion of "our house" was filled each season by repeat clientele. It was a plus for the family. Our guests' children and our own grew up together and looked forward each year to renewing their relationships. Our patrons developed an interest in us, not only as their hosts, but as people. Maybe that is why they forgave us, in the early times, our antiquated rooms, our less than imposing public space, and the lack of other amenities, which would not appear for many years.

We and our colleagues met more people in a season than most meet in a lifetime. That so many became our friends was compensation for what was sometimes an exhausting commitment.

An incident, which we often repeat, took place on one hectic Sunday during the check-in. The lobby was crowded and noisy with new arrivals waiting for their accommodations. "Last week's guests" had not yet left. One impatient arrival was told that his room was ready, but the bell-hops were all busy. He literally "lost it" and stood at the desk ranting, raging, and threatening to check out if he wasn't taken care of at once.

Suddenly two season guests came to my rescue. "Can we help you, sir?," they said to the shouter. The two volunteers toted the man's massive amount of luggage up two flights of stairs to his room. They accepted his tip. The story was complete when the irate check-in found himself seated at dinner that night with his two "bell-hops"!

VJ Day, which marked the end of World War II, took place during a season. Larry, my husband-to-be, was in the Pacific theater at the time, so my first surge of joy was personal. The occupants of our hotel were predictably euphoric. It was a time to be savored and commemorated. My folks served champagne to everyone and toasted the peace so long in coming. My father delivered a victory address to the assembled guests in the dining room, and the band played patriotic tunes. It was altogether a picture of celebration and delight. But in my memory of that special day, there is another scene that is indelibly etched. I had gone into the kitchen to announce the great news. The chefs whooped and shouted and we all embraced. I headed into the bake shop to spread the word. It was empty of the bakers who had already finished for the afternoon. But there, leaning against the cold, black bake oven, was our second chef, Matthew. A large and burly man, he seemed at that moment to be shrunken and withered. He stood with shoulders heaving, eyes squeezed shut, and silent tears flooding his face. It was then that I found out about his only son, killed just weeks before on an obscure Pacific island.

To anyone "on the outside," running a resort seemed easy. I actually had guests who commented on how lucky we were to be in the country and live in a hotel. It looked easy because that is how we wanted it to look. Now retired, and enjoying "time off for good behavior," I wonder how in the world we were able to do everything that was required. The hotel business was a huge undertaking, and would have been more appropriate for large corporations than for small families.

Before we entered into contract to sell Green Acres in 1975, we called both of our children to offer them the property. It was a time when the very hard times were already behind us and of course they would have been entering a ready-made business when they finished college. Their answers were unequivocal: "No way" . . . loud and clear.

We understand why the children chose not to follow in our footsteps. There could hardly be a more demanding way in which to make a living and a more difficult milieu in which to be a family. The joy is that Paul and Amy had a choice as to where they wanted to go, and what they wanted to do. Perhaps, reading this, they will have a better idea as to what it took to give them that choice.

*The Nevele, Ellenville. It is still operated by
the same family that began the hotel.*

Just Causes

IN OUR EARLY DAYS of hotel keeping, we were able to count on periods of relative leisure, essentially the winter months, to have time to participate in the life of our community and our world.

The family philosophy was one of activism, but participating in "causes" became more and more difficult as the format of our business moved inexorably toward 365 days a year.

My early memories of family "outings" were of meetings, rallies, fund raisers, and lectures. Even as children, my brother and I understood that we were very often in a minority position regarding political thought. We knew that "marching to the tune of a different drummer" with our Socialist father was going to be uncomfortable. Still, Elmer Rosenberg was the moving philosophical force in our lives, and we believed in him, adored him, and respected his logic and his fervor. We also enjoyed the great esteem in which he was held, and the real recognition he received for his considerable contributions to the world as a labor leader, an assemblyman, and as an organizer and innovator in local organizations.

Our dad was advised by his doctors to be relatively inactive, and was cautioned about the strain of public speaking and organizing on an already weakened heart. Being neither pliable nor self-protective, he rejected the advice and threw himself into leadership positions on a constant basis.

Not everything was controversial or political. He was a prime organizer of the Credit Union, a moving force in the Hotelmen's Federation, and an acknowledged leader in the Fire Insurance Company as a director and president of the board. He convinced our reluctant neighbors in Lake Huntington to utilize the WPA programs for construction of their first sewer system, and, though not religious himself, actively led the small Jewish community in the building of its first synagogue.

I was in grade school when the Civil War broke out in Spain. My father used his talent for oratory on behalf of the Loyalists, long before the world recognized that conflict as the beginning of World War II.

Bob and I accompanied him one night to a rally at the Nemerson Hotel in South Fallsburg to raise funds for the Lincoln Brigade, the American volunteers in Spain. As part of his address, our dad quoted from Abraham Lincoln's famous words on the people and the Constitution: "Whenever they shall grow weary of the existing government, they shall exercise their constitutional rights of amending it, or their revolution-ary rights to dismember or overthrow it." Suddenly the resort's casino, in which the meeting was being held, was plunged into darkness by its owner, Mr. Nemerson. "Rosenberg is talking Communist propaganda," thundered the angry hotel man. "But sir, that statement is a quote from Abraham Lincoln," replied a helper of my father's. "Oh, Abraham Lincoln?" The lights came on!

I'm not sure, after all these years, exactly what position was being sought, but I do remember one particular election cam-paign debate, that took place in Sullivan County. The candi-dates from the Democratic and Republican parties verbally demolished each other without mercy. Each attacked the other on every conceivable issue, and totally ignored the third participant on the platform, who represented the American Labor Party. When my father rose to address the crowd he drew huge applause with his opening line: "I find myself in complete agreement with both the previous speakers!"

One place that welcomed any and all views was the village of Woodridge. There, while there was certainly an assortment of political stances which brought forth passionate rhetoric, we rarely felt any personal attacks or back-biting. As in all things, there were exceptions to those who practiced benign tolerance for "way-out" thinking. My brother and I suffered a bit at the hands of our martinet high school principal, William T. McKernan, after our dad challenged him to a debate to which the educator failed to appear.

My husband and I entered the world of politics locally in the year that we graduated from college and came home for good. It was 1948 and Henry Wallace was running for the presidency of the United States. I had the experience, while in school, to be chosen for a fundraising tour with Lillian Hellman and O. John Rogge. We were heart-and-soul advocates for Wallace, and translated the activity to Sullivan County when we got back.

Larry chaired "Farmers for Wallace" and I was the leader of "Women for Wallace." Our most difficult task was finding halls in which to meet. We slated one rally for a hotel/bar in Jeffersonville that was threatened with destruction by the Veterans of Foreign Wars, the American Legion and the Fire Department. It was the mayor of the small community who came to our aid. Frederick Schadt was a man of fairness and courage. He arranged police protection for the meeting, which was held without incident. Those were the times in which violence toward dissenters was a very real possibility. We had heard about a peaceful concert by Paul Robeson in Peekskill which ended in a melee while troopers looked on. To discover a neighbor who didn't necessarily agree with our candidate, but who defended our right to do so, was heartening for those days.

It was a long and stimulating campaign, complete with a meeting in Monticello that filled a movie theater. An audience of a thousand came to hear author Norman Mailer and baritone Kenneth Spencer. Henry Wallace lost the election and went into obscurity, but Sullivan County brought in an 11 percent vote, which was remarkable for a third party in our area.

The following year I ran for the Senate (on the American Labor Party ticket) against Katherine St. George, who was endorsed by both the Democratic and Republican parties. There was no expectation of victory, but an election campaign was an opportunity to reach people with our alternate point of view on issues of the day. With McCarthyism in full bloom, there were few opportunities to voice any opposition to the powers that were. It is hard to know if we indeed changed any minds, but we certainly made the effort. When, some years later, the following story made the rounds, we identified with it: During the Vietnam War a lone dissenter appeared each night outside the White House in Washington. He carried a candle and a sign to protest the conflict. It is reported that he was asked, "Do you really think you can change the administration of this country?" "I'm not sure," said he, "I'm trying to make sure that the administration doesn't change me."

My mother, always the optimist, was a bit nervous whenever I participated as a candidate for elected positions. She wondered how I could assume a governmental job and do the hotel's spring mailings from Washington! Succeeding years found me in many campaigns but I never held public office.

We had another minority political entity in Sullivan County, the Liberal Party, which was often the kingmaker in local elections. Sam Chonin of Woodridge was its chairman for many years. The Liberals supported Franklin Roosevelt from the 1940s on. Years after her husband's death, Eleanor Roosevelt was a guest of honor at a reception to which Mr. and Mrs. Chonin were invited.

Rosie Chonin was a tiny, birdlike woman, who had spent years of long hours at intensive labor in the family luncheonette. Political receptions were a bit out of her experience, and she was understandably nervous as she waited on the receiving line to shake such a distinguished hand. Our delegate to the United Nations stooped down to greet her admirer. Rose Chonin looked up. "Oh," said she, "Mrs. Roosevelt, I've heard so much about your husband!"

In the years that we lived with our young family in Lake Huntington, Paul and Amy attended a central school in Narrowsburg, eight miles away. Our children, a generation after me, were in a learning institution that still had not been sensitized to the needs and rights of minorities. It was still a time when religious education took place during the school day, even though not on the school property. It was a time when school Christmas programs featured nativity scenes and were conducted by clergymen, and when only Christian holidays were celebrated with school closure. It was however, legal for us to remove the children from school for Jewish holy days. I must admit, having no one to check on me, I made up a few. I'm sure that the principal, Mr. Sullivan, is still trying to find out when and why "Shnikadick" is celebrated.

Our daughter, in the second grade, informed us that she was sure her teacher, Mrs. Bain, was Jewish. Her reason: "When the other kids leave for Catholic classes, only she and I are left in the classroom."

The principal of the Narrowsburg school was a decent man who was "doing business" as he had always done. When I complained about the religious nature of the Christmas festivities, he did what he thought was fair, and gave me equal time. That wasn't what I had in mind, but I scurried to put on a Chanukah program. When our son found a similar situation in the Boy Scout program, sponsored by the school, I complained once again. That time I was told by the scoutmaster to "pull him out" if I wasn't happy.

My really serious conflict with school officialdom came during the bomb shelter and "duck-and-cover" hysteria that was everywhere during the early years of the Cold War. I received a note from the school telling parents that since the school district couldn't afford a shelter, children would be "sent home in the event of atomic attack." The question I was to answer was where to leave my children if I wasn't at home. To make a point on the futility of making plans for a disaster that could not be contemplated, I answered that they were to "keep them." It didn't endear me to school administrators, but did lead to permission for me to address the P.T.A. about peace as an alternative. I was then president of the parent organization by virtue of a lot of hard work, and because no one else wanted the job.

A carefully written speech, garnered from the *Christian Science Monitor*, and without any buzzwords, regarding the absolute necessity of working for a world that rejected atomic weapons, resulted in charges by an administrator, of "giving aid and comfort to the enemy." I forced an apology for that one, and apparently reached the assemblage on some level, for I was reelected as president of the P.T.A. that same night.

My children did not suffer unduly as Jews. Anti-Semitism certainly existed but was not as overt as it had been during my childhood. Our firstborn came off the school bus one day during his first year at Narrowsburg Central and burst into tears. To our concerned questions as to what had happened, he replied that "one of the big boys called me names." To Paul's surprise, we smiled broadly to discover that the epithets were "stinker" and "little runt," totally acceptable to us instead of the religious slurs we had feared.

The atmosphere in western Sullivan County was one of extreme conservatism. Still, it was shocking to discover that the vice principal of the school our children attended was also the head of the John Birch Society. Larry and I determined that we would move the family to Woodridge for the academic year. We both remembered the extreme comfort and freedom of expression that existed in that small town, and we wanted our children to enjoy it as we had done.

While it certainly had many drawbacks as a means of making a living, a career in hotel keeping had one powerful plus. It allowed us to be politically independent. We were the customers in the area where we lived— the buyers of goods and services. The hotel's patrons came from other locations. Our "radicalism" or "eccentricities," if they existed, were quickly forgiven for the best reasons of economic opportunism.

At no time was that fact more appreciated than during the infamous days of McCarthy and his vigilante committees. The nation was in their grip from the late 1940s into the late 1960s. History records, during those decades, the destruction of careers and stringent application of economic sanctions against those who held and expressed so called un-American views. "Un-American views" were any philosophies that did not conform to the majority opinion expressed by those in office.

While we may have felt some social ostracism for minority political positions, including being "prematurely" against the war in Southeast Asia, our economic lives were never impacted.

The debacle of the war in Vietnam has finally been recognized, but those who opposed it at its inception were subject to the rage and disparagement of their neighbors. The mountain villagers were no less convinced than their urban counterparts that the "peaceniks" were unpatriotic.

A group in Sullivan County (Committee for a Sane Nuclear Policy) banded together to bring Benjamin Spock, the famous pediatrician/author and antiwar activist, to speak in our area. Once again, our largest problem involved securing a meeting hall. As fast as one was booked, its owners received veiled threats of violence or withdrawal of patronage, and the meeting place was canceled.

The Peace Committee decided to appear before the county's governing body, the Board of Supervisors, to ask for the use of a public building in which to gather. I was one of the speakers presenting the request. With me were two teachers from our local community college. They, not being natives, drew most of the fire as "outside agitators." After all, they hailed from New York City! We presented our request; then came the speakers who opposed our right to meet, at least in a public building. Most vituperative among them was a World War II veteran who appeared wearing his medals and overseas cap. Redfaced and angry, he questioned my patriotism, slammed my association with the "interlopers from New York," and suggested that I "go back where you came from." Having stated my case, that's exactly what I did.

We had recently begun business in Loch Sheldrake and were in the process of getting the "new" hotel ready. Among many other improvements, we needed to build a children's swimming pool. I was worried about being late for an appointment with a pool construction company representative who was coming from Monticello.

I sat at my desk. The pool rep arrived. Much to my surprise (and his), it was my opponent from the morning meeting at the government center, without his cap and medals this time. I invited him to have a seat, but got right to the point. "I really don't think you want to build a pool for us," said I. He reddened. "Well, business is business," he began, and added, "and we have great prices." "Would you believe that I don't want your pool... even if it's for nothing?" I answered. "That's taking economic sanctions," he thundered. "Damn right!" said I.

The Spock meeting was held, and successfully. We met in Rock Hill, at Bernie's Holiday restaurant, one ownership that did not bow to threats.

After our hotel fire, and in the turmoil of beginning again in a new location, we had for the most part, been politically inactive. I think we were repoliticized mostly by our children, who began to pick up the cudgels. They were in the vanguard of youngsters who put themselves on the line, taking a strong stand before their seniors caught up. To us, it was their finest hour.

So we found the time for the marches and the meetings, the trips to Washington and New York, and the demonstrations in our own towns----but never in full season and never on a weekend----and that was true for every like-minded hotel-keeper.

Our risk in being politically active against the war was really only a social one. It was embarrassing to sit down on the street in front of the Draft Board, and to be mocked by our neighbors. Dr. Spock shared with us his own feelings of discomfort at being physically carried away from a demonstration, and being accused of "betraying our troops" who were overseas. So pervasive was the patriotic fervor and the concept of "country right or wrong" that the nation was literally cut into two camps. The tide began to change as more middle-class youths were either drafted or in line to be taken into the army, and as hopes for a military victory dimmed. The atmosphere across the country eased a bit toward the dissenters. The marches became larger. Still, on an occasion when Larry and I appeared before the school board for permission to lead the young people on a town-to-town protest walk, we were accused of being against the conflict "too early"!

It is sadly ironic, in 1995, to have former Secretary of Defense Robert McNamara's confession that the Vietnam War was "terribly wrong." If we needed one, it could be called a vindication for the position that "the doves" took in opposing that conflict, and that the secretary of war did not voice when it could have made a difference. At this distance in time from all that took place, it is almost macabre to think of the lives that were lost or disrupted, the pain of a writhing nation, and the lost illusions of a generation.

We have never lost sight of the fact that our ownership of a hotel as a means of making a living created the opportunity to act on our beliefs even when they were unpopular, without fear of job or income loss.

Our father was a font of quotations, and many of them remained with us. One that he repeated often was from

Clarence Darrow: "As long as the world shall last there will be wrongs, and if no man objected and no man rebelled, those wrongs would last forever."

And so, while we hope that our decisions to speak out would have been the same, regardless of the consequences, we never did have to face that challenge.

"Challenge" may have been the key word to use for just living in this century of change and disruption. It didn't seem to matter much in which line of work people found themselves, there were enough inequities to go around! Still, whatever the problems happened to be, there was one half of the population that faced them along with an extra burden. Things were harder if you were a female.

I came of age in a society that had never heard of "women's lib." Not only was the phrase as yet uncoined, but even the discussions that took place around our kitchen table did not include or recognize women's problems, or the discrimination that they faced on a daily basis. This was in a socially conscious family, which agonized and empathized with the downtrodden of all descriptions. This was in a family that was fiercely proud of our father's history and of the "radical" legislation that he introduced in 1917, which became the law of the land during the Roosevelt administration.

The world in which I grew up boasted of only two women who were attorneys and one who was a dentist. To my knowledge there was not a single female physician within a two-county radius. In my mother's circle of friends, only one woman drove an automobile.

The hotel industry reflected the times by consigning almost all women to the nether world of the kitchen or housekeeping departments. Even if a woman had the "privilege" of working in the front office, it was inevitably the male member of the family who represented the hotel at the board tables of the insurance cooperative, credit union, board of education, hospital, and the Hotelmen's Federation. In every hotel there was a woman who was an integral part of the operation, but the trade organization was called the Hotel*men*'s Federation.

I do not point a finger only at the males of the time. The women, then as now, more than 51 percent of the population, categorized themselves. They did not visibly struggle against their second-class citizenship; they accepted what was a minority position. Perhaps most insidious of all was the female self-image that assumed that there was a *head of the household*, and she was not it.

In all of the business world of those days, women accepted less pay for equal work. Hotel workers were no exception. Janice Harrison (Brown's Hotel) told me of her experiences working side by side in the hotel office with men who received larger salaries than she, while both performed the same duties.

This resort community used its work force regardless of gender. Women "enjoyed" the same 12-hour days and 7-day weeks of labor, whether they were hotel women, shopkeepers, or farmers. "Help mate" had a special meaning in the area. So it was not work that was denied but status.

There were exceptions to the rule. A very few women were the "featured" members of their firms, even way, way back. Jennie Grossinger and Lillian Brown come to mind as the recognized owner-managers of their resorts.

Logically, given the time's mindset, even a woman's volunteer efforts were in the less prestigious organizations. It was the age of the Women's Auxiliary and the Ladies Aid—separate but not so equal. Most service groups, from church and temple, to hospital and fire department, followed the unwritten law: Men made the decisions and women supported them.

In the early days, Jewish doctors were unable to get placement on the staffs of the existing hospitals. It was a group of women from Monticello who pioneered the construction of the first county hospital to remedy that situation. Yet, once launched, and after countless hours of fundraising, the women were consigned to support organizations, and an all-male board directed the hospital's life for too many years.

It occurs to me that, even now, in this day of so-called liberation, I know of only a sprinkling of fire-women, and it is only in the last few years that the Rotary, Kiwanis and Lions, broke their all-male constituencies.

The women of my growing-up years were measured in terms of how white were their whites or how shiny their kitchen floors. Like their sisters in other areas of endeavor, hotel women expected of themselves that they would do any and all jobs that the inn demanded, keep a perfect home and be in full charge of the children. At best it was a killing troika of responsibility.

It was Ann Richards, former governor of Texas, who made the wonderful observation: "Ginger Rogers did everything Fred Astaire did----but backwards and in heels!" Certainly the hotelkeeping women did everything their husbands did.

The generation of women who preceded mine was nothing short of heroic. They waded into a strange hotel environment, mastered it, and grew with it. Like their pioneer foremothers, they walked where no one had gone before.

My own mother was a dress designer in New York City before her marriage. She had literally no experience with food preparation, staffs of rough men, buying in bulk, or systems of operation. By the time I was old enough to notice, she could cook for a crew in the spring, supervise the opening of the property, hire an orchestra, and handle reservations, along with a thousand other chores.

We knew from early childhood that my father was not well and that all things aggravating were to be kept from him. It was my mother who charged herself with solving any and all problems. And yet, her deference to my father was almost palpable. If she created an innovation for our operation, she managed to credit him with it. "Daddy says," or "Daddy thinks," was always her introduction to a new idea. It took a long time to recognize that my dad created master plans and dealt with community work, but it was my mother who was the backbone of the hotel. Like her, the women in the field had to fight for respect in their own bailiwicks.

I was most fortunate in that, to a large extent, my personal experiences were not a mirror of the times. Father, brother, and husband all encouraged my active participation and opinion in the home, the business, and the world. The world was not as accepting, and looked askance at a female in charge—a woman on a "man's" board," an "aggressive" woman. It was a time when men apologized for their weaknesses and women apologized for their strengths.

Popular wisdom of the time even suggested that it would behoove a woman not to appear to be too smart, lest she diminish her appeal to a future husband. The very qualities or talents that propelled men to successful careers were suspect when evidenced by a woman. It took many years for salespeople to acknowledge that a female could make decisions. Time after time they would come to the desk and, finding me there, would ask for "your father," or later, "your husband," when seeking our account. Such an introduction never got an order! After a while, salesmen got the message. It even took a long time to establish some authority with working men on the property. There were many incidents when my instructions were ignored until my husband seconded them.

I represented our hotel on the board of the Hotelmen's Federation when my dad passed away. I thought attitudes might be changing. At one meeting of the organization, after I had spoken, I was taken aside by Arthur Winarick, owner of the megalopolis Concord Hotel. "You are just the person I've been looking for," he said. "You are a decisive manager personality. I need people like you." Flattered, I suggested that since our hotel operated only in the summer months, I was available for the rest of the year.' 'Can you type?" was his instant response.

My one decisive victory for feminism came when I ran for a seat on the board of directors of the Cooperative Fire Insurance Company. After I had announced my candidacy for the

Lake Huntington territory, I was told that of a 24-member sitting board there were possibly two who would support me and that the others would actively oppose me. Not only had a woman never served, but there had never before been a female candidate. A committee visited our home to ask my husband to run instead . . . keep the job in the family! The group, composed of men in their sixties and beyond, worried about my ability to examine a property (too frail), or my powers of decision making (too young). What would happen if I became pregnant? How could I do the job? And how in the world could they conduct business with a woman in their midst?

One aged director met each member of the organization as he entered the hall where the annual meeting and the election were being held. "*Vote nisht for de madel, ze ist a reyte*" (Don't vote for the girl, she is a red), he cautioned. Who else would run for a "man's job"?

Fortunately for me, the decision lay in the hands of the membership, and among them were some active supporters. I will not soon forget the wonderful Mrs. Celia Meyerson, who stationed herself on the road between Woodridge and Mountaindale, stopped cars that she recognized were on their way to the meeting, and asked the occupants to "Wote fa Cissie"!

My ace in the hole was the annual meeting itself, packed as usual, and the uncommitted voters, many of whom were women. I can't say that I was elected by a landslide, but elected I was. So great was the consternation at possible defeat by a female that I was never again opposed in an election. I serve to this day.

There was a sweet ending to my opposition by the board, however, and I knew that I would be accepted after I attended my first board meeting. Joe Posner (Brickman) was the chairman. He had known me all my life and, once I was elected, made sure that I would feel welcome. He opened the meeting with: "Gentlemen . . . and lady darling!"

I have been comfortable with my fellow board members since that day, and have always been gratified at how well we work together. They soon discovered that I would not turn their world upside down. Even though I insisted that they must not call the women who worked in the office "the girls," and proclaimed that I would never serve the coffee, I was accepted. Our differences, such as they have been, never involved the question of gender.

No one doubts that the only constant in our lives is change. While the battle for equality is by no means won, the changes have been monumental, in the nation and here in our mountains. What has changed most is women's view of themselves. The consciousness raising of the 1970s and 1980s led to struggle against a chilling status quo and it brought results.

Eleanor Roosevelt said that "no one can make you feel inferior without your consent," and that consent is no longer given. Many doors have swung open. The professions now accept both sexes, denigrating humor is passe, and old definitions of femininity have been discarded along with girdles and spike heels. Women are learning to support each other and to break down barriers in the work place, the home, and the community. Yet, with all the victories that have been won, it is still true that: "Whatever women do they must do twice as well as men to be thought half as good. Luckily that is not difficult!"

The struggle for equal acceptance continues on many fronts, but during my lifetime a new "ism" emerged that continues inexorably. Ageism, aside from the waste of talent and wisdom that it causes, is yet another divider of our population, and is difficult to combat. One wonders if perhaps the problem lies in fear. The biased are not afraid of turning black or Jewish, but they know that if they are to have a future they must get old, and the aged are a reminder of that inevitability. Of course, this culture has put a mighty premium on youth. It is the time of hair dye and the facelift----for goodness' sake, don't look your age! My father used to ask, "Is it some kind of virtue that you were born after I was?"

Part of the answer, I think, lies in the attitude toward work and status. While my mother, for instance, was still in the hotel business, she was accepted by everyone around her as the senior member of the firm. When we left the hotel she lost the authority, the involvement, and some of her self esteem. There was a subtle difference in how the world treated her, and her comment was an old Yiddish adage: "If three people tell you that you are drunk, you have to lie down!" Hopefully, there will be enough of today's mature citizens who refuse to "lie down"!

Dr. Benjamin Spock and the author.

Photo courtesy *Times Herald-Record*

Let Us Entertain You

THE ENTERTAINERS who started their careers in the Catskill Mountains had a lasting impact on the entertainment industry in the United States and in the world. Dore Schary cut his teeth in the theatrical world as a member of the social staff of the Flagler Hotel before he became chief of Metro-Goldwyn-Mayer. His boss at The Flagler was the producer and playwright-to-be, Moss Hart. Don Hartman performed skits and led activities at Grossinger's in his youth. His later career wasn't too shabby; he headed Paramount Pictures!

Dory Schary, Moss Hart, and Don Hartman were not alone in finding an early proving ground at the Catskill resorts. Danny Kaye started at White Roe, Jerry Lewis at Browns, Sid Caesar at the Avon Lodge, and the Ritz Brothers at the Ambassador. The list of comedians who honed their craft at Catskill hotels includes Red Buttons, Alan King, Jackie Mason, Milton Berle, Buddy Hackett, Billy Crystal, and Robert Klein. Of course when they played those hotels, they were far from household names.

But guests didn't come to the small hotels to be entertained by stars. They looked forward to the prospect of being diverted,

Above:
Danny Kaye
and Red Buttons
with Jennie
Grossinger, early
1960s.

Left:
Jerry Lewis with
Lillian Brown.

amused, and having just plain fun. Only the biggest resorts, like Grossinger's and the Concord, built their reputations on shows featuring nationally known entertainers.

I can count on my fingers the calls from prospective guests asking who would be singing or telling jokes during their vacation. Vacationers expected that their evenings would be full, and they were. The young singers and comedians who entertained our guests already had the talent, but they didn't yet have the famous names. Danny Kaye was merely one member of the social staff at White Roe, not a featured player. Mack Weiner of White Roe remembered arguing with his father over the $10 per week that Kaye was paid. His father thought it was too much. Danny Kaye offered to entertain at John Weiner's bar mitzvah; Mom Weiner vetoed the suggestion. "Too dirty," said she.

When the boardinghouse business first emerged in the mountains, entertainment was impromptu and self made by the early guests. Just plain good talk on the front porch evolved into charades or a bit of dancing to a phonograph. Owners organized mock marriages for their patron's amusement, or hayrides or campfires. Always anxious to make sure that the population who visited them were diverted, the hotel people began to seek professionals who would create memorable evenings. Members of the trade in Fallsburg remember an African-American fiddle player who would go from place to place providing Yiddish music for a small sum. Little by little, entertainment as a concept developed, and the Catskill resorts initiated full-blown programs that became synonymous with the area. By the early 1930s, most hotels advertised nightly shows and dancing to live orchestras.

Social staffs, in those early days, were hired for the entire season. Hotels would hire a comic, a straight man, a soprano, a tenor, a dancer or two, and sometimes even a scenic designer. A social director pulled it all together and very often brought some of the staff with him. He was at once the emcee, director, actor, producer, and very often the comedian.

Talent was developed to its fullest in our mountain resorts. After all, diversions had to be provided seven nights a week. The small staffs had to call upon all their creativity and ingenuity. If something worked, it couldn't be repeated----guests stayed for many weeks and would remember the first success. The accomplishments of those social staffs were monumental.

Shows were first performed in simple surroundings; the theater could have been the barn. When the barn was painted, it became the "Casino," a little more renovation and it was the "Playhouse." Finally, night clubs were built as the days of the resident social staffs were coming to an end. In the larger resorts they were elaborate and highly touted. There was the Moulin Rouge at the Ambassador and the Fiesta Room at the Flagler. Brown's had the Brown Derby, the Waldemere featured the Oval Room, and the Nemerson boasted the Penguin Club. The Pines called theirs the Bamboo Room and at the Raleigh, the night club was simply the Raleigh Room. For the smaller establishments, which were the greatest in number, casinos sufficed.

Early entertainment included concerts, plays, revues, dance recitals, champagne hours (dance contests involving guests), amateur nights, hayrides, game nights----all directed by talented, ambitious little troupes. When additional actors were needed, everyone was pressed into service. My father once starred in Odet's *Awake and Sing*, and I was thrilled to take any child part available.

There was always "a band music," as my grandmother termed it, and the hotelkeepers were ingenious in adding to the possibilities for talent from other departments. My mother told me that when she did the hiring she rarely asked a prospective waiter if he could carry a tray. "Can you sing?" was the question.

For vaudevillians, out-of-work actors, and aspiring performers, our mountains provided a rare opportunity to work, to learn, and to practice. Auditions were conducted in New York City at a place called Nola's Studios. There, the Sol

Nite club at Green Acres.

Huroks of Fallsburg, Swan Lake, Hurleyville, Lake Huntington, and all the small towns, were tested in yet another endeavor for which they had no preparation.

When my turn came to be an audition *mavin*, resident staffs were a thing of the past, and only the orchestra remained to be hired. I still recall my absolute discomfort sitting in an empty hall and requesting the few dance tunes with which I was familiar, while attempting to look knowledgeable. That my mother and father, and their contemporaries, who were without any background for the job, could put together a social staff, and do it so well, remains one of the great mysteries for me.

In time, the casts my parents chose became predictable. If a blond singer tried out with any song in Hungarian, she was sure to be chosen by my father. If a comic told an off-color story, he was rejected· by my mother. She, incidentally, had the dubious distinction of turning down Danny Kaye in his bid for the social director's job. Pointing out that he had not yet met

Sylvia Fine, Kaye's wife and his writer, my mother was unrepentant.

Always starstruck, I spent a myriad of summer afternoons in the Casino watching rehearsals. I remember our social directors, Murray Rumshinsky, of musical fame, Michael Rosenberg, the remarkable actor from the Yiddish stage, DeMay and Moore of the nightclub circuit, Arthur Lessac, now famed as the creator of new pathways in voice and speech, and Herby Faye, an old-time vaudevillian who years later had a new career in television on the *The Phil Silvers* [Sgt. Bilko] *Show*. They shared the stage with memorable singers, dancers, and musicians who brightened our resort world.

People often talk about the hotel *tummlers* (the word derives from the German *tummel*, "tumult"). The image that comes to mind is that of a slapstick and ever-present entertainer doing pratfalls or falling into the pool fully dressed. That may have been an apt description of a few of the social directors, but it certainly is not what I recall. Such personalities existed, but they were hardly standard for every hotel. Social directors and those with whom they entertained were memorable for their versatility and diversity of style, just as the resorts were as different as the personalities of their owners. The hotels' entertainment reflected the tastes of the people who ran them. What we all had in common was the desire to please our clientele, to make them feel special, and to send them home with wonderful vacation memories. That was the universally accepted definition of hospitality, and hospitality was the hallmark of our business.

The casinos, early entertainment halls of my youth, were an attraction to the populations of the local bungalow colonies who had not yet begun their own programs. Some bungalow colonies even advertised the facilities of the hotel next door! Since seating space was limited, a member of the hotel owner's family stood at the door to make sure that the hall was not inundated with "outsiders." As a teenager, that was my assign-

Eddie Cantor discovers Eddie Fisher at Grossinger's in 1949.

ment. There was one sure sign of the nonguest: the bungalow colony "crasher" carried the definitive dead giveaway—a flashlight!

In the 1940s, the social staffs of my childhood were abandoned in favor of acts booked by agents for single performances. The Charlie Rapp Agency, Beckman and Pransky, Leonard Jacobson, Henry Stern, Jack Siegal, Phil Cutler, Aaron Totter, Jack Fink, and many others sought out the talent that would grace our stages. A hotel owner planned the summer's entertainment, selecting from the names submitted by the agents, but it was rarely possible to really know who would actually appear until the agents' lists were complete and they could accommodate all their accounts. The singers, dancers, and comedians circulated among the many hotels. Once the bungalow colonies became large enough to add their own casinos, they too used the talent agencies for their shows. There were always the tried-and-true acts, but the newer and younger "stars to be" filled out the resorts' vast entertainment schedules. The proving ground tradition that began with the early resident staffs continued. Some hotels, including the Brickman, featured late-night shows where new talent was showcased.

"Unknowns" including Bette Midler, Billy Crystal, Alan King, Robert Guillaume, Orson Bean, Melba Moore, Richard Belzer, Steven Landesberg and Freddie Roman, performed on the Green Acres stage. At the Olympic, my brother remembers "trying out" Lenny Bruce and Jackie Mason. The composer of television and movie scores, Billy Goldenberg, was Bob's band pianist as a teenager. Paul's had Van Johnson on staff, Jan Peerce was at the Commodore (Swan Lake), Robert Alda was at the Plaza (Fallsburg), and Jerry Lewis started as a bellhop before going on stage at Brown's.

There were over 500 hotels, each with at least one band, whether it was a 3-piece combo or a 10-man orchestra. Every hotel had some form of entertainment. It was an unprecedented opportunity for the showbusiness world to find work. Davey Karr, a popular comic of the time, kind of summed it up: "Laugh," said he, "it's good for you . . . and it will help me finish my basement!"

During the late 1940s and 1950s, when the House Committee on Un-American Activities reigned in the headlines, many performers were blacklisted. Deemed unhireable by most filmmakers, club owners, radio stations, and other media, those performers found that they were welcomed on Catskill hotel stages. They were willing to work, at that time, for what we could afford to pay.

Established stars such as Zero Mostel, Hershel Bernardi, Larry Adler and Paul Draper, Irwin Corey, Martha Schlamme, Bernie West, Jack Guilford, Ellie Stone, Phil Leeds, and a host of others, brought us top-of-the line entertainment.

We enjoyed a touring theater company with stars like Howard da Silva, Kurt Conway, Kim Stanley, Lionel Stander, Loretta Leversee and Phoebe Brand, who presented productions of Broadway caliber.

Entertainment continued in the mountains even after the hotel shows and dancing were over for the night. There were clubs such as the Wonderbar in Old Falls which featured gay revues, the Rainbow Gardens in Monticello where Sadie Banks and Roy Gobey reigned in midnight splendor, the 52 Club in Loch Sheldrake, and the Cozy Corners in South Fallsburg where Belle Barth shocked audiences——and packed them in.

With the arrival of the 1950s, hotels added late late shows to their own schedules. Started by the Roxy in Loch Sheldrake and the Laurels in Sackett Lake, the idea caught on and spread.

For entertainment, much as for food, the Catskills were subjected to preconceived notions. It wasn't so much the performers, but rather the agents who determined that our audiences were to be treated as a special group. The talent agencies were convinced that no singer's repertoire was complete without a Jewish song for a Jewish audience. If the performer happened to be an African-American, and he donned a *yarmulke* (skullcap) for a rendition of "Yiddishe Mama," we were supposed to be swept off our feet.

Our audiences were essentially urbanites. They were the same people who patronized Broadway theaters and nightclubs. Treating them with that kind of condescension was just not acceptable to some resort owners. Our guests did not need or want special entertainment for their ethnicity. When I made that point early on, there were those agents who accused me of being anti-Semitic. It was difficult to explain to them that I loved Yiddish when it was part of a program, but that I objected to its being "pulled in" as a ploy. I literally "lost it" when a

A word from the world's foremost authority, "Prof." Irwin Corey.

singer announced, "I'm a *shikse* (Gentile woman), but I will do a number in Yiddish." Audiences have heard non-Italians sing in Italian, and Americans sing in French and they were never surprised. Why then should it be "cute" for a non-Jew to sing in Yiddish?

The new system of booking through agents was to produce a *kupvaytik* (headache), which every owner experienced. While there was no great demand during the week, on Friday and Saturday nights all the hotels competed for the same pool of singers, dancers, and particularly for comedians.

To meet the need, the practice of "doubling" or in some cases "tripling" was born. That meant the entertainers did two or three shows in one evening, commuting across Sullivan and Ulster counties. The trouble was that the agents who made the arrangements were not necessarily skilled traffic managers. Very often they were completely unrealistic about the actual distances and too optimistic about the time needed to travel between hotels.

Jackie Horner, a dancer, describes harrowing trips at breakneck speeds over country roads, changing costumes in the back of the car, while on the way to a second or third performance. It borders on the miraculous that any "third booking" was performed according to schedule.

When the shared entertainment was a "natural"—let's say from the Ambassador to the Hotel Levitt (a scant half-mile apart in Fallsburg), the scheme made sense. When, however, the double came from Chester's in Woodbourne to Green Acres in Lake Huntington, about 35 miles away, we were in trouble. If the comic was a huge success, he found it difficult to leave a cheering audience. Encores became just one more problem.

On one occasion, in Lake Huntington, comedian Eddie Schaeffer "tore the house down," and he stayed on and on. The double that night was the Waldemere Hotel in Livingston Manor. He arrived at midnight for a 10 o'clock show.

We all took our productions seriously, and we were spending what seemed a fortune. A delay between performers was excruciating, so we asked the first act to stall while the second was on its way. Those opening acts hated outstaying their welcome. Singers could do an extra song or two, but a dancer

Van Harris

had a set routine and couldn't simply throw in an extra dip or twirl to stretch the time.

My brother had booked Morty Gunty on a Saturday night. Opening for him was a tap dancer billed as "Little Buck." Gunty would have been on time but for a breakdown of a freight train in Fallsburg that blocked the way. Little Buck, tired from his routine, did find a way to stall—he told every story in Morty Gunty's act!

In many of the hotel clubs, guests danced on stage before the show began, and a closing curtain was no longer used once that setup was adopted. Again at my brother's hotel, as the crowd danced one Saturday night, a gentleman suddenly keeled over in the middle of the stage. There was a physician in the audience who rushed up to give the man emergency help. The guests stood by as CPR was administered and every effort was made to revive the patient. It was to no avail; the man was dead.

No one left the nightclub. An ambulance crew removed the body from the stage, and within an hour, the show was on! Van Harris was the featured comedian that evening, doubling from another hotel. He arrived in the usual rush, and asked the usual question: "How did the opening act do?" My brother replied truthfully, "He died."

Booking entertainment and spending time with entertainers may have been my happiest time as a hotel owner. After the shows, a hotel coffee shop would be like a scene out of the Woody Allen film, *Broadway Danny Rose*, with owners, agents, and performers sitting around a table exchanging stories. The guests loved the opportunity to *kibitz* with the acts; truthfully, so did I.

When I first began booking talent, my personal preference ran to the more cosmopolitan entertainers. Agent Aaron Totter had his own interpretation of my tastes. He once phoned to tell me of a "find." "Miz Blumberg, I have for you a very intellectial ect. She takes off her clothes, but while she's stripping she reads Shakespeare!"

Myron Cohen.

I very often went overboard in my search for a sure-fire success. Harry Adler, a personal representative for many entertainers, was one of our season guests. His clients, among others, were Myron Cohen and Alan King, and we were offered their services at a discount. While not yet nationally famous, those comedians were part of a coterie of acts who had established reputations as "mountain stars." I could never resist the temptation of presenting such big names and often spent two weeks' budget on one show. Paying large sums for big names and housing their entourages, in the hope of attracting more guests, was a practice that was to hurt many hotels in the years to come.

Booking the Steves and Edyes and the Bob Hopes, rarely generated sufficient income to justify the cost, unless the resorts were among the biggest. The bottom line was that most guests didn't choose a vacation location based on the Saturday night star.

Nonetheless, a bad show seemed a disaster and failures were painful. When a performance was a hit, we were ecstatic, particularly when experimenting with innovative performers who had not yet made their marks, even in our circuit. The time would come when those entertainers appeared in movies, on television, or on the New York stage. It was a certainty then that we could no longer afford them.

Steven Landesberg played Green Acres the summer before he made it big in television as Dietrich on *Barney Miller*. My mother, always a harsh critic, asked me who he was, when Landesberg arrived in our lobby. I told her that he was our featured comedian that night and she turned up her nose. "He looks more like an accountant than a comic," was her judgement. Unfortunately, many of our guests agreed. His style of humor wasn't what they were used to. I booked him again, and again he faced a silent, laughless audience. Steve and I sat down for coffee after his second appearance. Visibly shaken by his dismal reception, he asked, "What's the matter with you? I died here the last time, and you brought me back." I said I knew he was funny and hoped that my audience would have learned something in a month. One year later, his success on TV told me I was right.

Our judgements were not always right, however, and yet we all considered ourselves impresarios. One hotelkeeper is purported to have watched Paul Draper warming up in rehearsal. "Only one dancer?" he complained. "We generally prefer a team."

In all my years of hotelkeeping, I don't think I ever missed a show. It got so that I memorized the routines of many of the comics, but somehow I never tired of them. It surprised me, therefore, when one night, I watched Mrs. Myron Cohen sitting with her back to the stage, knitting during her husband's performance! "I can't watch him one more time," said Miriam Cohen.

The recent resounding success of *Catskills on Broadway* (starring Mal Z. Lawrence, Marilyn Michaels, Freddie Roman and Dick Capri) was an accolade not only for its talented stars, but for all the entertainers, on all of the hotel stages in our mountains. Seeing the four Catskill comics on stage was nostalgic for the former guests, who were more than willing to see it, one more time.

There were some who never did the same show twice. "Professor" Irwin Corey, The World's Foremost Authority, was as unpredictable on stage as off, and always brilliant. On one occasion my mother rose to leave the club while he was performing. She thought she was being unobtrusive, but he spotted her. "There she goes, Rose Rosenberg," said Irwin, "under indictment for creative accounting."

Anne Chester (Chester's Zumbarg) told her own story about Corey. Irwin had arrived early for an evening performance and decided, in his own capricious way, to replace the maitre d' and seat the guests. A particularly heavy lady arrived alone at the dining room door. Corey greeted her, "Good evening, madam. How many are you?"!

From the very early days when D. W. Griffith made his first films in the Catskills, through the decades of social staffs and the agent-produced shows, "the mountains" has been synonymous with entertainment. When our "graduates" became stars and shared their memories of Catskill hotel appearances on television, our national reputation was insured. It remained however, for one dramatic gathering to put us on the international map. If I have one big regret about our 16-hour days as hotel operators, it lies with having missed the biggest entertainment event of the century—Woodstock!

In August of 1969 the assemblage of an estimated 700,000 young people in the small town of Bethel, just miles away from our original location in Lake Huntington, electrified the area. A protest against the Vietnam War, and a phenomenon of its time, such a gathering had never before been seen in ours or any other county.

The symbol for the "Aquarian Exposition" was a dove of peace sitting on the neck of a guitar. The promised entertainment included the biggest names in protest rock and folk music. Joan Baez, the Who, Jefferson Airplane, Janis Joplin, Joe Cocker and Credence Clearwater Revival were an unbeatable combination, all in the country setting of Max Yasgur's dairy farm.

The original announcement was that 50,000 tickets had been sold, but the powerful lure of brilliant advertising across the nation made that early figure a more than vast understatement. By bus, by car, in trucks, on motorcycles or bicycles, and on foot, America's young converged on Bethel, now dubbed Woodstock.

When the crowds continued to arrive, choking the roads and making egress or exit virtually impossible, when the news came of lack of food and medical supplies for the concert goers, the hotel operators and the citizenry rose to the occasion. Food was flown in, doctors volunteered their services, we all sent blankets and other supplies with good samaritans who somehow negotiated the back roads and carried them to the site. Churches and synagogues had crews of volunteers who met the need by preparing portable edibles to feed the vast crowd.

I must confess that my primary concern at the time was that our staff was taking off for the scene, that our guests were having trouble reaching us, and that I was missing it all!

The reports were of great music, nudity, rain, garbage and mud galore, "free love," lots of drugs, and with all that, peace, love, and an absence of the feared crime and violence associated with mass gatherings. If there was one sour note it lay with the inevitable gougers who took advantage of the situation by attempting to overcharge the multitudes for everything from water to a piece of fruit. Happily, they were very much outnumbered by the generous and the concerned, and I venture to say that the vast majority of those who came to the festival remember our citizens with fondness and gratitude.

We innkeepers, so close to the excitement, could only hear and read about it. There was no event important enough for us to leave our hotels. The common wisdom was that if you looked in the dictionary under "workaholic" you would find a picture of a hotelkeeper!

The sentiment for Woodstock, after all these years, remains so powerful that without any invitation

Pat Mareto when he was a standup comic.

or planning at all, thousands come yearly to spend time on what has become almost hallowed ground.

At our resorts, entertainment was not confined to the evening. Hotel owners were determined to amuse and divert their guests during all hours of the day and night. Even the scant hour and a half between dinner and the show had to be filled. In whichever inn you stayed, after dinner the interim programs began. Generally they were conducted in the lobbies.

One lobby favorite, artist Morris Katz, is still on the scene. Armed with paints, an easel, a canvas, rolls of toilet paper, and a sense of humor, he creates "Instant Masterpieces," accompanied by a barrage of patter. His technique has not changed in a quarter of a century, and the works of art are remarkably

*Group calisthenics and poetry readings were among
the many activities for guests at Green Acres.*

similar: perhaps the Wailing Wall, or the New York skyline, a Talmudic scholar or dancing children, all created and framed in minutes and all for sale.

We also had mini art "auctions" after dinner. The innovative entrepreneur who ran the events (with a percentage to the management) has left us with a phrase that we often repeat. He extolled the beauty of a print or etching, and to make sure the sale was made, he added, "The frame *alone* is worth the money!" So much for art appreciation.

Entertainment, in all its forms, was a 24-hour commitment. Our resorts had every sporting facility, and many included indoor pools and health clubs, but still, a rainy afternoon found us scrounging through our files for potential indoor events. Antique dealers, leather workers, flower arrangers, stockmarket analysts, and makeup artists lectured, sold, and added another kind of entertainment to the vacation. Depending upon the hotel, afternoons could be filled with poetry readings, art lessons, or chamber music to while away the hours. Hotels had dance instructors, art teachers, lecturers and storytellers in residence, all doing daytime programs.

On one occasion our teenage son was having a heated political argument with a season guest. "Look," said the guest, "this hotel has a resident physician, a resident artist, and a resident lecturer. Think of me as your resident fascist!"

When the weather was good, sports were the main activities. An athletic staff kept everyone involved. Guests enthusiastically participated in tennis, volleyball, baseball games, hikes, calisthenics, Simon Sez, handball and paddle ball, shuffleboard, swimming, boating, ping pong, and basketball. Everything was available without ever leaving the premises. In later years, individual and community golf courses were added. The hotels were summer camps for adults.

One would think, having grown up with all those sports programs, that I would have become a superior athlete. I never did. I was one of the adherents of George Bernard Shaw's credo,

"Whenever I feel the urge to exercise, I lie down until it goes away!" On the other hand, when we were young, my husband spent whatever time off he could manage on the sports fields. In truth, there was precious little time for owner/operators to partake in the vacation world. After all, we were responsible for providing that world.

In the years since we left the business I have yet to meet a guest who doesn't fondly recall his or her days on our sporting fields and in our entertainment halls. When we have the occasion to visit former patrons, we find prominently displayed, the small trophies won at Green Acres for a sporting tournament or a dance contest. We talk about the acts they saw on our stage, and which of them have become stars.

Guests recall the entertainment, the leisure, the fun, the friends . . . and they all remember the food!

Kutsher's, Monticello, 1990s.

Three Times Daily
Plus Snacks

*P*ART OF THE MOUNTAIN MYSTIQUE in our counties was the delicious and abundant feasts with which hotelkeepers feted their guests. The food service was tangible hospitality. It represented an eagerly anticipated part of our guests' experience, and was a vital segment of any hotel's reputation.

Because, each in it own way, the resorts did such a remarkable job of creating culinary delights, I am particularly stung by the snide criticism that has been applied to our mountain hotels, in current literature, and in the press. One has only to compare the popular view of the "lavish cuisine" served on luxury liners with the critics' word pictures of overfeeding and gluttony at Catskill tables to understand that our best efforts were viewed with prejudice. I am not sure exactly who coined the term, but "Borscht Circuit" was never an accolade. No writer ever called the Italian section of the mountains the "Minestrone Circuit." Sadly, many of our own people accepted that thinly veiled anti-Semitic title, which went a long way to isolate us from the mainstream of New York vacationers. Stigmatization, we are told, is fully realized when those who are being characterized identify with the stereotype.

That several generations of comedians took our groaning boards as a base for humor allowed us to laugh at ourselves. It did not, however, define us, nor was it gospel, nor should it have become a means of proving us to be declassé. It is true, of course, that we never adopted "nouvelle cuisine," which means small portions at large prices. That would never go over in the Catskills!

An article in the *New York Times* once featured a yuppie commentator's poor attempt at humor. She was describing a weekend at one of our resorts to which she brought her child and his nanny, although the poor soul feared that "she would be served beet soup for breakfast." The writer slammed hard at the cuisine: they were served "industrial strength Jell-O" and "the food arrived 6 minutes and 30 seconds after we placed our order." Her complaints included being sent a piece of birthday cake from a neighboring table. My only reaction to those kinds of negatives would be *"a chasora, the calle is tsu shain"* (What a pity, the bride is too beautiful)!

It seemed that no editorial writer for any section of the *Times* could resist a small poke in the eye if the story was about a Catskill resort. Even when one creative hotelkeeper founded a Shakespeare Festival of high quality, the *Times* called it "Borscht Circuit Shakespeare."

I have often wondered if the "outside world" is aware of what was (and is) produced in our mountain hotel kitchens. The same crew, seven days a week, turned out nine meals a day with myriad choices for adults, children and staff. Holidays such as Memorial Day or July 4th added cocktail parties and/or midnight suppers, all proffered in strict time slots. Once Continental breakfast (anything cold after the regular breakfast hours) was added to the schedule, the kitchen virtually never closed. Since many of the hotels catered to long-staying guests, menus could not be repeated weekly, or at least had to contain "surprises" to keep the dining public's interest. The creativity, organization, and intense labor required of the culinary department was mind boggling. What made it even more so was that underlying the production was the absolute need for buying well and avoiding waste, if the hotel was to remain in business.

We had enough hotels to proffer a variety of styles of cooking and degrees of religious observation of dietary rules. There were the Orthodox places that offered Glatt kosher regimens supervised by rabbis and that featured two kitchens for the separate preparation of meat and dairy dishes as well as the closest of attention to the religion's dietary regulations. You could also select kosher hotels which observed the laws, but not to the same degree. Both types of kitchens used meats and fowl which were slaughtered ritually, one set of dishes for serving meat and another for dairy, as well as the absolute avoidance of any prohibited food such as pork products or shell fish. Neither style allowed for cooking on the Sabbath.

There was a third category of food service which was called "kosher style." Again, the laws were the same, but interpreted in a more liberal manner. They didn't use supervision by a *Mashgiach* (supervisor of kosher practices), very often did cook on Saturday, and used one kitchen for all food preparation.

Until my husband and I took over at Green Acres, my parents used a kosher look-alike kind of dietary presentation, but didn't follow many of the rules. What it actually meant was that the food was Jewish-American, that bacon, and ham were not served, and that meals were planned to separate dairy and meat products, even though we never had more than one set of dishes.

Larry and I decided that the regimen had little or no meaning. Anyone who really followed the laws of *Kashruth* would not stay with us, and those who did not were being denied the variety that many people sought. Our change of style lost us some of the older clientele but proved to be a tremendous plus for attracting younger families who had themselves abandoned the dietary restrictions of their parents. It served as well to open the doors for non-Jewish clientele. Our ads read: "Everything from lobster to the traditional Friday night meal."

We served all the delicacies my grandmother made, but added seafood, bacon, Italian and Chinese dishes, and as many other interesting culinary treats as we could produce. It became necessary to find chefs versatile enough to handle all kinds of menus. We found those talented people, but some of our guests had strange reactions to the mixed styles. An angry patron sought me out after breakfast one day. "There's bacon on the menu," she said. "You didn't tell me you served bacon." I tried to reason with her. "You enjoyed the lobster last night," said I. "Lobster I eat," she snapped!

With the exception of the Brickman and Olympic which pioneered a modified American plan (breakfast and dinner only), all of the hotels were on the full American plan. We literally served three banquets a day. Hotels featured certain "standards" that were common to all. You could find baked herring, blintzes, borscht and schav, gefilte fish, tsimmes, kasha varnishkes, matzoh ball soup, chopped vegetables with sour cream, brisket and flanken (boiled beef), and a host of other "ethnic" dishes on every hotel menu in our area. Each hostelry then added its own specialties to provide a diner's dream.

Not every guest, and certainly not every employee, was familiar with what we in the trade, and brought up on the diets of our fathers, took for granted. We had patrons who looked askance, for instance, at the delicious *pitcha* (jellied calves' feet, resembling aspic) and were loathe to taste it. *Kishka* (stuffed intestine) was considered a delicacy in my home, albeit an invitation to acid indigestion, but just didn't go over with our newer clientele. There were many specialties that required "growing up on" to be enjoyed.

Robbie Riesenberg, the son of a friend, and a native of these parts, had never spent any time at the hotels. While still in high school, he eagerly sought and was hired for a waiter's job at Stier's Hotel. On his very first day in the dining room, a guest requested a glass of buttermilk, something Robbie had never heard about, much less tasted. Still, he rushed into the kitchen, found the bottle labeled "buttermilk" and poured a glass. It was obvious to him that the milk was spoiled! It was heavy and didn't smell so good either. He poured it out, emptied the "stale" bottle and reached for another. When he had gone through the process of emptying six bottles of buttermilk, he was finally stopped by the hotel's owner, Frank Stier, who, witnessing the process, literally believed the boy had lost his mind!

Generosity was a given from the smallest to the largest of our resorts. If it was humanly possible, no guest was refused anything. "Choice of" were only words on the menu; in our Catskills you could have it all. Service to guests, whether they were patrons or visitors, was a mandate that came from Jewish custom. My mother's instruction, which I later discovered was codified as a proverb, was: "*A krank'n fregt men, a gesunt'n git men*" (you ask a sick person what he would like, but you just serve a healthy one).

If a client had a problem with our regular menus, "special" foods could be and were prepared. Hotels all catered to salt-free and sugar-free diets and to any and all dietary restrictions or requirements that might exist.

Hilda Cohen (Kanco Hotel) catered to her own visiting mother's medically indicated dietary needs, and told me of the interest guests took in the covered dishes that she delivered personally. There are those in any assemblage, I suppose, who fear that someone is getting something wonderful, which they are denied. So Hilda was often called to the tables and questioned about the food she was carrying. The hotel's maitre d' noted her discomfort with the process. That same maitre d', one afternoon, brought a hamburger back to the chef in the kitchen. A client had rejected it. "There's a hair in the meat," he told the chef. "So what do you want me to do about it?" raved the temperamental culinary expert. "Well, don't tell anyone, or the whole dining room will want it," was the reply!

In small hotels like ours, one baker handled everything—
rolls, danish, cookies, pastries, pies, and challah for Friday
night. Even with a helper, the job was monumental. As years
went on, a skilled baker became harder and harder to find. One
season we found a most desirable candidate for the job. He had,
however, a problem. His wife was expecting a baby during the
summer and he would have to leave for a few days when she
gave birth. The baker offered to teach my husband to make
sponge cake, challah, and rolls, and he would prepare a few
choices for the freezer. We determined it could be managed.

On the first Friday night of the baker's absence, I opened
the dining room doors and saw what I took to be colorful
centerpieces on each table. It seemed that Larry had inadvertently added too much food coloring to his batter, and though
delicious, the guests ate their first bright orange challah! Once
Larry had mastered the art of making breakfast rolls, we
envisioned that the family would enjoy those treats all winter
long. It was not to be, for he could bake them only in batches
of 300.

When the world became diet conscious, low calorie dishes
were added to every menu. We all know that there are a dozen
rationales for someone on a diet. They include: "a broken
cookie doesn't count," "if you have a snack while standing up
you consume fewer calories," and so forth. Our guests figured
out a new one. If you dine off the regular menu and then eat
the diet platter, they will cancel each other out.

Our breakfast menu was standard and preprinted, but the
hotel office staff was responsible for lunch and dinner menus
each day. Our daughter, Amy, was in charge of creating the
stencil from which mimeographed copies were made. The bill
of fare that she received from the kitchen was bare-boned and
unadorned, so that she had the additional job of creating
descriptive adjectives to jazz up the offerings. "Roast Philadel-
phia Capon" was a standard, along with "Long Island Duckling
Orange," and then there were "Au jus," "Monte Carlo," "a la
Ruse," "Jardiniere," and when in doubt, "a la Maitre D'

Hotel." Menus were expected to be ready for the dining room by 12:45, and their production was, of course, only a small part of the office work. It followed that mistakes were inevitable. Two memorable ones were: "Boiled Young Girl" (fowl), and "Cold Sliced Crap" (carp). Miracles do happen—no one noticed.

It seems amazing that the thousands of meals prepared and served over the years generally went off without incident. From the guests' point of view, they always were trouble free, but no hotel kitchen was without its emergencies. Chefs quit in the middle of meals (but owners and the remaining staff took over), dishwashing machines broke down and dishes piled up to the ceiling, deliveries of food were late and improvising on the menu took place instantly, power failed and meals were served by candlelight, fights broke out in the kitchen, but no matter what the problem, the meals were served. Sometimes it was remarkable ingenuity that made that possible.

Sherwin Harrison was the steward at Brown's Hotel on an off-season weekend when the entire premises was booked for a wedding party. The nuptial dinner included soup. Just before the meal was to begin the dishwashers were asked to run the soup plates through boiling water in the dishwasher to make sure that the receptacles were warm for service. As luck would have it, the kitchen worker carrying the plates to the service area tripped and broke half the soup plates. It was a horrific moment . . . no way to serve soup to the whole crowd.

Harrison solved the problem. "Turn off the air-conditioning in the dining room," he ordered. Predictably, the dining room turned torrid. No one wanted hot soup. Then they turned on the cooling system!

We had only one dining room for adults. I don't think there was a guest who didn't know the schedule for meals. And yet, is there a mountain hotel vacationer who doesn't remember hearing over the public address system, on every day of his vacation: "Attention Please . . . Ladies and Gentlemen, the *Main Dining Room* is open and dinner is being served."

New Roxy Hotel, Loch Sheldrake, before and after rennovation.
The New Roxy became Green Acres in 1967.

Part 4:
Turn, Turn, Turn

The best way to see the future is to appreciate the past.

----Stan Raiff, President
Institute for the Development of Entertainment Arts

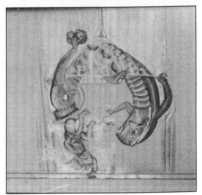

Lively, but eccentric, murals adorned the walls of Maud's Summer Ray in North Branch.

We Called It "Eclectic"

DECOR FOR OUR HOTELS varied with the taste of individual owners.

One thing was certain. The innkeepers who ran small hotels had neither the time nor inclination to study *Better Homes and Gardens* or *Architectural Digest*. Their experience was more with living rooms than lobbies, so that the overall effect for early resort public space was casual and cosy, but it certainly followed no rules.

Since the relatives were part of hotel life, in our case at least, they added to the furniture supply with their own castoffs. Aunt Leah's tier table and cousin Bella's wing chair found their way to Green Acres, making "eclectic" very much the word of choice.

Furniture store owners fancied themselves to be decorators, so when the hotelkeepers felt inadequate for the job, they relied on those "experts" to help them select the lobbies' furnishings. Salesmen being salesmen, the sellers envisioned what had been sitting for ages in their warehouses and then pushed "the perfect purple couch." The results were, to say the least, not always wonderful.

In the early days at least, individuality was the keynote, as each place created a look of its own, sometimes surprisingly charming and always different. In some resorts the creativity was memorable.

Paul's in Swan Lake (now Daytop Village), broke the pedestrian building mode with a low-rise Spanish stucco building and Mediterranean style furniture. The Olympic presented a totally deco lobby complete with blue glass on side tables, and drapes in the geometric prints of that era. Chester's, in keeping with its population of the intelligentsia, featured fireplaces and a profusion of books and paintings. Maud's Summer-Ray of North Branch, was owned by artists and populated by guests of like tastes. Their walls were covered with marvelous frescoes, the furniture was carved, and objects of art were everywhere.

Quick to employ what was at hand, hoteliers used the services of talented staff members. At Green Acres in Lake Huntington, we had a casino decorated by a children's waiter/artist in 1932 who gave us murals, on view for almost 30 years.

Some of us second- and third-generation innkeepers turned to antiques and collectibles early on to create an interesting look for our public areas.

It is hard to believe that there was a time when pitchers and bowls sold for a few dollars, round oak tables were available for the picking, and pier mirrors, dry sinks, and portmanteaus could be picked up for the proverbial song.

The modern furniture that many of us would have preferred was not affordable, and so we found an inexpensive way to be different. You didn't have to be an antique expert in those days to compare the cost of a new sofa with a Victorian one, or the price of a Danish modern coffee table with an old oak one. It would be 20 years before those artifacts would be in demand.

Living on the Pennsylvania border, we found a veritable treasure trove with which to decorate. I often think that had I bought up all that was available, and filled a few barns, it would have been a more profitable enterprise than the resort.

When, as purchasing agent for our hostelry, I began to bring home all those old goodies, I ran into my father's wrath. The original homestead, when he bought it, had been furnished with the very sort of things I was buying——dry sinks, pitchers, bowls, slop jars and the like. "I just threw out that junk," was his comment. My husband was equally negative about my discoveries. "Don't give it a fancy name," he said. "What you have there is used furniture!"

I, however, had found a new love, and am a devoted antiquenik to this day. Among the finds I brought home was a round oak, clawfoot kitchen table, with four leaves and in mint condition. "I hate it," said Larry, "it has toenails!" Not at that or any time was a kitchen table to seat 10 available for $5. I was insistent, and it has been in our kitchen ever since.

A few years ago an appraiser came to place dollar values on the antiques that we took with us when we left the hotel. She sat at that kitchen table with my mother, spoke into a tape recorder, and assigned amounts to each object. For the table, her estimate was $750. "Sold!" said my mother.

During the middle 1930s, hotel people of our area discovered the joys of Florida vacationing. Depending upon their finances, they were either hotel guests or rented the efficiencies that abounded.

So enchanted were they with the south land, that the Catskill resort owners sought to emulate the newly discovered styles. Our mountains soon boasted an array of colors never seen before. All at once the landscape was dotted with pink and salmon and sky-blue buildings. What was lovely against an azure sea and ecru dunes, and on new deco buildings, was ludicrous when applied to the tilting bungalows and the original architecture of our mountain milieu. Fortunately, the fad did not last. However, it did illustrate our hotelkeepers' quest for a new look, and their willingness to experiment.

When Green Acres built its first new eight-room guest building during my tenure at the hotel, I was determined to avoid the "stock" colors that my parents and their peers had favored for decades. As if by pre-arrangement, all the owners painted floors with "porch and deck gray," bedrooms in off-white, and, because the color was always on sale, used a particularly nauseous aqua for pool buildings and the like.

For the new rooms I wanted decorator colors and a distinctive look.

The painters we used were an old-time partnership from Hurleyville—Burstein and Shapiro. We had a conference. "I'd like the bedrooms walls to be a champagne color," said I. "Cissie," Mr. Shapiro explained patiently, "champagne is a drink, yellow is a color!" In the end they humored me, mixed the paints, and champagne it was.

Within a few years of that first addition, we were launched on a half-million dollar renovation that would bring us into the twentieth century.

Decorating "from scratch" for the new lobbies, indoor pool, entry, and so forth, of the new construction, became a heavy responsibility. We sought professional help. As it turned out, the decorators who had been recommended brought in schemes that we rejected as cold and institutional. It was suggested that we tour other and larger hotels that had been renovated years before, to see how it was done.

As strange as it may seem, that was the first time I saw many of the hotels that were in my backyard for a lifetime. Summer found us all completely tied to our own resorts and in the winter many of our colleagues were closed. I had been to Grossinger's and the Concord for a few events, and to the establishments of our personal friends such as the Pauls, Rosenblatts, and the Horowitz family (Olympic) into which my brother married.

So I went out scouting. Brown's, the Pines, the Tamarac, Sha-Wan-Ga Lodge, Kutsher's, Stevensville, and a host of others were all examined. But our final decor was the result of a collaboration between my sister-in-law, Harriet Rosenberg, and myself, guided by our architect, Kenneth Goldfarb. It was original and reflected our own tastes, much as the early lobbies reflected those of their "decorators." The furniture was starkly modern, designed by Eames and Stendig, and upholstered in fall colors. Antique pieces were kept to add warmth, as was the collection of old paintings that we had accumulated. The results were outstanding. The renovation was featured in *Interiors Magazine* and we felt as if we had won a Pulitzer Prize!

No matter how we redid the public space and added new buildings with modern rooms, we never could afford to retire the large number of accommodations with which we started. There were no hotels of our size that could emulate the leader in our field, Arthur Winarick of the Concord, who had the wherewithall to turn old structures into staff quarters or destroy them entirely.

If hotels were in the business for 50 years, they had, of necessity, 50-year-old buildings. "Simple" would be a kind adjective for most of the rooms, even after our attempts to modernize them. The original farmhouses (ours was 100 years old) had not been built for luxury, and the bedrooms were small. In their case, old did not mean charming. Time had taken its toll on the floors, which were never even. As buildings settled, the windows took on a tilt and doors did not fit flush with the sills. Walls were finished in a material called craftex or papered in patterns prone to exaggerate flaws. The ceilings were tin, which only in the last few years has returned to fashion. Flooring very often was merely painted, or covered with linoleum. As for the "newer" construction such as the main buildings that went up in the mid-1920s, they, too, had rooms that were far from what the latter-day guests expected. Our fathers, unschooled in both construction and decoration, suffered the additional problem of lack of familiarity with posh establishments in the hotel world of their own day. Their original guests came from the tenements or at best simple homes, and accepted the country lodgings without complaint. As guest circumstances improved, the hotelkeepers' attempts at "catch up" were difficult to accomplish.

When guests entered the new and wonderful lobbies and entries we eventually constructed, it was their expectation that the accommodations would be equally up to date. We suffered from the contrast, as did our colleagues.

Even the newly built bedrooms that were our idea of real luxury did not measure up to accommodations provided the world over by motels and up-to-the-minute resorts created by the chains.

The constant changing of furniture to accommodate families did nothing to add to room appearance as a season wore on. I waged a constant battle with the chambermaid staff to make sure that at least the bedspreads matched when the room was readied for new occupants. I didn't always win the battle.

Never, during my years in the business, was I able to open the door to a bedroom and have it "sell itself." Our emphasis, of necessity, remained on services rather than accommodations.

Interior of the renovated Green Acres, Lake Huntington.

Hooray! We Owe
A Half-million Dollars

ARCHITECTS were professionals rarely, if ever, employed by the small resorts in the early days. They did not appear on our scene until the era of mass expansion, which began in the late 1940s.

My father's version of an architectural rendering was a sketch on the back of an envelope or a napkin. He was a brilliant organizer and speaker, a student of economics and history. An architect he was not. He shared his ignorance of that art with his compatriots, but it didn't stop him or them from doing some of the worst planning in the building business! Maybe that's what prompted one of our guests to observe that our main building was the only one he knew of where you climbed up three flights of steps to find yourself in the cellar!

Our Catskill resorts were a rarity in the business community. Most enterprises have an initial investment for a building and inventory, and the debt is then amortized over the ensuing years. For hotels, the investment was continuous---a pool, tennis courts, a children's pool, camp buildings, nightclub, new lobbies, more rooms, elevators, air conditioning, connections for the buildings and indoor pools. Redoing was never over and the property was never "finished."

An initial mistake that all the early builders of hotels made was the construction of what were, for those days, highrise buildings. Land was relatively inexpensive, so it is hard to know what made them build straight up with three- and four-story buildings, which were without elevators in most cases. They created a problem from the beginning, and that error was to plague them, along with their failure to have a long-term plan for what might be needed in the future. Chances are that there wasn't one hotel of the early era that wasn't built, renovated, renovated again, and yet again.

Initially, the main buildings (ours was built in 1925) had no rooms with private baths. Closets were constructed to hold one suit (if it was hung sideways). Inevitably, hotel people discovered, on completion of main complexes, that they needed a card room, a children's dining room, a staff dining room, or additional office space. So our area's buildings have juts and more juts to take care of what was initially overlooked.

As the guest population became more discriminating, owners were forced to redo their accommodations to produce rooms with baths. The rooms with baths on floor were cut up to produce rooms that shared a bath (semi-private) and rooms with private baths.

To be fair, it wasn't all the lack of planning that was to blame. Almost without exception the hotelkeepers were poorly financed, so the "afterthoughts" were added when the funds were available.

While the first series of renovations done on hotel buildings built in the 1920s certainly improved them, they all reflected the years in which they were accomplished. Semi-private bath accommodations were out of date almost as soon as they were created, and even the rooms that had private facilities were not large enough for the standards of the day.

Necessity, the well-known mother of invention, forced the hotel owners to use what was called a "hotel double," which was a three-quarter bed with a new name. One day, my mother was attempting to register a couple who objected to that lone "double" bed in a room that could not hold another. "We don't sleep together," exploded the husband. "Force yourself," replied my mother!

Green Acres' main building was built on the top of a hill, overlooking Lake Huntington. The view, which entranced my dad, was magnificent—if you were still alive after climbing the mountain from the swimming area. The guests called it "cardiac hill." My father drove up.

The wonder was that those early buildings did indeed get built, albeit with the many errors with which their owners were forced to live. The early hotelkeepers' approach to construction was just another example of incredible naivete, coupled with what can only be described as *chutzpa* (nerve) to the nth degree.

In many cases, the first contractors of our region were carpenters who were learning on the job. Florence Neukrug of Avon Lodge described the gentleman who did their building as unable to read a plan, measuring with his hammer rather than a tape measure, and "winging it" as the building progressed. Avon Lodge ended up with one room in their main building that measured 6 feet by 8 feet, held one bed, and had no bath. It resulted from a "slight" error in calculation by the builder, making it forever necessary to find a friendly patron on the same floor who would share "the facilities"!

The builders were very often at least the partial financiers of the buildings they constructed. Mortgages, however, were the vehicles for expansion, along with notes, which came to be known as "Sullivan County currency."

Every early hotel had at least one "unfixable." When one considers that our fathers did not employ engineers in the process of construction, it is understandable that there were

The original Green Acres, Lake Huntington, undergoing renovation.

flaws. Some of them were bedeviling. At Green Acres, water pressure for the upper floors was our cross to bear. When, at 6 P.M., all the guests hit the showers, rooms above the first floor were without water, particularly if the house was full.

On one packed week in July, we were hosts to a state senator, his redheaded wife, and their small son. It was Mrs. Gittleson who called, promptly at six, to inform us of her "malfunctioning" shower. We had a standard answer, "It is being worked on," knowing full well that the only cure for the water problem was seven o'clock, when the usage was finally down. "I'm in the middle of dying my hair," said the distressed lady. "It must be washed out."

Our only solution for her was to suggest that she go down to the lake to complete her rinse. That evening, at dinner, a visiting friend asked me to point out where our celebrity guest, Senator Gittleson, was sitting. Without turning around, I told her to look two tables down for a white haired gentleman sitting with a redheaded woman. "I see the white haired man," was her response, "but the lady sitting with him has *green* hair!"

I believe that the arrival on the scene of the mammoth Concord Hotel (Kiamesha Lake) in the late 1930s spurred the vast renovations that changed the hotel business for all time to come.

Arthur Winarick, the Concord's innovative and enthusiastic owner, took over an old property and created one of the

The Concord, a complete "today" resort.

world's largest, most modern, and best equipped hotels. The rumor was that he did it with cash, certainly something his colleagues were unable to even think about when they were starting out.

In the years that followed, the Concord added banks of tennis courts, an indoor pool and health club, not one but two outstanding golf courses, and even a ski lift. To accompany those great attractions, Winarick built enough brand new rooms (some with *two* bathrooms) for thousands of guests. He reported to us "little guys" that he was buying carpet "by the mile." Winarick innovated in every aspect of the business. He built a magnificent nightclub, brought in famous names in entertainment, and orchestras of national reputation.

Even before the Concord impacted on the area, a group of hotel properties had grown, improved, and outstripped the vast majority of the small hotels of which I write. My father, then secretary of the Mountain Hotelmen's Federation, noted that the new large hotels had little in common with those with 100 rooms or fewer. By mutual agreement, in 1939, the large properties formed a separate trade group, calling themselves the "Big 21."

The names are legend, and include Grossinger's, Young's Gap, the Evans, Morningside, White Roe, the Stevensville, the President Hotel, Paul's, the Flagler, Raleigh, Laurel's Hotel and Country Club, the Brickman, the Waldemere, Edgewood Inn, Stevensville Lake Hotel, Swan Lake Hotel and, of course, the giant of them all, the Concord.

One of our guests, at check-in time, told us that he had called his uncle to say goodbye before leaving on his summer vacation. "Where are you going?" asked the uncle. Upon learning that it was to Green Acres, a small hotel in Lake Huntington, he commented: "Well, for me, when I go to the *country*, it's only the Concord . . . it's a regular *city*."

The coming of that "regular city" marked a new era. Certainly the larger hotels had to keep up. Extensive building

The Olympic, Fallsburg, before and after renovation.

Grossinger's: the original farm house and the hotel in its prime.

programs to provide "indoor everything" were begun. Modernization and winterization became absolute necessities.

The small hotels were hard pressed to be part of the new expanding resort world. They still had the old rooms with bath on floor, the semi-privates, and less-than-luxurious rooms with private baths which showed their age. The properties lacked the capital improvements that were part of the new picture, and many were still not able to operate for extended seasons, since they didn't have heated accommodations.

The smaller hotels tried to compensate for what was lacking in facilities and modernity by creating new services. The addition of children's day camps was one innovation. Some hotels became dude ranches, others "sold" the smallness and homey atmosphere that were still an attraction, still others appealed to the intellectuals with avant garde entertainment, lectures, and the like. We, at Green Acres, tried an amalgam of approaches to attract young families, featuring all of the above and adding lobster to our menu.

Our rates were a good deal lower than those of our larger competitors; it made a difference to the guests, particularly to those who stayed for weeks at a time. But we, and our colleagues, were pressed to add, each year, to the attractions of the resort.

The first letter of the season, to former guests, contained an enthusiastic description of what those improvements were. Not always being able to report big additions made writing that initial pitch for reservations a challenge. As the composer of the spring letter, I was liberal in my use of the ambiguous word, "refurbished." Sometimes it meant that we had painted the public bathrooms.

Returning guests asked one question: "What's new this year?" Once, when that question was posed to my dad, he responded with, "Did you have a good time last summer?" "Yes." "Did you enjoy the food, the entertainment, the ambience?" "Yes indeed." "You'll be glad to know," said my father, "we didn't do anything to make things worse!"

Eventually, changing guest expectations and competition from modernized hotels made building an imperative. Hotels began major transformations and huge capital improvements. Once convinced that it was "build or die," the hotelkeepers had to find a way to fund the changes.

Even local banks were unable to handle the whole load. Some of our friends in the business were able to work with insurance companies or other institutions. For us, and for many, the answer came from an agency of the federal government, the Small Business Administration (the SBA). In cooperation with Sullivan County banks, and after tons of paperwork and duplicate sets of attorneys (homegrown and out of New York City), the mega mortgage came to the mountains.

When Catskill hotelkeepers entered into the era of reconstruction, they were of necessity involved with a whole series of variables, impossible to predict. "Projecting" for the lenders what additional improvements would bring in business became a fancy name for guessing. More than that, the guesses were very often built upon wishes.

For some, the time of expansion and restructure was a bonanza. Certainly the attorneys, creative accountants, architects, and contractors enjoyed a golden age. Small family operators, however, found themselves in gilded, debt-ridden enterprises, attempting to survive projections of 95 percent occupancy! I will never forget my mother's reaction when, after a year of delay, I excitedly announced that our SBA loan had been approved. "Hooray," she said, "we owe a half-million dollars!"

Mark Twain once described American houses as having Queen Anne fronts and Aunt Mary behinds. Nowhere was that more true than in the modernized resorts of the Catskills. Our own project at Green Acres, for example, involved removing the front of the main building and then creating new lobbies, dining room, an indoor pool and health club, as well as a card room and assorted decks, all of which were tacked onto the front of the structure my father built in 1925, 38 years earlier. A separate building with new guest rooms went up at the same time.

Our good fortune came in choosing a talented and dedicated young architect, Kenneth Goldfarb of Monticello, who listened carefully to what we wanted, understood exactly what we expected to spend, and ensured that the planned renovation matched our finances. Others were not as lucky. Not every architect or builder was on target with the proposed costs. When costs ran over, hotelkeepers lived with the professionals' mistakes.

There were hotels where expenses on building "extras" were almost as large as the expected initial costs. Caught in a web of short term loans to cover moneys expended, in some cases it buried them.

Green Acres was among the few whose building program came in within budget----with minor exceptions. No one could anticipate the state of the structure to be redone. On one devastating morning, our general contractor, Al Adler, informed us that the existing dining room was being held up by the wallpaper! Time and weather had eroded the wooden beams and it was steel beams that were needed to shore up the building. That was an unexpected expense. Fortunately, in our case, the extras were minimal when compared to the size of the project.

Once the building was torn open and exposed, there was no turning back. Time was of the essence and the time frame for building was perilous. Construction could not begin until the fall, went on through our famous bitter winters, and all work needed to be completed before the onset of the summer season.

We all learned the hard way about materials that didn't arrive, tradespeople who failed to coordinate, and moneys from the Small Business Administration that, though due at predetermined times, were inevitably late.

Every building site attracts some "sidewalk superintendents." Among ours was the local grocer. He arrived daily, inspected the works, and informed us that we would never finish on time! He never knew how often I considered pushing him off a scaffold.

There were those who had faith. We had good friends who booked Green Acres for their son's bar mitzvah celebration, and that event made June 15th the target date for completion of the project. As Hiram and Clemence Frank wandered through the indescribable mess of mud, exposed timbers, and building materials on the construction site, they somehow were able to envision the finished product that I described. They were sure we would be ready. I had my doubts.

Our family was living a commercial version of "Mr. Blanding Builds His Dream House," only it was infinitely larger, vastly more complicated, and our economic lives hung in the balance. There must have been some humor there too, but at the time it escaped us. And yes, we did open on schedule. So, to my knowledge, did every other hotel that renovated.

Our new building was genuinely beautiful. It was a symphony of cedar-shakes, brick, and glass, perfectly attuned to its site. It was an artistic coup.

Once launched into a larger facility, intense personal labor was no longer the answer to "making it," although the labor continued. The small family owners were forced to add management employees such as stewards, convention managers, superintendents of service.

Overhead, in the form of taxes and insurance and advertising, grew exponentially. The tight control that was possible before expansion was no longer a given. While, by this time, most businesses had incorporated, the mortgages and notes bore owners' signatures, so that they were burdened personally with debts in amounts never before imagined.

Conversation at our home dinner table ran to finances. Suddenly we were talking in telephone numbers—hundreds of thousands of dollars. The children were listening. Our 11-year-old son, in the year that we were building, suggested that he would like a 10-speed bike. When he mentioned what we considered to be an astronomical price, he was told that it was unaffordable.

It was difficult for Paul to fathom that his folks, who were always talking about spending for the project in high figures, could be short for anything. It was then that we delivered the lecture about the difference between having money and borrowing money! Neither the offspring nor the community could believe the personal penury in the midst of so much business plenty.

Too many hotelkeepers were unprepared for the expansion undertaken. There had been too little allowance made for empty times caused by economic dents, gas shortages, or changing vacation patterns.

Construction costs ran over budget while optimistic projections for income fell short. Notes once again replaced currency to cover those shortfalls, and notes were always cast for too limited a time.

The industry landscape had already begun to show alarming changes. Small operations that were not able to modernize were also unable to compete. Many were sold, foreclosed, or abandoned.

Faced with spiraling overhead, all the hotels recognized that the short summer season was no longer able to carry the debt load. With income measured by rooms and days, it became obvious that those days needed to be extended. Catskill Mountain hotels were on their way to year-round operation.

Nothing Stays the Same

OUR FAMILY left the hotel property in Lake Huntington because of a disastrous fire in 1966. Fate's oblique sense of humor decreed that it should occur only three years after a huge renovation, and on the eve of a season.

While I can rail against fate for the fire, it was I who left the hotel a quarter of a million dollars underinsured. Larry had spoken over and over again about proper protection, but insurance was an area of the business that lay in "my department," and I was unwilling to spend the kind of money required for full coverage. Optimism about having been on our hill for 45 years without incident, and unwillingness to further indebt us, plus looking forward to the sprinkler system that was due for installation the following year, seem more than foolish reasons in retrospect. We paid heavily for my mistake. Larry never once said, "I told you so."

The fire took place as a result of a lightning storm in early June. In the midst of a violent downpour, the newly redone main building was struck multiple times and burned from the inside out.

We had purchased a home in Woodridge just months before. It was there, with a direct wire to New York City, that I could work during the week while the children attended school and my mother and Larry saw to the spring opening. We were all at the hotel for the weekends.

Summoned by a midnight call, I arrived in Lake Huntington to witness an inferno. Larry had removed my mother from the building moments before the roof collapsed. He stood, singed and barefoot in the pouring rain and watched the futile efforts of the local fire company.

Our magnificent new construction and our years of labor and saving and care and dreams were going up in smoke. I ran to Larry who put his arms around me. As we both looked toward the blaze and wept, he said, characteristically, "Easy come, easy go!"

That was in 1966. Just recently I received a letter from a former employee who was at the hotel on that fateful night. She reminded me that Larry, on the very next day, set out to get jobs for every member of the staff who had been hired for the season. Fran Rifkin Weiss was placed at Sha-Wan-Ga Lodge where she worked until graduation from college. She never forgot Larry. There were a myriad of people who didn't forget us.

They say that life's emergencies divide the men from the boys, or, to be politically correct today, the women from the girls! I'm not sure who "they" really are, but it has been my experience that cliches become popular because they're true. At any rate, without recounting every detail, what is significant is that there were friends, tradespeople, acquaintances, and even our congressman, John Dow, who tried to help us get back into business.

It would be too much like a fairytale if there were not those (to whom we were in debt) who sent summonses in order to be "first on line," or if there were not those who were less friendly when we were no longer "Mr. and Mrs. Acres." Some people truly believed we had a secret store of cash, or implied that the fire was profitable. To add insult to injury, we had neighbors who robbed the remaining property. There were indeed those people. It was never a perfect world.

Still, there were enough of the "lifesavers" to keep the faith: Guests who drove up in the middle of the night, while the building still burned, with signed blank checks; our friend, Benjamin Cosor, who went to work immediately to find us a property and offer a mortgage; and other friends and family who proffered whatever they could spare. There was the travel editor of the *New York Post*, who called from a vacation trip in Europe to assure us of our credit with the paper, an endless number of creditors who accepted our notes and our word, and our 14-year-old son who found a job to add his help.

At best, we knew that we were starting all over again, and it was anybody's guess as to whether or not our operation was transferrable to another location. The days of that summer were filled with a million and one details. We had to reach all those guests who had reserved, contact staff who had been engaged and try to secure other positions for them, find a new location and restructure our debt load. The saving grace was our home in Woodridge, which still had the New York direct wire on which we could be reached.

We remain forever grateful that there was no loss of human life and no physical injury as a result of the fire. Our children mourned their pet collie who succumbed, but aside from Taffy, what was taken from us was material.

After any disaster there are so many who wish to offer comfort. Unfortunately, there is little that anyone can say, and the constant repetition of "it could be worse" begins to wear on already frayed nerves. One day, after a parade of visitors repeated the same phrase, my mother finally snapped: "Sure it could be worse," she said, "it could happen to you!"

With a lot of real help, and by taking partners in the new property (old friends from Woodridge, Joy and Jack Studley), we made the big move. We purchased what had been the New

Roxy Hotel, in Loch Sheldrake. It had failed several years earlier and was in the hands of the bank. I don't know what the old Roxy looked like, but the new one had disintegrated into a swamp. It took fully nine months to renovate.

It took the family just as long to adjust to a totally new premises. In Lake Huntington we could have drawn a picture of every room, and knew how many it could hold, and where it was located. In Loch Sheldrake we wandered the structures in complete bewilderment. For some reason the numbers did not conform to the floors. You took the elevator to "2" and the room numbers started at 300! Rooms in the same category were of different sizes. The place had twice the number of accommodations as did the property we had left, and indoor corridors connecting the buildings added to the confusion. Periodically I would get a call from my mother from some-where in the halls, with the plaintive question, "Where am I?"

Our children, when we first viewed what were to be our new premises, had a wonderful time exploring. All at once we heard shouts of delight. "We've found a lake," they reported excitedly. Their father was quick to answer: "Don't jump in," said he, "it's the sewer system!" Paul and Amy were not alone in their misconception. For years after our first season, we had one guest who always reserved a "lakeview" room!

Most difficult of all was that the family ego was assaulted by the flashy colors, lack of style, and tawdriness of our adopted hotel. Aside from the neglect the premises had suffered, it was not originally done in our version of "taste." Amy, small as she was, dubbed it "early ugly"! The architectural errors were legion. My first view of a cavernous lobby with its upper balcony perched on what looked like spindly legs, brought me to tears. In truth we were spoiled, having so recently renovated in Lake Huntington to achieve what was for us a place of beauty and a source of pride. We missed the lovely lake we had taken for granted, the wonderful views, and even "cardiac hill" on which our former main building was located.

From a practical point of view, we gained new facilities that were sorely missing in the original Green Acres, even after it was redone. The connected and winterized buildings, the larger capacity, the sprinkler system throughout, the elevator, large nightclub and bar, which the Loch Sheldrake property offered, were tremendous pluses we would not have achieved in Lake Huntington for the foreseeable future. We gained, too, in having a new location that was right in the middle of the county's most popular resort section rather than far out on the western end of the county.

The flaws were addressed, and the decor redone. It was with the help of the same architect who planned our original renovation that we succeeded in recreating a look that was our own. Once the lobby was paneled in walnut, and the "skinny legs" fleshed out into columns, and once my partner, Joy Studley, and I filled the public space with the antique pieces and art for which we had always been known, the new hotel began to feel like home.

We added too, a complete children's campus with its own pool, new tennis courts, and all the accouterments needed to operate Green Acres "East"!

The Roxy, while the bank held it, had been rented to seasonal operators who stripped it clean and left it filthy. It took weeks to merely remove the accumulated garbage, longer to put the kitchen back in shape and equip it, and to see to the refurbishing or replacement of all the mechanicals that had been sorely neglected. The oversight of all the above was Larry's work. He literally spent every waking hour at the hotel, and if anyone wanted to see him, it had to be while he worked on the property.

That's where a favorite story emerged during the creation of our new premises: Larry was up to his ears in the mess of the kitchen when a gentleman we knew arrived to speak with him. "I was the *mashgiach* (guardian of kosher practices) for the former owners here," said he, "and when I heard you were taking over I knew you would have a job for me." "I'm awfully sorry," my husband explained, "but we don't observe the laws of *Kashruth* and much as I would like to have you working for us, the job just doesn't exist." "That's certainly understandable," the man replied. "But, Larry, you would appreciate what happened to me here. It was already two years after I first began the job, and I was still at the original salary. So I approached the former owner and put it to him that I wanted a raise. 'Listen,' said the owner, 'if I have to give you a raise, I may as well buy kosher chickens!' "

Since our fire took place in June, we spent that first summer out of Lake Huntington getting the guests who had reservations settled in other hotels. My brother's hotel, with an operation similar to our own, was the first choice, and most of the clientele from Green Acres were willing to transfer their vacations to the Olympic.

The names and addresses of those guests were all that we had in the way of a mailing list, since our guest file had been destroyed in the fire. It remained then to reach the "rest of the world" and let them know we were back in business with a new location.

The help that we received from Bill Sonnenshein of the *New York Post* was of inestimable value. In addition to our own paid ads, he gave us terrific coverage in the vacation columns that the paper ran. Bill came up with the idea for a "Missing Names Contest." We invited all former Green Acres guests to send their names, and the names and addresses of their friends, promising a free weekend to the family whose name would be picked from a hat. We were more than delighted with the response and were initially launched by that effort.

We were able as well to gather many of the staff who had been with us for so long, so all was not strange in Loch Sheldrake. Even some of the Lake Huntington natives who had been in our employ joined us on our new property.

The grand opening took place in June of 1967. Harry Adler, our long-time guest in Lake Huntington, used his influence in

The Green Acres Missing-Names Contest brought results.
Larry Blumberg, Rose Rosenberg, Cissie Blumberg.

the entertainment world to persuade Jackie Mason to preside over the festivities. It was a successful gala and a successful summer!

The move to Loch Sheldrake changed our lives. We became a four-season resort, open for business 12 months a year.

When the need to extend the short Catskill season became evident, hotels had to find vacationists for every part of the year. Even those resorts which were not open for twelve months had slow periods with which to deal. The hotelkeepers met the challenge with their usual ingenuity. They sought, found, and encouraged new kinds of customers----those who traveled together and were not limited by the season of the year: senior citizens, clubs, fraternities, business seminars, family circles, church and synagogue organizations, retreats, bridge groups, and college orientations, to name a few. It wasn't only self-contained groups, however, who helped fill in those many slow periods. The hotelkeepers created groups by organizing special events planned to attract like-minded clientele and worked with tour bus companies who helped put them together.

From placing display advertising in appropriate press, to putting salespeople on the road or going themselves, owners literally beat the bushes for new guest populations.

For Green Acres, now located in Loch Sheldrake, there was another reason to extend the season. Our new purchase was sprinklered throughout with what is called a "wet system." That meant that it was necessary, at all times, to keep the heat going or the water in the system would freeze. We now added the cost of heating the buildings to the rising costs of taxes and insurance and were committed to operating not only in the spring, summer and fall, but in the winter as well.

The difficulties of filling a resort that had never sought anything but a summer clientele are obvious. Families who had been our stock in trade for so long, were just not available in numbers once school began in early September.

Summers, in addition, had found us as a "unique" hotel. We were known as the place with the quintessential day camp and the "special" young crowd. We called our guests the cognoscenti and they believed us.

All at once we were unique no longer, and in direct competition with every year 'round establishment. We were also late in developing the fall and winter group business which others had been cultivating for years.

We faced an uncertain future, saddled not only with the debt of our new property, but with the responsibility for paying off the debts of the first Green Acres.

The family was fortunate at the outset in being able to negotiate a three-year contract with Sullivan County Community College, located just a few miles away. The school was prevented by law from providing dormitories (community colleges were supposed to service local students only), but in order to survive financially in a sparsely populated county, the college had to seek additional registrations from out of the area.

The school got around the statute by setting up a dormitory authority which functioned independently, thereby creating a solution for housing out-of-county students. We became the "boy's dorm," providing rooms and two meals a day for our young guests.

The allowed rates were very low, and we had to design a completely different system from the one with which we were familiar for the "care and feeding" of guests. It allowed us to cover our winter operating costs, but was hardly a money maker.

The student population of that drug era precluded our fond dreams of being "Mr. and Mrs. Chips." The war in Viet Nam was raging at the time, and many of the students had no wish to be in school, but were less interested in being in the army.

Nonetheless, the experience was a valuable one. Tutored by my brother Bob and his wife, who ran the "girls dorm" at their Olympic hotel, we created a whole new approach to innkeeping.

What emerged was an operation which we could translate for the future. It was a scaled-down, low-rate, cost-effective business. We used buffet lines, served wholesome and plentiful but simple menus, and employed a skeleton staff.

When the contract was up with the college, we became a ski resort. Tour operators supplied the "sportsmen," we worked out an arrangement with nearby Davos ski area (Woodridge), and we were launched in a winter business. It bore no resemblance to hotelkeeping as we had known it.

The groups arrived by chartered busses and were checked in without benefit of front desk registration, bell-hops or seating arrangements. Housing was three or four or more in a room, achieving an occupancy heretofore unknown. Entertainment was provided solely by DJs or rock bands, and the population consumed more liquor in a week-end than our "regular" guests did in a season!

For the first time in our history, we were catering to ethnic groups who had never before visited us in significant numbers.

It was a time to lose one's preconceived notions and prejudices. The African-American and Hispanic guests with whom we dealt, were essentially easy to please and pleasant to deal with. We had little or no trouble having white and people of color under the same roof.

But we still suffered from our diverse accommodations, particularly since everyone paid the same rate. On one weekend we were approached by an angry committee of Queens College students who were sure that the hotel was discriminating against them as African-Americans. They were housed in older rooms. My protestations included the evidence that other groups of the same skin color were in the newest sections, but I wasn't convincing them.

It was then that I remembered a friend, born in Ghana, who helped finance his college career by working for us as a bell-hop. Wentworth Ofuete-Kojo had become a professor at Queens College, and, happily, was visiting nearby. I sent out a call for help. When he got to the hotel desk, he put his arm around my shoulder and questioned my angry guests: "Are you giving my cousin a hard time?" he asked. The situation was diffused.

Green Acres in Loch Sheldrake.

To the delight of any and all guests who shared the weekends with them, one Hispanic group returned repeatedly, and always brought along their own Salsa band. The weekend was spent with more dancing than skiing, and all of the guests participated. As a matter of fact, real skiers (on any weekend) were few and far between. The tours served more as an excuse to get away on a holiday with other young folks.

We grew accustomed to the sweet aroma which permeated the premises. On a Sunday afternoon as the crowds waited for the busses which would take them home, you could get high just walking across the lobby!

On one such check-out day, several women clients who were not part of the tours but had driven up independently, were among the crowd. They inadvertently locked their keys in the car and asked for help from those gathered in the lower lobby area. No one volunteered.

Finally, one of the Hispanic young ladies who was having the key trouble, jumped up on a table and demanded: "Don't tell me that with 200 Puerto Ricans here, nobody can open my car!" I held my breath, shocked at the implied slur. The keys were retrieved and I learned the lesson that only a member of the same ethnic group can make jokes about that group and get away with it.

Hoteliers have always been plagued by minor theft. For some reason our summer guests figured that the rate covered towels, silverware, blankets, pictures, et al, which they "adopted" as souvenirs. Just for the record, we lost those items abundantly to our summertime Long Island clientele and never to our winter population. So much for popular wisdom.

The winter season had its own hazards for hotelkeeping: Not enough snow, too much snow in which to travel, freeze-ups, groups that came up short, alcoholics creating damage, to name just a few. But all in all it was a most satisfactory way to fill the hotel in what had been a barren time.

Ski season was relatively short, however, and there were other seasons to fill. We, and every other hotel operating on a 12-month basis, needed to look for other groups which traveled together. We found them.

There were Polka weekends and folk dance festivals. We catered to meditators, veteran's groups, organizational fund-raisers, family wedding parties, and the ubiquitous senior citizens.

Of them all, it was the traveling seniors who kept the hotels busiest in the spring and fall. Logically, they had the time and the disposable funds to make trips possible. Through churches, synagogues, social clubs and other interest groups, they were a line of business on which to count.

They were, in addition, a delight to serve. Appreciative, lively, optimistic, are three adjectives which seemed to apply

universally to our older guests. Perhaps it was only those who
had those attributes who were ready to move themselves out
and about.

We began to develop new methods of entertainment for our
seniors which we had never used before. They were pleased
with shopping trips to local emporiums, bus rides to view our
beautiful countryside, and formal entertainment which our
summer-time young families would reject. We presented sing-
a-longs, one-man shows, and "lectures" by anyone we could
find who was a bit different. Their acceptance of the simple was
fortunate, since the key to the groups was a low rate!

We all used speakers who worked for little or nothing,
sometimes because they were selling a product. Representatives
of brokerage houses were happy to send someone who would
speak on "investment for retirees," and local people gave
demonstrations of flower arranging (and sold inexpensive sam-
ples of their work). We tried to be as inventive as possible. I
told stories of how my folks got started. We even drafted a
young friend, Paul Nishman, who kept bees and spoke to our
groups about his hobby.

When groups were not forthcoming, we organized and
sought out a source of clientele which other hotels had discovered much earlier—singles' weekends. We had a lot to learn.

First of all, it seemed sensible to attempt to get people of
like ages to attend. It didn't take long to discover that mention-
ing the parameters was futile. In addition, the field had an
arithmetic all its own: 28 to 40 meant 50 and up! Over 45 meant
senior citizens!

Now that I am safely removed from hotelkeeping, I can
confess that the singles business endeavor was my least favorite
in the crazy-quilt of groups handled.

My original picture of "a single" was one of a person
relatively the age of my children. Imagine my surprise when,
on the very first weekend we put together, our initial arrival
was the grandmother of one of the bell-hops! "Poor lady,"

thought I, "she will be so out of place." She turned out to be amongst the youngest of the crowd!

Inevitably, in my experience, women outnumbered men by 2 to 1. With those demographics, the male of the species had his choice. It was the way that the choice was exercised that really offended me.

"Open seating" in the dining room meant that no one was assigned to a table. It was the established custom to handle dining in that way, and theoretically gave patrons a chance to meet many people over the course of the six meals served. The gentlemen always arrived in the dining room a bit later than the women. They wandered through the tables, eyes busily assaying, searching and rejecting. The procedure had all the elegance of a half-price sale!

The prizes which the females had come to find were not my idea of Prince Charmings, but in that atmosphere they were suddenly desirable. The whole process was demeaning. Furthermore, in the many weekends which economics determined that we must have, I can't think of a single couple who found each other.

The pursuit of group business necessitated a new staff member. We hired a convention manager. In actuality, the title was a misnomer for us. We had few conventions, and the gentleman did not "manage" anything. What we had was a person who could seek out the groups, something now too time consuming to add to my other duties.

In a place our size, such an employee worked essentially on commission. Unfortunately, the man we hired was not known for being unduly concerned with business ethics. It followed that we had some conflict over his predilection for "promising too much" and his willingness to book anything.

One afternoon he found me in the dining room and launched into a passionate pitch: "Please don't say no out of hand . . .you've got to realize that business is business . . . you can't tell customers how to think . . it's a large group and if we don't take them, someone else will . . ."

By this time he was breathless. I finally determined that he had received a message on our New York line. He was to call back a North Carolina exchange in reference to a weekend for 400 members of The White Citizens Council!

Now my brother Bob, who had his own New York line, was a constant joker with the phone. Since a quiet afternoon was prime time for him, I knew immediately who had set the trap. It took a while to convince my convention man that he had been had.

Certainly, one of the no-nos of the hotel business is involving yourself in guest politics. It behooves the host to stay away from any hot topic. There was one time when I couldn't resist.

The Disabled American Veterans held a gathering at Green Acres every June for three or four seasons. We may have been worlds apart in political philosophy, but we were personally fond of the committee who managed the outing, and impressed with the love and gentleness the entire entourage showed to each attendee. The group consisted mostly of World War II veterans, many of them terribly disabled. We became good friends in the course of their stays.

On one visit, at the height of the war in Viet Nam, I decided that I could speak with them about my anti-war convictions. My concerns and opinion were received with patience and respect, so I went a bit further. "How about a statement from this convention," I suggested, "on opposition to the conflict."

To my surprise they agreed to place the matter before the assemblage during a business meeting. I'm sorry to report that the proposition as I had outlined it went down to a rousing defeat, but I could discern no anger with me for having suggested it.

Anxious though we always were for business, my sophistication failed me when a couple arrived at the hotel one day to arrange a particular weekend, which they specified would be closed to the general public.

The visit was preceded by a phone inquiry. They asked initially if the hotel catered to "swingers." At that time, my definition of a swinger was someone who drank a lot and stayed up late, so I had answered "of course" and gone on to tell them about our wonderful night club, bars and super facilities.

After I showed the committee around the place and they were pleased with what they saw, we returned to my office to conclude the arrangements. It was then they began to ask some strange questions. Would we have all-night towel and linen service? Could extra mattresses be placed on bedroom floors? Would extra keys for exchanging be provided? And finally, albeit late, I began to see the light.

Having figured out the nature of the weekend, I knew we wouldn't be able to conquer our distaste. Even if Larry and I could have summoned the strength to accept the business, I couldn't imagine explaining the lifestyle to my children and my mother! We refused to book the group and settled for a "dark" weekend. Dark, in the trade, means empty, rarely a decision of choice for innkeepers.

As for the judgmental side of my character, I figured once in a lifetime I was entitled!

The group business provided us with a liberal education in Americana and experiences otherwise almost unattainable in the average lifetime. We met gays and girl scouts, bowling league members and master bridge players, folks with developmental disabilities and Mensa groups. Although our acquaintance was of necessity fleeting, we formed impressions.

I wonder now if my colleagues in the field might agree that: Folk dancers were always more politically liberal than square dancers----senior citizens on day trips went home with all the Sweet and Low packets----Unitarian groups were 3/4 Jewish---- male singles over 50 had a penchant for gold chains and pinky rings----the handsomest men showed up at gay weekends----state troopers were the most obstreperous guests----polka dancers

arrived with their own liquor supply----and our most appreciative guests were the physically and mentally challenged.

Having said all that, I apologize for the generalizations and
stereotypes. The difficulty with weekend business was that we
rarely got to know individuals very well, and so the impressions. . . well, they are just impressions.

The operation of a hotel on a 12-month basis was our
salvation economically, but it certainly impacted on our personal lives. We were "on tap" constantly, fought for family
together time, and missed a lot of the world outside our own
domain. We did have quiet mid-weeks in the winter months,
built a home from which we did not move with the seasons,
and even had weeks where we could get away for a vacation.
But the bulk of our days found us immersed in work and
responsibility, and we began to tire.

Still, we never expected to be able to sell the hotel. We knew
of few successful sales and thought we were in "for life." It was
my assumption that I would die at my desk. . .hopefully not on
a busy weekend!

In the mid seventies, a favorite sport for visitors to the area
seemed to be "hotel shopping." Our place wasn't listed anywhere, but that didn't stop the committees who toured the
grounds. We laughed about the "buyers" who never flinched
at a good stiff price. The price was fine; the down payment
they offered was a dollar ninety eight!

The point was reached when I took none of the prospective
buyers seriously and rarely moved from my desk when approached. If anyone wanted to see the hotel, I suggested they
take a tour on their own. When the "real buyer" arrived, he
was treated in the same cavalier manner!

Sell we did, and well, in 1975. The resort was purchased by
David and Leon Scharf of New York, who planned and opened
a residential school for mildly retarded adults. The Scharfs, after
15 years, sold it to the parents of the residents there. Green
Acres is now called New Hope Community and we are grati-

fied to have the property used so well and for such a good purpose.

We were very successful at Green Acres/Loch Sheldrake. There were times I thought it would never happen, but the day came when I was able to send a letter to a banker that ended:

"Sincerely----but no longer----yours"!

Interior of Green Acres at Loch Sheldrake.

So This Is Progress?

$\mathcal{I}$ DO NOT WISH TO SUGGEST that only Jewish immigrants and their offspring can be good hosts. Still, I am constantly surprised at what I find in the resort field, now that we have finally arrived at "guesthood" ourselves.

All across the country, million-dollar properties staff their front desks with greeters who telegraph disinterest and impersonality. Only on TV hotel ads does one find warmth and charm applied to a visitor's first moments. It is the rare hostelry that has a visible owner, and those in charge toss a registration slip across the desk without any real recognition of the guest who receives it.

Once roomed, one may literally never again be spoken to by anyone in management. The 1990s innkeepers seem to completely overlook the hospitality that was so basic to our mountain hotel operations. We followed every one of our patrons throughout the days of their vacation. Florence Neukrug (Avon Lodge) told me of her father's unbreakable law: "The family walks the floor in the dining room to make sure that their guests are happy, not only with the food being served, but with every part of their stay." So it was for all of us. We knew

248

if guests liked the show, if their children were adjusted to day camp, and if the menu pleased them. Most important of all, we got to know them----they were people who were living with us.

I've been told that I am living in the past, and things have changed. The Sheratons and Hiltons don't intrude on their guests, so why did Catskill hoteliers?

I'm accused of not accepting "progress." Maybe things have changed, but I don't believe that people have. I don't think that there is anyone who did not or would not appreciate a personal welcome and an interested, visible host. Besides, I liked it better the old way!

Maybe it's a sign of age, but lately I have some real questions as to the relative value of what we call "progress"! I will freely admit that my questions apply to the trivial as well as to deep-seated philosophy.

Phone company progress, for instance, took us from operator answered calls to dials and then push buttons; and the replacement of the old "exchanges" to a world of pure numbers. I liked the exchanges. Maybe it was because they were easier to remember, and were useful in other ways as well. We had a relative who bemoaned her inability to remember names. She was particularly concerned about remembering her granddaughter's fiancé. It was our suggestion that she associate his name with a familiar telephone exchange. "Aunt Anna, you certainly know your son's number----Jerome 6-1347. Just think of Jerome, that's the young man's name."

Well, not every plan always works. Imagine the consternation when Anna approached the groom warmly at the wedding reception: "Endicott, darling, *Mazeltov!*"

When I was growing up, our world had no "senior citizens." We did have people who were old, but no one had yet coined the phrase which I believe serves to separate our society. Of course, neither was it an imperative for grandparents to spend the winters in Florida and take Spanish lessons.

It was only progress that brought us the phenomenon of nursing homes and "golden age" retirement villages. In the days that were, most homes had a *bubbe* and *zeyde* nearby or in residence for at least part of the year. Unlike today's child of the suburbs, or our own exurbians, we were not denied the society of mixed ages and experience.

In Woodridge, we knew not only our own grandparents, but the grandparents of our friends as well. We were exposed to their language, their food, and their stories of another world. We were influenced by their philosophies, and they were not intermittent visitors, but an integral part of the fabric of our lives. We basked in their certainty that grandchildren were "perfection."

Just down the road apiece, maybe as far as New York City, were uncles and aunts and cousins by the dozen. The world had not yet achieved the mobility that took extended family to the far corners of the world.

If there is one outstanding difference between our lives and those of our children, it is the vast array of technical advances that they handle with ease. Grade schoolers operate computers, word processors, calculators, and the like, while some of us look on in awe.

Our adult children have dragged me, kicking and screaming, into the twentieth century. They have brought unsolicited additions to my life in the form of microwave, Cuisinart, VCR, CD player, and computer. I, who considered myself a "modernist" when I abandoned my manual Royal typewriter for the IBM Selectric, fought them all the way!

It is easy to understand how much business, government, and medical life have benefited from the use of the computer. That I am struggling to master its complexities, and have an unreasonable resistance to its wonders, is surely one of my shortcomings, and I regret it. I understand as well, pluses for those on medication in the codifying and easy monitoring of prescriptions in the microchip file. I am told that this system provides greater safety as well as efficiency. Who am I to argue? That's progress with a capital P. So why do I miss the days when the drugstore owner was called "Doc" and always discussed your condition. In our little town, pharmacist Meyer Lebed had a standard quip on receiving the doctor's instructions: "I had a friend, *aleve sholem* (rest in peace), who used to take this medicine."

Maybe we've lost something in the maze of technology. You can take your own blood pressure by machine while you wait for the potions, but you can't get a hot chocolate or a "two-cents plain" and the chain drugstore employees have no time to talk, much less make you laugh.

In the resort world, progress was most noticeable (and welcome) when technology made life easier and more comfortable. One could hardly complain, for instance, about the demise of the old "icehouse" which preceded modern refrigeration. It was a large, frame, barn-like structure, usually located as close to the kitchen as possible, that housed huge blocks of ice. From the icehouse, the blocks were transferred as needed to an indoor walk-in box in which perishables were kept. Literally buried in sawdust, the ice, I seem to remember, lasted most of the summer. It was cut, during our frigid winters, from the lake on which the hotel property fronted. As children, we eagerly anticipated being spectators at that ice harvest. Cars were driven onto the lake, and with a tire removed, a belt on the wheel powered the cutting saw. My brother and I considered the process to be great entertainment.

According to John Weiner of White Roe Hotel, his family hotel also had an icehouse. "The cutters, all locals," he says, "were tobacco chewers. This became painfully evident when, later in the summer, someone drinking a highball at the bar would note a speck of dark brown in a piece of his ice. 'That's the iron in the water,' the bartender would explain. 'Very good for the blood!' " John remembers that the severity of a winter was judged by the thickness of the ice: 10-12 inches——mild, 15 inches——average, and 18-23 inches——very severe.

When its day had passed, our icehouse, and every other hotel's similar structure, was renovated, usually into sleeping quarters.

There were other progressive changes that made less sense to me.

Hotels, originally, served soup in heavy silver cups that waiters carried into the dining room and then emptied into bowls at the guests settings. They were able to serve piping hot soup. That procedure was abandoned in favor of minute vessels that held a thimblefull, which was tepid by the time it arrived at its destination. They are still serving soup that way. Maybe the miniature portion is more *aydle* (refined), but the soup is cold, and there isn't enough of it!

I sound like the standard ancient joke that seemed to be a part of every stand-up comic's repertoire in our area: Two guests return from vacation. One asks, "How was the food at your place?" The answer: "Pure poison----and such small portions!"

Among the changes that I applauded was the retirement of the heavy crockery, standard for hotel dining rooms way back when. In those days it took real strength to lift a coffee cup. The dishes were practically indestructible but graceless and homely.

With the advent of the automatic dishwashing machine to replace hand washing, it became possible to use finer china. Lo and behold, that same clumsy service is now appearing as "collectible" in smart antique shops! So are the bentwood chairs that were universally used in hotel dining rooms. They were strong, very inexpensive, and we couldn't wait to replace them with something more modern. Progress.

The world has become so accustomed to communicating with high-tech machines, that I have noticed a marked decline in person-to-person skills. Corporate America must have noticed it too, for bank clerks and receptionists have been trained to use rehearsed patter. They think they are "reaching out" when they tell you, with the world's most overused phrase, to "Have a nice day."

Today's progress has brought us machines that talk. I've already mentioned that I'm not too choked up about machines, but I really hate it when one of them thanks me for using AT&T!

In this "advanced" society, even the fine art of matchmaking is being handled by newspaper "personals" or commercial outfits that use technology to measure compatibility.

At our hotel, we had a resident artist, tennis pro, physician, and discussion leader. We had as well an unashamed resident *shatchen* (matchmaker) in the form of my mother. It was her favorite indoor sport, and she was very often successful. Even though the hotel clientele was predominantly family, there was always an unattached bookkeeper, desk clerk, or salesperson on whom she could concentrate.

When one summer our house physician was single, my mother invited a succession of unmarried cousins to visit. Since none of the relatives struck his fancy, she decided that our secretary should leave the staff table and join the doctor in the dining room. That maneuver was a winner. Taking no chances with time, mother made the wedding at the hotel in August!

I particularly remember the year when her potential couple were our widowed auditor and a member of the accounting firm with whom we did business. She "ordered" the bachelor accountant to service our books, even though another member of the firm had been handling the account. It was hard to refuse my mother.

He did indeed come from his office in Woodridge to Lake Huntington. My mother's "compatibility" antennae were in good working form—Ben Kantzler and Evelyn Morris married in the fall. We had the best accounting service in our history.

I am sure that it is true for every form of career in which one has spent a lifetime, but hotel people, at least, retain their interest in the industry. In the safety of retirement, I find myself scrutinizing surviving establishments and comparing them with the way in which we did business.

On a recent visit to Kutsher's Country Club, I noted an absence of microphone paging. The use of personal beepers and a modern phone system keeps their public space and grounds in delightful stillness. I wish I could have said the same for our premises of yore.

Our telephone setup was at best primitive; some rooms didn't even have phones. We were also missing the instruments that had lights to alert occupants when there was a message. Beepers, of course, had not yet been invented. The grounds were extensive, and it was hard to hear the crickets as handymen, housekeepers, and the management were interminably called. Part of the noise pollution resulted from summoning guests to phone calls.

On one opening weekend, we determined to keep the paging to a minimum. It was decided that the solution would involve putting guests' messages into the cubbyholes at the front desk which held their keys and mail. As luck would have it, one lodger's broker was trying to reach him on that Friday afternoon, relative to a large block of stock to be sold. The guest picked up the note in his box after 5 P.M., apparently suffered a severe loss as a result, and there was hell to pay. We abandoned the attempt for silence and resumed paging.

Kutsher's, very much a "today" hotel, has an abundance of state-of-the-art equipment for the use of performers. Monitors; standing, sitting and walking around microphones; banks of spotlights; deluxe sound equipment; portable video machines; and skilled technicians to run them are all in evidence.

It was with retroactive shame that I remembered our own attempts to provide "high tech" for the very same stars who were entertaining there.

We did have one microphone, and a spotlight. The latter's only versatility was the possibility of amber or magenta. Our sound system's capability was for "on" or "off"! Comedians teased me, in those days, by proclaiming on stage that when they complained about the piano being out of tune, I had it painted.

Most of us hoteliers really loved "the acts" and wanted to please them. Our size, the shortage of money, and another set of priorities severely limited our ability to provide them with the niceties.

When Green Acres was in Loch Sheldrake, we took full advantage of our proximity to and friendship with the Posner family of the Brickman hotel. We entered the age of technology through the back door. When a convention group needed video equipment, a screen or slide projectors, we borrowed them!

I'm forced to the conclusion that progress is a mixed blessing, in the innkeeping business as well as in every segment of life. But as I said before, maybe that's age speaking.

Watching the ice harvest in the days before refrigererators replaced ice boxes was great entertainment for my brother and me. Originally done largely by hand, ice harvesting in the 1930s became mechanized.

Changing Populations

DURING THE 1890s, New York City's death rate as a result of tuberculosis, or consumption as it was called in those days, rose at an alarming rate. It was higher there than any other city or town in the United States. Particularly vulnerable to the disease were the residents of the overcrowded slum sections like the Lower East Side, where homes and places of work were poorly ventilated, person-to-person contact was continuous, and the population was overworked and undernourished.

The city's best known authority for lung diseases was a Dr. Alfred Loomis, who, using the newest wisdom in the field, planned to raise money to build a rural sanitarium where indigent sufferers could be isolated and could, at least in the early stages of the disease, find a cure in the fresh air of the mountains. The "fresh air therapy" that found such favor in those days is deemed now to have no medical basis as a treatment for the bacterial lung infection. If nothing else, it helped limit the spread of the disease by isolating those who were infected.

Dr. Loomis died before he could execute his plan, but he left many friends among New York's rich and powerful, who carried out his dream as a memorial. Among them was banker J. P. Morgan, who had lost his first wife to tuberculosis.

In accordance with Dr. Loomis' wishes, the sanitarium was built in Liberty. It was a magnificent structure, more like a mansion than a charitable institution, and set in the picturesque hills, just outside the town.

The Olivia in Loomis, a tuberculosis sanitarium.

Loomis Sanitarium itself, and the "word" of fresh air's curative powers, brought a stream of people to our mountain boardinghouses, and a host of others who remained as permanent residents. We had a new industry, which was to flourish for a long time.

So pervasive was the area's reputation as a haven for the tubercular, that Grossinger's hotel, in Liberty, changed its mailing address, first to Ferndale, and then to "Grossinger, N.Y.," to avoid the stigma.

Our mother, in those days, cautioned us that we were not to drink from glasses or use restaurant utensils in the Liberty area, for fear of contamination. But we were to see her medical "knowledge" at work years later as well, at a time that she decided our hotel should not take people from the Bronx, when an outbreak of polio was centered in that borough!

With the advance of medicine and the discovery of wonder drugs, tuberculosis was conquered, and health care, as an industry, declined in the area. Interestingly, several decades later, with the demise of many resorts, it has returned once again, but in a very different form.

Our diminishing tourist industry, from the late 1970s on, created a bonanza for organizations that were seeking properties in which to locate rehabilitation centers for those afflicted by the new scourges of the times. Drug and alcohol addiction, when it became a national problem, was the target for cures in many different modes. Among them was the theory that involved separation from an original community to enclaves where the individual could be treated for given periods of time. The bargain price of hotels was just what the New York nonprofits were looking for.

Paul's in Swan Lake became Day Top Village, Logos took over the Young's Gap Hotel in Liberty, the Valley View Resort in Kauneonga Lake retained its name but exists now to treat addicted populations. The Delmar Hotel (Liberty) became Re-Directions, Murray Hill Hotel (Fallsburg) is now Dynamite Youth Center and there are many more.

When the national conscience was pricked by revelations of abuse and overcrowded, inhumane conditions at facilities for the developmentally disabled, the "Willowbrook Decree" was passed by the New York State legislature during the early 1970s. The long-overdue philosophy that it promulgated, that the stricken among us were entitled to "the least restrictive environment," was translated into law. The Department of Health began a plan to move the populations of state institutions out into the community. They called it "deinstitutionalization."

Once again, it was to the Catskills that the state and private not-for-profit organizations turned for inexpensive properties.

This time they were to be used as more equitable residential settings for the disabled.

The Flagler (Fallsburg) became the new home for Crystal Run Village, our own Green Acres (Loch Sheldrake) was converted to New Hope Community, Greenwood Inn (Greenfield Park) was adapted for treatment of the developmentally disabled, and the New Brighton (Parksville) emerged as the Hebrew Academy for Special Children. These larger, mini-institutions, were only part of the picture. Homes were bought up as well, to serve as an even more "normalizing" housing option for the developmentally disabled as well as the mentally ill.

For those suffering from serious and persistent mental illness, the discovery of psychotropic drugs allowed a new door to swing open. It was no longer necessary for them to languish in the asylums of old. They could live in the community, with help and a support system, and do so successfully.

The arrival of these new and vulnerable populations was a double-edged sword. There was no question that the establishment of all of those disciplines created a new industry. Both the larger and smaller units employed staffs who lived, bought, and spent their salaries in our towns. Indeed, their payrolls alone pumped millions of dollars into the local economy. The facilities were, in addition, purchasers of goods and services for their consumers, and the renovations and improvements that they undertook gave sorely needed work to all the trades. The fly in the ointment was that, being non-profit, none of them were required to pay taxes. For local businesspeople and homeowners, the missing tax dollar had to be divided and absorbed.

The health-care agencies are not alone in their tax-free status. Meditation groups, ashrams, and other quasi-religious entities seized on the opportunity of available properties at a fraction of their replacement value, to become another part of our scene. The Waldemere (Livingston Manor), the Gilbert and Windsor and Brickman (Fallsburg) were all converted to new uses—and off the tax rolls.

It can be argued that there was no line of prospective buyers waiting to buy all those former hotels, but the effect on the economy is evident.

Twenty-odd years after the nonprofits arrived here, I think that the locals have finally been convinced that the new populations are good neighbors. The fear and doubt that was volubly expressed in the early days has been put to rest by a virtually unblemished record that reflects none of the horror stories projected.

The NIMBY (Not In My Back Yard) syndrome espoused every prejudice and myth about people with disabilities. It was reminiscent of the kind of blind defamation to which our early Jewish settlers were "treated." Only the specifics differed. We heard talk of possible rape, fear for the safety of local children, concern that the tourist industry would be affected by the very sight of those who were not exactly the same as the neighbors. And the bottom line was always "Property values will go down"!

In order to sell our hotel to those serving developmentally-disabled persons, it was necessary to go before the zoning board of the town. So naive were we as to prevailing public opinion, that we didn't even attend the meeting. We merely sent our attorney to present the case, and we were turned down! The next step was the zoning board of appeals.

That time, needing a unanimous vote, we did our homework. It was necessary to convince each member of the seven man panel, and we took our time.

Somehow we were able to get the vote needed, and the sale went through.

It is heartening to report that today the villagers of Loch Sheldrake firmly support New Hope Community (the former Green Acres) which now serves a developmentally disabled population.

This area is proof of the fact that every original fear was unfounded. Though property values did indeed go down, it was for very different reasons than the presence of the new populations. Those with disabilities were responsible for no increase in crime, their individual homes are well kept; the truth is simply that they have become part of our communities without incident.

Not every village opposed the new community residences. Both officials and townspeople in Woodridge, Fallsburg and Monticello, made their newcomers feel at home. They attended open houses, did business, and accepted the differences in their neighbors which are visible. I think that can be a new definition for *menchlichkeit* (humanity).

When members of the Hasidic community (ultra-orthodox Jews), who had vacationed for years in our mountains, began to arrive in greater numbers, the area experienced yet another wave of "immigration." Former hotels were purchased to become Yeshivas (religious schools in which secular subjects are also taught), and a small year-around population developed. The availability of parochial schools became an attraction for ultra-orthodox and orthodox populations, adding to the diversity in our county. The vacationers among these religious groups were essentially bungalow colony dwellers and our neighbors, for the most part, only on a seasonal basis. In many cases they bought bungalow colonies for their exclusive use, creating condominium and cooperative enclaves. To cater to their special needs and tastes, many business sprang up, particularly in Woodburne and Woodridge. Kosher bakeries and meat markets, fruit stores and bookstores, notion shops and restaurants are all geared to the population they serve. Most are open for business only during the summer months.

The new arrivals, much like the orthodox adherents of any religion, are clannish and bound by their own world of belief and ritual. Many look different in their special clothing and have customs with which our local people are unfamiliar. The world has changed enough so that there have been no overt incidents of bias such as their predecessors experienced years ago. While their is no joy in the arrival of the Orthodox, neither was there anything but "talk" about this new wave.

The largest groups of Hasidim are centered around Wood-bourne. On Saturday nights in the summer, when Sabbath is over, the streets of that hamlet are filled to overflowing. Stores catering to the group offer everything from kosher pizza to falafel----the scene is vibrant and colorful, as a crowd of all ages shops and visits. Conversations in English and Yiddish fill the night. My friend, Elizabeth Berman, reported the charm of a tiny tot wearing a *yarmulke* and *tsitzes* (skull cap and prayer shawl) asking his mother, "Kafe fa mir a keevee." (Buy me a piece of kiwi fruit.)

We were to receive yet another wave of "immigration." In this case, they were welcomed with open arms.

Proximity to the urban areas and our natural beauty were certainly part of the attraction for the huge numbers that decided on Sullivan County as their second home destination. I believe there is a further reason. Many of those who purchased here were our guests and staffs of old. They remembered the mountains as the scene of the "best times of their lives," and it was a magnet for them as a vacation destination and a place of retirement.

So when the Pines (Fallsburg), the Kutsher's (Monticello), and Brown's (Loch Sheldrake), among others, created veritable villages with all the facilities of a hotel in close proximity, the houses sold like proverbial hotcakes. Independent builders created other enclaves in all the communities, Vacation Village (Loch Sheldrake, on the Evans property), Davos (Woodridge), which was once the site of Kleinberg's hotel, and Camelot Village (Sacket Lake), to name just a few. Those communities feature pools, entertainment halls, athletic facilities, day camps, and the conviviality of "friends next door." The beautiful Brown's hotel is the latest spot to be purchased and renovated as studio and one-bedroom apartments. Potential purchasers are the thousands who trek south for the winter and return north for the summer. For those who seek single homes, real estate in our area remains a country bargain and a mighty attraction.

I'm not sure how old the concept of "bed & breakfast" is, but it was unknown in my days as a hotelperson. In the last years we have seen this new form of vacation possibility really taking root here. Essentially dealing in small numbers of rooms, the B & Bs are uniformly charming in decor and welcoming in spirit.

They are totally unstructured and conducive to the traveler who gets away for a short period. For the guests who choose them, the panorama of things to do includes the nightclubs of the hotels, the summer theaters, the small entertainment clubs as well as the public and private golf courses, the antique shops, the ski hills, the trout streams, and our countryside, rich in history and unexplored byways.

Perhaps most unexpected for me are the changes that other "new populations" have made in the western part of the county where I grew up. Narrowsburg, restricted and provincial in my memory, is now the home of an opera company. Callicoon, which in my day was steeped in reaction, has attracted young people who are making unexpected changes: supper clubs, artists and artisans abound. Jeffersonville boasts new citizens who are painters and sculptors; and Lake Huntington, the town of my childhood, features string quartets and folk singers in the entertainment center that was once a bar and bowling alley. I should have known to never say never!

The Story Doesn't End

LEGEND TELLS that a biblical king was searching for a phrase that would be forever applicable to any event or life situation anywhere. He presented that conundrum to suitors for his daughter's hand in marriage. The successful swain was the one who presented the truism, "This too shall pass."

For the resorts in our Catskills that were successful for decades, and that flourished and grew and developed a world-wide reputation, changing times brought a diminution of the crowds and the passing of an era. It didn't happen all at once, but slowly and surely we began to see a changing business landscape.

Earlier on, when expansion and improvements were the order of the day, the small hotel units that could not afford to modernize were unable to compete with their neighbors. They were the first to fail.

When it became obvious that there was an imperative to "keep up with the resort Joneses," that endeavor led other hotels to take the gamble of short-term financing and the acceptance of unrealistic debt to produce the improvements that the buyer/guest expected each season. It became a sad joke in our family that next year we would be asked for an indoor mountain.

For those who did keep up, there were an assortment of additional reasons for decline. When added together the results were devastating to the resorts themselves and to the community at large.

The base of our original tourist population were women and children who spent a good portion or all of the summer in the mountains. It was a given for husbands to commute on weekends to the bungalows or hotels of choice where their families escaped the city. Once the society changed so that women worked full time, a full summer in the country was no longer an option.

The metropolitan population, which was our stock in trade, was already less desperate to leave the urban area when air-conditioning made the city bearable during the summer months.

With upward mobility, increasing incomes, and a change in the city, many of our former guests moved to the suburbs. There, beach clubs, pools, and day camps burgeoned, providing another way to spend July and August. Vacations in the Catskills continued, but stays became shorter.

Airlines had already lowered their fares to the point where the middle class could afford to see more of the world. Travel to the Caribbean and Europe was a powerful lure and provided all the cache and excitement of a more sophisticated form of recreation. Additionally, vacations no longer needed to be confined to summer. Warm climates like our own south and west were accessible during the snowy months, and winter vacations became popular. Not to be discounted, in the loss of business, was the second generation's desire for more multi-ethnic settings.

The hotelmen here neglected to respond to changing tastes. It has always been my feeling that we waited too long to court the non-Jewish world that lay at our doorstep. Advertisements that featured the kosher menus could easily be interpreted as another kind of "restricted" stipulation.

There existed too, an unwillingness on the part of the hoteliers to make changes in formulae that had succeeded in the past. The three-meal regimen, which we clung to, was no longer in favor with the younger tourist. Aside from the Olympic and Brickman, no hotel innovated with the modified-American plan, which was used in other areas.

The consistent attitude of the press toward this area and their relentless stigmatization added fuel to the fire and was a significant reason for those who stayed away.

It is important to remember that while our business was falling off, so was business in the rest of the nation's resort areas. We had always been vulnerable to economic dents, recessions, and depressions because we were engaged in a luxury industry. That many hotels were unable to withstand drops in business was due to the immense debts the properties carried, financed poorly with unrealistic time frames in which to meet the obligations. Because the hotels were family owned and, in the vast majority of cases, a sole source of income for those owners, they were unable to absorb the losses from poor seasons. I can't think of one hotel that was part of a conglomerate and could count on other income to tide it over difficult times.

An additional blow for existing resorts came with the establishment of a gambling empire in Atlantic City, New Jersey. Now group business, which had become a significant source of income, particularly in our off-season, was attracted to the lush casinos and brand new hotels established in our reachable proximity. We had no like activity with which to compete.

For some inexplicable reason, the citizens of this area did not appreciate the industry that lay at the core of the economy. One had only to look at the growth of allied businesses in every single village of the counties to realize that as the hotels went so went the financial life of every citizen. Yet the community as a whole never entered the spirit of solving problems together. Year after year the budget to promote tourism was a source of rancor and dispute for our governing body.

When times changed there was no organized attempt to support tourist destinations that would attract the crowds and help not only hotels, bungalow colonies, and motels, but by so doing would bring the entire area to life.

The hue and cry locally was for "industry." We had an industry, but no one seemed to recognize that it was the lifeblood and the underpinning for economic life. A myth emerged, which somehow still exists, to the effect that it was the hotel business people who discouraged manufacturing from coming to the area. No one has yet given me any hard evidence of an incident that would prove the allegation.

The fact that hotel properties bore the brunt of property taxes here suggests that they would have welcomed any business to share the load. Realistically, there are a host of reasons for General Electric et al. not locating in our back yard— distance from a metropolitan center, lack of rail transport, and a weak skilled-labor pool, to name just a few.

The reasons that led to defamation of the resort owners are multiple. They include an underlying anti-Semitism that never seems to go away. In addition, the perception of great wealth squirreled away, or purposeful bankruptcy, or mean-spirited failure to meet bills when business fell off, added to declining friendship with the community.

The charges, in the vast majority of cases, were just not true. There were cheats in our business as there are in any other endeavors, but most of those who failed found themselves dispossessed of everything for which they had labored.

For too many years our local populations resented the waves of tourists we resort people courted so avidly. The city folks filled the streets and the supermarkets, created traffic on the country roads, and by their very numbers created waves on the bucolic scene. It was almost as if the citizenry wished that the New Yorkers would stay at home. . . and just send the money!

When the resorts became the dominant industry in this corner of the mountains, a host of businesses sprang up. Some of them became synonymous with the Catskills. Singer's in Liberty and Kaplan's restaurant in Monticello were de rigeur for a meal sometime during the season. Marcia's (Liberty) was the premier women's clothing salon. Sullivan's (Liberty) was our answer to Macy's and the Wunderbar (Old Falls), Frank and Bob's (South Fallburg), the Kentucky Club (Woodridge), as well as Herbie's and the 52 Club (Loch Sheldrake) were the late-night places to be. Katz's Bakery in Liberty had them standing on line in the morning. So it should have been obvious that there was more to the tourist industry than just hotels, bungalow colonies, and camps, and that every trade connected directly to them. The "we" and "they" attitude that existed for too long prevented the obvious need for the entire community to seek solutions to failing business.

When Green Acres' newly renovated main building burned in 1966, we tried in every possible way to find a means of rebuilding on the premises that had housed us for a lifetime. The half-million-dollar improvement project was only three years old and we were disastrously underinsured. The fire took place just two days after the "grievance day" that the town held on taxes each year. Taxes are levied in advance, so that it seemed reasonable for us to receive some adjustment to help the hotel to get going again. The town refused, and considering all the factors, we had no choice but to leave the homestead on which the family had labored for 45 years. We purchased in Loch Sheldrake where another Green Acres would be financially feasible.

Lake Huntington, which would have happily provided a tax abatement to any new "industry" that employed eight people, only missed us when we were gone. The drugstore closed, the notion shop went out of business, and even the post office was reclassified.

Individually, there are stories that any hotelkeeper can tell about help, encouragement, and cooperation from community members, and not only on a self-seeking basis. Perhaps the answer to relationships is connected to the verity that people respond to each other in one way and to a business in another. When a business is in trouble, and everyone bears some of the effects, what develops is a scapegoat attitude. Problems have to be "someone's fault." Solutions require a coming together and an abandonment of recrimination.

Not only did owners of properties that were failing suffer the predictable personal results, but there was a lack of sympathy, and more, an anger at those who were in trouble. I hear to this day the criticism of the former owners of properties that were abandoned and fell to ruin, or succumbed to fire.

"Why don't they clean up the property, take down the disintegrating structures?" is repeated and repeated. The answer should be more than obvious. When property owners left those hotels, or colonies, or farms, or houses, they left because there was nothing with which to continue! In most cases it was neither sloth nor indifference that caused their neglect. There just wasn't the money to accomplish the clean up.

Today when you pass a closed, decaying resort, know that in the sagging grey timbers and weed-choked pool are buried the dreams, expectations, and prodigious labor of a family. The faded signs and crumbling entrance gates are a mute memorial to the herculean efforts of real people who struggled and eventually lost.

We regarded as a truism the fact that "everyone thinks he can run a hotel"! It took the experience of watching new owners of mountain properties to prove that we were right. Entrepreneurs from any and all enterprises who took over hotels here uniformly failed. Even though most had bought "huge bargains," and were then operating with a fraction of the debt load of their predecessors, they reckoned without the immense amount of expertise that Catskill hotel people developed over the years, and the inordinate skill required to manage a resort.

The Flagler and the Tamarack were both successful properties at the time they were sold. The new owners, who came from other careers to become hoteliers, failed in a relatively short period of time. The Laurels, Morningside, Brown's, Majestic, Olympic and Nemerson and Stevensville Lake hotels were among those who could not survive the change to new owners. Between failures and sales, our 500-plus hotels have been reduced to a scant dozen. The chapter on the golden days of the Catskills is closed. We speak with nostalgia of the days that were.

That is not, however, the end of the story.

Beginning in the 1930s and 1940s, when hotel people vacationed, their destination was Florida, specifically Miami and Miami Beach. Depending upon their circumstances, and length of stay, the mountaineers stayed in hotels, homes, and the southern equivalent of our own bungalows, the ubiquitous efficiencies.

Indeed, some of our more successful colleagues were themselves the builders and/or owners of properties, predominantly on what is known as South Beach.

The proprietors of the Gibber Hotel ran the Cadet; the Levinsons who owned Tamarack Lodge, created the Algiers; The Olympic's Horowitz family were part of the Avalon; Meyer Weiner and his sons of the White Roe, operated the Plymouth; the Evans family ran the Seagull and the Governor; The Novaks (Laurel's Country Club) were the owners of the Sans Souci; Stevensville Lake's Dinnersteins owned the Ritz Plaza and the Lucerne; the Kutsher family had the Beacon and Haddon Hall; Gartenberg and Schecter of the Pioneer owned the King David. . . and on and on.

South Beach, in its heyday, was as posh and lovely as it could be—and it was busy! The late forties and fifties, and even the sixties, were the decades of success, very much like our own history in the mountains.

Decline began when airfares to the Caribbean and Europe became affordable, and when young vacationers abandoned their fathers' spas for the flavor of overseas travel.

I last visited South Beach in the early eighties. At that time only the very old tourists remained. Seeing them lined up in rows on the front porches of the resorts, one felt that the average age was—deceased!

Starting in the seventies, the area experienced a drastic loss of business. Hotels changed hands, the clubs and fashionable shops were closed, the atmosphere was radically changed. Properties showed signs of neglect, as hurricane and other weather damage went uncorrected. The "snow birds" (those northerners who went south for the winter, including the mountain folks), purchased condominiums in the northern suburbs, where self-contained communities gave them everything they needed for extended stays.

South Beach became seedy, Lincoln Road lost its haute couture shops and became the home of second-rate stores and fast food restaurants. It seemed as if that golden land was gone forever. But today, that section has undergone a renaissance! It is back in all its glory, and has become a kind of Riviera in the United States.

The hotels have been restored to their former deco beauty and color. Cafes spill out to the sidewalks and music is everywhere. The young and the beautiful are in evidence as photographers use the beaches as backgrounds for international models.

Tourists come from every corner of the globe, creating a diversity of age, national origin and dress. Galleries, museums, and smart shops have returned to Lincoln Road and Washington Avenue. The entire area has been designated as an historical one, and renovators are closely supervised to make sure that any addition is in the style of days gone by.

Entertainment is the order of the day. During my visit in 1995, Luciano Pavarotti did a concert on the beach. The Miami Beach Convention Center was host to a huge antique show. A wonderful old building had been turned into a symphony hall on Lincoln Road, part of which is now closed to traffic. And the mountain acts of yore were playing the condos! It was hard to find a table at charming bistros which abounded. On Ocean Drive, the promenade was shared by rollerbladers and elderly folks with walkers! In short, the area is very much back.

It is my belief that the Catskills has the same possibility of rejuvenation. When I was a hotelkeeper, guests came specifically to a resort of their choice, and they remained on the grounds of that hotel for the length of their stay. Vacationers of today do not follow that old pattern. They travel, rather, to a destination, and that place is chosen based on "things to do and see." The veritable reincarnation of South Beach was accomplished by a very few people——a consortium of the business community, grassroots supporters, and government, working in concert. It is my hope that we here can find that combination. It is my certainty that we still have the ingenuity and the will to do what others have done.

There is a new and exciting stirring of understanding in the community now that recognizes a revitalization of tourism, our answer in the past, as the path that can lead to success in the future. There is a new and concerted effort by townspeople and government to work toward that end.

There is a groundswell of support for gambling in the county. There are groups working to restore the Catskills as an entertainment center, whether it be in theater, country music, symphony halls, or nightclub variety shows. Interest is alive in making the old Woodstock site into a new concert park, and the Laurel's property into a home for a symphony orchestra.

We are privileged to live in a dramatically beautiful part of the world. Our lakes and streams await the avid fisherman. We have a plethora of outstanding golf courses, and our surviving resorts remain a "best buy" in the tourist world. We are still less than two hours from New York. We can create the needed tourist destinations.

In 1994, a not-for-profit organization was born in Sullivan County that seeks to restore the mountains to their former glory. IDEA (Institute for the Development of Entertainment Arts) is involved in creating once again the vibrant programs that distinguished the Catskills of yesterday. Stan Raiff, the group's visionary sparkplug, produced that year the first of what have become annual entertainment festivals.

He called it "Remember the Catskills" and featured entertainers like Eddie Fisher, and Irwin Corey, who began their careers here. With them he introduced new and aspiring young stars to be. Publicity releases were sent to the press in nearby eastern states. Along with the announcement of the event, Raiff solicited mountain recollections of former guests and staff members. Offering prizes to the winners of the contest, he asked for "a favorite Catskill memory."

Hundreds of letters poured in. It seemed as if anyone who had ever visited this area had a story to be told! Here is one from an enterprising former hotel employee, now a physician in Dresher, Pennsylvania:

> While a college student during the early forties, I worked one summer as a bellhop in a Catskill hotel.
>
> The first complaint I received from a guest involved a squeaky bedspring. I promised to take care of the problem, and exchanged it for a spring from the room next door. A generous tip was forthcoming for my efforts.
>
> The next day, the complaint came from that room next door ----the same squeaky bedspring. Again I took care of the problem — and in the same way. That brought another good tip.
>
> For the next month or so, I continued to move the offending bedspring, making money each time. It was a wonderful way to augment my check-in and check-out income! ---Dr. Leonard L. Lit

Another Pennsylvanian, Bettyanne Gray, tells of her favorite "souvenir" from the hotel world:

> We used to tell our children that they behaved well enough to go to the White House, but as a reward we'd take them to the Catskills. One vacation stands out above all the wonderful times we had at places like Grossingers, the Concord, Kutshers and the Nevele.
>
> It was to the Nevele that we took our family for Thanksgiving in 1966. The kids were enthralled with the ice skating, the new friends made, and the amiable counselors. We hardly saw them. But we did notice, as we wandered from activity to activity, the toddlers and infants carried by adoring parents—and we drooled.
>
> We both realized then that our son and daughter, both in school, were becoming independent, and that we just weren't finished nesting. Nine months and one week after our vacation, our third child was born. She is our "Catskill kid," and our favorite souvenir from the Nevele!

Letter after letter, filled with humor or nostalgia or both, convince me that this corner of the world remains alive in the minds of those who experienced it. There was something special here for millions of people. We are remembered as the green and lovely spot where life stood still for just a little while—where there was laughter and music and youth.

Nothing lasts forever and the hotel business as we knew it is no exception. But we can be again the center for tourism and hospitality. It won't ever be the same, but that doesn't mean it won't be good!

We've only come to the end—of the beginning.

An Afterword

$\mathcal{I}$ TEACH ELDER HOSTEL CLASSES on the Catskill experience. At one session a man attending the course introduced himself as a Protestant from New England. Anxious to discuss the humor that was part of my anecdotal history, he wondered if its source was ethnic. He told of his experience when attending a lecture on the subject of Yiddish comedy. After the program, the speaker had invited the audience to recall some moment in their lives when laughter defined the day. My "student" was distraught to realize that he had nothing to contribute.

"Do you suppose it has something to do with the religion?" he asked. "Do I lack humor because I'm a Protestant?"

I didn't then, and don't now, have a definitive reply. What I do guess is that the answer does not lie in religion, but in culture, custom, and experience.

You have been traveling with me through recollections of what was a unique period. My memories, distilled by time, were triggered by the wry and the gently comic. For me, it was humor that underlined events. I suspect that saving moments of laughter (sometimes through tears) is universal for all people.

If there is one thing that binds us, it is the ability to find the ridiculous in the serious. For the Jewish people of the world, humor was a necessity for bearing the many sorrows that befell them. Can it be different for any minority that has known discrimination? When others tell their stories, it is probably only the accents that differ. I can imagine that what happened in our hotel office one summer may have had counterparts anywhere that immigrants vacationed.

A letter arrived containing a money order. The signature was illegible and there was no return address. The text read: "Two kahples kahming!" We, who handled reservations, could figure out that four people were expected, but the important "when" was missing. For days and days, every time a party of four entered the lobby, we thought we had found the expected guests, but it was not until late August that the mystery was solved. A single lady came to the reservation area, and she announced: "The others are in the car . . . we are two Kahples!"

"Aha!" we said in unison.

There is an absence of chronology in my memoir because recollection arrives unbidden and not in neat little packages. I cannot place a particular event in anything but a general time frame, nor can I remember in which season I met a particular guest or member of the staff. The pictures of the past have formed an amalgam for me. And yet, the panorama of it all retains its shape and its meaning.

It is the stories, the *meises*, that are the glue. I have always loved the stories —— they seem to survive the times, long gone, that spawned them.

I wonder if you were ever a visitor, or worker, or resident of these hills.

Did you have an experience that moves you still? Do you tell your tale when family or friends gather? How do *you* remember the Catskills?

I set out to tell the story of a special time and place, to present the Catskills as they really were, and to applaud the achievements of those who labored there. Our immigrant fathers were not angels, but they had the courage to found, the vision to build, and the strength to maintain a resort industry and a vacation haven—and they did it against odds. In a century when so much has been lost, it is important to remember achievement. Then our children and their children can look back with wonder and with pride.

Appendix:
Roster of Hotels

I AM INDEBTED to Mr. Benjamin Kaplan, former executive director of the Sulllivan County Resort Association and to the *Sullivan County Democrat*, a bi-weekly newspaper published in Callicoon, N. Y., for the use of the following list of hotels. A directory of hotels appeared in the *Democrat* as part of a four-part series by Mr. Kaplan called "The Who's Who of Sullivan County Hotels." Hotels in Ulster County—indicated by an asterisk (*)—- were taken from an index in Catherine Terwilliger's book, *Wawarsing: Where the Stream Winds.*

It must be understood that such lists can never be totally accurate or complete. Smaller establishments came and went, were unrecorded, and changed hands. Other properties not only changed hands, but also had more than one name. The list from Sullivan County was published in the *Democrat* in 1991. The Ulster County resorts reflect the membership of the Ulster County Resort Association in 1953, according to Ms. Terwilliger. I have added names found in the 1935 vacation guide published by the New York, Ontario & Western Railway and from the recollections of my colleagues.

Where it was possible, I have listed the owners of the hotels; they are not necessarily the names of the last owners. Some were garnered from a 1932 *Journal of the Hotelmen's Federation*, some from Ms.Terwilliger's index, and others from the memories of friends, colleagues, and neighbors.

ACCORD*
Chait's Hotel	*Alex Chait*
Kutay 's Lodge	*Morris & Ethel Kutay*

BEAVER BROOK
Beaver Brook House

BETHEL
Emr's Hotel
Liff Hotel

BLACK LAKE
Brown's Lake View
Levine's

BLOOMINGBURG
Coronet Lodge

BRIDGEVILLE
Hotel Kinne

BRIGGS HIGHWAY *
Echo Hotel	*Sam Wagner*
Epstein's Villa	
Greenwood Inn	
	M. Bucholtz & Sons
Highland Hotel	*Krevat & Panich*
Jockey Country Club	
	Standard & Keller
Luxor Manor	*Weinbrott family*
Maple Leaf Inn	*Shapiro & Godfrey*
Melbourne Hotel	*H. Drucker*
Sashin's Hotel	*Morris Sashin*
Ulster Lake House	*Rosenberg family*

CALLICOON
Callicoon Inn	
Delaware House	
Olympia Hotel	
Polster's	
Villa Roma	*Martin Passante*
	(orig., Ernie Vindigne)

CALLICOON CENTER
Hahn's	
Hill's	
Mootz Lone Pine	
Tumble Inn	*Harry C. Schuler*

COCHECTON
Erie Hotel

DeBRUCE
The Homestead
St. Brendan's Hotel

DIVINE CORNERS
Neversink Inn
Riverside Hotel
Schildkraut's House

ELDRED
Tallwood Lodge

ELLENVILLE *
Arrowhead Lodge	*Slutsky family*
Breeze Lawn Hotel	*Ephraim Yaffe*
The Cathalia	*Joe Tso*
Evergreen Manor	*Jerry &Max Slutsky*
The Fallsview	*Ben Slutsky*
Nevele Country Club	*Joseph Slutsky and Sons*
Overlook Hotel	*Louis Drucker*
Rande's Hotel	*Rande family*
Robin Hood Inn	*Rogow family*

FALLSBURG and SOUTH FALLSBURG
Alpine Hotel	*Uffel family*
Avon Lodge (formerly House of Joy)	
	Arkin & Kasofsky; Mayer & Florence Neukrug
Ambassador Hotel	*Hyman Merl*
Barlau Hotel (formerly Branlip Hotel)	
	Laufer family
Biltmore Hotel	*Vogel & Nochatevitz*
Blue Eagle (formerly Hotel Wadler)	
	Silver family

Brickman Hotel (now Siddah Yoga
    Dam Ashram)   *Joseph Posner & Sons*
Cedar Hill   *Wohl family*
Claremore   *Nachatovitch family*
Commodore   *Louis Cohen*
Didinsky's Villa
Elm Shade Hotel   *M. Kaufman*
Fain Lodge   *Feinbeg family*
Fallsburg Country Club   *Pollack family*
Flagler   *Fleisher & Morganstern*
Flamingo Hotel   *Honig family*
Hotel Furst   *Harry Furst*
Gilbert's Hotel (now Siddah Yoga Dam
    Ashram)   *Anne Gilbert*
Grand View House   *Selden family*
Heiden Hotel   *David Heiden*
Hoffman House
Irvington Hotel (orig. Hotel Glass and
    Hotel Lisss)   *Charlow family*
Lakeside   *Goldberg Bros. & Schilit*
Laurel Park Hotel   *Abrams & Kane*
Leifert Hotel
Levitt Hotel (formerly Lakeside, then
    Senate)   *M. Levitt & Sons*
Lorraine Hotel
Majestic Hotel   *Philip & Bernard Cohen*
Mayflower   *Uretsky family*
Mohawk Hotel   *Saslow & Bernstein*
Mountain View
Murray Hill   *J. Malman*
Nemerson Hotel (Later, Deville, Belfiore,&
    La Vista)   *Abraham Nemerson*
New White Rose   *Goldberg & Rashansky*
New Prospect   *Pellman, Becker & Loitz*
            (later Max, Dave & Willey Forman)
Oakland House   *H. Kunis*
Olympic   *Wm. & Betty Horowitz*
            Robert & Harriet Rosenberg
Pancrest Lodge   *A. J. Pantel*
Peckler Hotel   *Peckler family*
The Pines (formerly Moneka Lodge owned
    by Karp)   *Philip Schweid family*
Pine View Hotel   *Leibowitz family*
Plaza Hotel   *Patt & Orlansky*
Premier Hotel
            Harry Schwartz & Bessie Sussman
Raleigh Hotel   *Nettie & Manny Halbert*
Regal   *Bernstein family*
Riverside   *Benski family*
Riverdale   *Rozman family*
River View   *Silverman & Shapiro*
Rosaler House
Russell House
The Saxony (formerly Hotel Glass,

    Hoenig's Nassau, later The Polonia)
Schenk's Paramount   *Schenk family*
Summit Hotel   *Yetta Sandler & Dave Forman*
Tree of Life Hotel
Windsor Hotel (now Siddah Yoga Dam
    Ashram)   *Sidney & Theresa Sussman*
Zeiger's (Later El Dorado Hotel)
                          Zeiger & Stern

FERNDALE
Avalon   *G. L. Hornbeck*
American House   *Gross family*
Balfour Hotel   *Lefkowitz & Goldsmith*
Blue Paradise   *J. Strawitz*
Brook Spring House   *A. Haber*
Bush House   *S. Bushlowitz*
Bushville Paradise
Capitol Mansion   *Waxman & Case*
Chelsea House   *D. Flamenbaum*
Crystal Lake House   *N. Berkman*
Dan Bee Lodge   *Irving Cantor*
Deluxe House   *Luxenberg family*
Eager Rose Garden   *Eager family*
Empire Hotel   *Lillian Brown and then*
                  Gartenberg and Schecter
Fairmount Hotel
Ferndale Manor *Ehrenreich, Orber & Eisenberg*
Ferndale Mansion   *Max Wexler*
Ferndale Palace   *S. Weissberger*
Greening House (later the Lilmore) *J. Seinfeld*
Hysana Lodge   *Chessler & Sons*
Kanco Inn   *Kantor & Cohen*
Lakeside Inn
    Mendelson, Baxt & Fish; Sold to Grossingers
Lakeview Farm House   *Katzelnick & Fragin*
Leader House
Leffler House
Marko Palace   *M. Markowitz*
Mongaup House   *E. A. Gregory & Son*
New Majestic   *R. Goldfarb*
Orchard House   *Goodman & Forman*
Overlook Hotel   *Susser family*
Pine View House   *H. Wexler*
Plaza Hotel   *Silvermintz family*
Pollack's Hotel   *Elias Pollack*
Queen Mountain House   *Meyer family*
Royal House   *L. Tannenbaum*
Seiken Lake House   *M. Seiken*
Shady Grove Hotel   *B. Goodman*
Shelbourne Hotel and Country Club
    J. Benkowitz , sold to Leibush Goldberg
Stier's   *Frank Stier and Sons*
Spring Wood
Terrace Hotel

Upper Ferndale Mansion
    Golant, Smith, Brown & Davidson
Yarish House   *Charles Yarish & Sons*
Walnut Mountain House   *Katz & Bergreen*

FORESTBURGH
Forestburgh Inn
Kleb's
Klein's Halfway House
Leininger's
McCormick's Sunset Farm
Martin Miller's
Theimer's
Humphrey Toomey House

FREMONT
Gamrak
Mountain Laurel Farm

FREMONT CENTER
Central Hotel

FOSTERDALE
Recreation Farm

GLEN SPEY
Bel Air Resort

GLEN WILD
Central House   *B. Katz*
Empress Hotel   *Lucas & Stein*
Glenmore   *D. Berkman*
Grand Mountain
    L. Bernstein, J. Dobzinsky & M. Gold
Hotel Frederick   *Joseph Frederick*
Jaffe House   *Rev. S. Jaffe*
Rosenblatt's   *Louis Rosenblatt*
Zucker's Glen Wild C.C.

GREENFIELD PARK *
Beerkill Lodge   *Kamfer family*
Birchwood Lodge   *Zalkin family*
Bookbinder's Hotel
Cherry Hill   *Trachtenberg & Cooper*
Claremont Hotel
    Schweid family, then David Chorney
    & Abe Weiner
Grand Mountain   *Steinhorn family*
Gruber's Seven Gables   *Hyman Gruber*
Kerness House   *S. Kerness*
Maple Court Hotel   *Jonas Nass*
Pioneer Country Club   *Gartenberg & Schecter*
ReisReit Hotel   *Reiss & Reiter*
Roseville Hotel

Tamarack Lodge   *Levinson family*

GROSSINGER
Grossinger Hotel
    Jennie & Harry Grossinger family

HANKINS
Delaware Valley Inn

HARRIS
American House
Grossman's Inn
Lakeside Inn
Primrose Mansion
Resnick's
Turey Hotel

HIGHLAND LAKE
Bertram's Lodge
Fern Cliff Lodge
Green Meadows
Highland Lake House
Highland Lake Inn
Highland Villa
Deer Head Lodge
Lake Shore
Lake View House
Lakewood House
Manor House
Mills House
Pine Grove House
Pinehurst on the Lake
Pine Beach Inn
Pine Hill Lodge
Olympic House
Sand Beach
Singing Pines
Sunset View

HIGH VIEW
Bonnie View
Eagle's Nest   *Michael Spiegl*
Sha-Wan-Ga Lodge   *Atlas & Dan*

HORTONVILLE
Hortonville Hotel
Haeling Hotel

HURLEYVILLE
Arcadia Lake
Astor Hotel
Brookhaven
Butler Lodge   *Cohen family*
Columbia Farms Hotel   *M. C. Knapp & Sons*

Columbia Star Hotel
Forest Inn
Garden House
Golden Hotel
Holiday Hotel   *Shlessinger family*
Hotel Wellworth   *Charles Panzirer*
King David Hotel
Kramer's on Luzon Lake   *Jack Kramer*
Lake Shore House   *Henry Diamond*
Majestic (later Dunwoodie)
Pollack's Grand View
Purvis House
Seldin's Grand View   *Seldin family*
Salon's Lodge   *Salon family*
Sunset Hotel
Wayside Inn   *Schindler family*
Richmond Hotel

JEFFERSONVILLE
Charles Arndt's
Ander Von Bergen
Frank Hess
Franklin House
Roy Hess
Lake Jefferson Hotel
Likel's
Mall's
Mansion House
Sohl's
Smith's Maple Gove
Sunnyside Farm
Wahl's
Welch's
Tonnison's White House

KAUNEONGA LAKE
Arlington
Balcony House
Block's Mansion   *J. Block*
Buckner's
Carlton
Columbia Hotel
Finneran's
Flag House   *H. Lipschitz*
Fur Worker's Resort
Glenwood
Golden Eagle   *Max Kutik*
Hurd's
Kenmore Hotel   *E. I. Glass*
Kensington Hotel   *M. Adler*
Kroner's Ramsay House
Kushner's
Lynn's
New Empire Hotel   *Max Calvin*

New Kensington   *M. Adler*
Panzer
Rita Hotel
Rosedale Hotel
Sylvan Inn
Tieger Inn
Woodlawn Villa   *A. Plotkin*

KENOZA LAKE
Adler's
Alexander's
Apple Gove Cottage
Armbrust's
Chautauqua Cottage
Dell House
DeLap's
Edgemere   *Feinberg family*
Fern Hotel
Gedney House
Goldsmith's
Heidt's
Heschle's
Kenoza Falls Lodge
Kenoza Lake Hotel   *Kantrowitz family*
Lake View Country Club
Luckey's
Miller's
Moran's
Mrs. Schwenger's
Rosner's
Sackman's (later Season's)
Valley View House   *Bacarziak family*
Waterfall's House
Weiss'

KERHONKSON *
Colonial Hotel   *Kitia family*
Granite Hotel
        Henry Zabatta (orig. owned by Geller family)
Hillside Mountain House   *Charkosky & Son*
Kerhonkson Lodge   *Z. Nachman*
Millbrook Lodge *Martin Frank & Howard Bern*
Peg Leg Bates   *Peg Leg Bates*
Pine Grove Hotel   *Betty & Jack Schloss*
Rubin's Maple View   *H. Rubin & Sons*
Ukranian National Association

KIAMESHA LAKE
Concord Hotel (formerly Ideal and Glucks)
                       Winarick, Parker Families
Columbia
Evan's Kiamesha Hotel   *L. & I. Evans*
Fairmont
Flaxman's

Hotel Gibber	*Abe Gibber*
Gluck's Hillside	*L. Gluck*
Hotel Gradus	*Gradus & Hammerman*
Kiamesha Ideal	*Jacobson Brothers*
Kiamesha Inn	
Kiamesha Lodge and Country Club	*D. Scherer*
Kiamesha Overlook	*Harris Goldberg*
Kiamesha Pine Hotel	
Lakeside Inn	
Mayfair	*Kesten & Cooper*
Mapledale	*Wm. Coleman*
Pine Tree Villa	
Rosemont Lodge	
Savoy Hotel	
Solnitsky's	

LAKE HUNTINGTON

Alpine Hotel	*Newman family*
Belmont Hotel	
	Fruchter family, later Levant family
Bischoff's Villa	
Crestwood Hotel	*Kleiner family*
Furk's Farm	
Green Acres (formerly Huntington Lakeside)	
	Elmer Rosenberg family
Hillside	*Braverman & Korash*
Hillcrest Cottages	
Huntington Lodge	*J. Broudy*
Laurel Cottages	
Lorraine	*Morris & Celia Ferber*
Lotus Lodge	*Shavitz family*
Mansion House	
Mountain Glen	*Glinner family*
Nutshell Hotel	*Fergussen family*
The Lenox	
The Pines	*Lager & Dworkin*
Pine Park House	*Julius & Clara Falchook*
Prospect House	*Mrs. J. Schiffer*
Rialto Hotel	*Chavitz family*
Rose View	*Kopel & Mindlich*
Schmidt's	
Sunny Hills	*Tumilowitz family*
Viola Hotel	*Nathan & Molly Vogel*
Wayside Hotel	*Weiss family*
West Shore Hotel	*Sarah Bernstein*
The White House	*Nelly White*

LIBERTY

Barkley Hotel	
Buckley Hotel	*A. P. & Mary Buckley*
Champlin House	*Champlin family*
Clements House	*J. N. Clements*
Darbee House	*Darbee family*

Evergreen Manor	*Jaffe family*
Fernwood House	
Four Corners Inn	
Grand View Heights	
Hall House	
Lancashire Inn	*F. W. Lancashire*
Lenape Hotel	*Frye family*
Lennon House	*Lennon family*
Liberty House	*Thomas Houlihan*
Mansion House	*Addison Clements*
Melody Country Club	
Sunny Crest Inn	*Isidore Tauber*
The Swannanoa	*Fred Schrader*
Washington Inn	*Washington family*

LIVINGSTON MANOR

Arlington Hotel	*Arthur Schwartz*
Beaver Lake Lodge	*L. Lichtman*
Beaverkill Valley Inn (formerly Bonny View)	
Camp Livingston	*Benjamin Lipschutz*
Chan-Al (Lanza's)	
Edgewood Inn	*Alex Wittenberg*
Hollywood Country Club	
Hotel Capitol	*Isidore Goodman*
Kenmore Lake House	*Jack Muravchick*
Lorraine	
Mansion House	*Clarence Wolk*
Menges Lakeside	*Della Menges*
Mountain Crest	*Jack Keiser*
Mountain Lake Farms	
	Max Sheckner (orig. owned by Jack Keiser)
Murray Hill Farm	*M. Murray*
Parkston Hotel	*M. Friedman & Sons*
Rainbow Lodge	*Theodore B. Golub*
Sand Lake Hotel	*Dave Switko*
Shandalee Lake Farm	*Charlie Huber*
Sunrise Hotel	*Barney Hodesblatt & Sons*
Tempel Inn	*Gus & Lou Tempel*
Trojan Lake Lodge	*MichaelSteinman family*
Waldemere	*Rosenthal Brothers*
White Roe Lake Hotel	*M. Wiener & Sons*

LOCH SHELDRAKE

Algier's Country Club	
Bell House	*Rubinstein family*
Brookside Hotel	*B. Protas*
Brookside Inn	*Isadore Brooks*
Brown's (formerly Black Appel Inn)	
	Charles & Lillian Brown
Capitol Hotel	*Kesis, Listitzky & Motzkin*
Delmar Hotel	*Max Jacobs*
Evans Hotel	*Ike Evans family*
Ganz Hotel	

Gold's Lakeside — *Gold family*
Green Acres (now New Hope Community) — *Larry & Cissie Blumberg*
Jewel Country Club — *Tannenbaum family (orig. Mergler family)*
Karmel Hotel — *Ben Jacobs*
Lakeside Hotel — *S. Rochefsky*
Laufer's River View — *Schorr & Laufer*
Hotel LeRoy — *S. Kranass*
Loch Sheldrake Inn — *Max Yavorofsky*
Loch Sheldrake Lake View — *Babitsky family (formerly owned by Goldberg)*
Loch Sheldrake Rest — *Mermelstein & Lieberman*
Midwood Hotel — *Pohl family*
Monterey Hotel — *Mishkin & Gordon*
Morningside Hotel — *Golembe family*
Newman's Villa
New Edgewood Hotel — *Joe Garfinkel*
New Roxy Hotel (became Green Acres) — *Moskowitz family*
Normandie — *Sam & Dorothy Srulowitz*
Overlook Hotel — *Mrs. Rose Saltzman*
Park Manor Hotel
Pine Grove Hotel — *L. Kove*
Pine View Country Club — *L. Lipman*
Rapkin's Hilldale
Riverside Palace — *Benkski & Mass*
Riverview — *Altman family*
Sadowsky's Mountain Cliff Hotel
Schlesinger's
Shady Nook C. C. — *Max Levine family*
Sunny Lake Lodge
Victoria Mansion — *Kupermith & Kelman*
West End Country Club — *Cohen family*

MASTEN LAKE
Mamakating Park Inn
Mount Prosper Manor

MONGAUP VALLEY
Greisberg's
Riverdale
Polaris Lodge
Sapir's
Morris Shapiro's
Sunnside
Wolf Spring Farm

MONTICELLO
Anderson Hotel — *Anderson family*
Arcade Hotel
Blackman's Inn — *Samuel Blackman*
Block's Hotel — *Ben Block*
Blossom View

Capitol
Carlton Hotel
Chernick's
Clover Hill Hotel
Coli's Maple Grove
Colonial Park Hotel — *Streisfeld family*
Cooper's Corners
Delano Hotel — *Schect & Rappaport*
Donde House — *Sam Donde*
Esther Manor — *Goldstein family*
Eusner's — *R. P. Eusner*
Frank Leslie Hotel
Goldblatt's
Goldenberg Hotel
Hamilton Farms — *Gordon family*
HarmonyCountry Club (now Kutsher's Sports Academy) — *Leshner & Regalson*
Imperial Hotel
Joyland Hotel
Kahaner's Inn
Kotney Manor — *Ben Kotney*
Kutsher's Country Club — *Kutsher family*
Lander's Brookside
LaTourette Hotel
Little Hungarian Hotel
Locust Inn — *Wlodower & Bernstein*
Maple Shade Hotel
Maplewood Inn
Maple Grove
Melberg's
Monticello Inn — *Machson family*
Monticello Overlook
Norman House
Palatine Hotel
Park View Hotel
Patterson Farm
Pine Lodge Hotel — *S. Brams & Son*
Rockwell Hotel
Rosery — *I. Aks*
Royalton
Skliar's — *Skliar & Newman*
Slatkin's
Spring Lake Hotel
Star Mountain Hotel
The Swan
Victoria Hotel — *Albrecht family*
Washington Farm
Western View
Willow Lane
Wolf's Corner Hotel

MOUNTAINDALE
Chester Hill House — *Sidney Glick*
Cold Spring House — *W. Greenberg*

Evergreen Hotel   *H. Bedik*
Grand Central Hotel   *Boim & Glick*
High Cliff House   *Friedman Brothers*
Hilltop Lodge
Linden Lawn Hotel   *Silver family*
Little Falls Hotel   *Helen Rashkin & Sons*
Kirshman House   *Kirshman & Rothperl*
Mountain Peak Lodge
Nasso Hotel
    Nesslowitz family; later Sam Slobodow
Paramount Hotel   *Glickman & Hanzelick*
Pioneer Country Club   *Gartenberg & Schecter*
    (orig. Cohen & Walterman)
Rosemond   *L. Kopp*
Royal Mountain Hotel   *H. Schlosberg*
Rubinstein's Hotel
Star House   *Perlin family*
Wilsonia Hotel   *William Greenberg family*

NAPANOCH *

Breeskin Hotel   *Breeskin family*
Napanoch Country Club   *Ben Feinberg*

NARROWSBURG

Century Hotel
Hillside Inn
Peggy's Runway Lodge
River View Farm
Silver Lake Farm
The Rustic
Zehner's

NEVERSINK

Kee's Resort Hotel
Klein's Hotel
New Age Health Spa (formerly Begun's
    Neversink Inn)   *Dr. W. Mendel*

NORTH BRANCH

Antler's Hotel
Maple Hotel
Maud's Summer Ray   *Zuni Maud*
Woodland House   *Hiram & Clemence Frank*

PARKSVILLE

Ambassador Hotel   *Sam, Sadie & Lena Levitz*
Avigail
Belmont House
Breezy Hill House   *Louis Pachanik*
Brookdale Hotel
Charam Hill House   *Charam family*
Conklin Hill House
Earlington Hotel
Fiddle House   *Harry Fiddle*

Flamenbaum Hotel
Fleisher's Hotel
Flower House   *Treiber family*
Fox Mountain House
Glory Hotel   *Louis Eisenberg*
Golden House
Grand Hotel   *Max Schmidt*
High MountainView House *D.Tanzman & Sons*
High View Mountain House   *Louis Seinfeld*
Highland View House   *B. Schwartzman*
Hillcrest View House
Ideal Summer Resort   *Benjamin Tanzman*
Kaufman House
Klass Hotel   *Joe & Anna Klass*
Klein's Hillside   *Hymie & Nat Klein*
Lake Plaza Hotel
Lash Hotel
Lincoln Hotel   *Louis & Harry Peltz*
Malachowsky's Hotel
Maple View House   *Max Siegel*
Merker's Tip Top
Mountain Pleasure Farm
New Brighton Hotel
    Archie & Eleanor Morganstein
New Mountain House   *Guttman & Weiss*
Overlook Hotel
Paramount House   *Gasthalter family*
Park Villa Hotel
Parksville Mansion
Perl House
Pine View House
Prospect Inn   *Orseck family*
Ridge Mountain Hotel   *Max Welkowitz*
Rose Hill House   *Mrs. M. Sisselman & Sons*
Shady Grove House   *A. Novick*
Spring Lake Hotel   *Horowitz family*
Spring Grove
Sunny Brook House
Sunnyland Hotel
Sunrise Hotel
Tanzville Hotel   *Nat Tanzman*
The Park Inn
Wallach Farm House
Weinreb Hotel   *Joe Weinreb*
Westin Hotel
Young's Gap Hotel
    Holder, Okun, Senate & Spector

ROCK HILL

Lakewood House

ROSCOE

Antrim Lodge   *Frank E. Keener*
Campbell Inn   *Wood family*

New Alpine Hotel — R. S. Sanders
Rockland House — Mrs. Joseph R. Taylor
Tennanah Lake House — Anthony N. Wolff

SACKETT LAKE
Belmore Hotel
CongressHotel
Laurel's Country Club — Novak family
Sacket Lake Lodge

SWAN LAKE
Commodore Hotel — Tuchfeld, Chorofsky
& Weissman (later Sol Siegal family)
Cromwell — D. Siegel
Fieldston — Jack and Martha Levine
Goldwasser's
High Mountain House — Rotterman & Goldman
Horshoe Lake House
Kramer's Hotel
Lana Hotel — S. Siegel
Langer's
Lennon's Farm House
Locust Grove House — Relis & Relis
National Hotel & C. C. — Max Bochner
Pine View Hotel
Paul's (now Daytop Village) — Emanuel Paul
President Hotel — Abraham Ellner, Max Leshnick
and Irving Podolnick
Shagrin House — Joe Shagrin
Sherwood's
Springwood House — N. Hibscher
Stevensville Lake Hotel (later The Imperial)
Dinnerstein, Weiner and Goldstein
Swan Lake Hotel — H. Levine
Swan Lake Inn & C. C. — Miller, Schraff & Davis
Swan Lake Mansion — Rieg, Steiger, Tykot & Lipp
Vacationland — Cohen & Cohen
Wilshar Hotel
Wasserlauf's
Woda's
Young's House
Wellworth Hotel

SPRING GLEN *
Homowak Lodge — Irving Blickstein
Hotel Rieger — S. Rieger

SUMMITVILLE
Mountain View Hotel — Charles Jeboltosky
Sokoloff's Hotel
White Rose Hotel — Judah Altman

SWISS HILL
Forest Glen

TENNANAH LAKE
Holp's Lodge
Huff House
Lupo's
Tennanah Lake Hotel
Wolf's

ULSTER HEIGHTS *
Brookland Hotel — Sam Sieman
Brustein's Hotel — Herbert Brustein
Central Hotel — Tucker family
Lakeside Crest — Morris Zamore
New Alpine Hotel — Sapkowitz family
Rosedale Hotel — Brown & Noble
Surise Manor — Dickman & Kramer
Western View — Jerome Hirschon
Woodbine Hotel — Dole family
Woodleigh Hotel — Berman & Wengrow

WALKER VALLEY
Jeronimo's — Jeronimo family

WAWARSING *
Jefferson Hotel — Levine Brothers

WHITE LAKE
Brown's Hotel Royal — Brown family
(orig. Max Waldman)
Camp White Lake
Hellman's
Lake Shore Chateau — Jack Eckstein
Laurel
Lenox
Mansion House — J. Block
Pontiac Hotel — Abraham family
Prospect House
Racine's
Shanghai Lodge
Sunny Glade
L. F. Taylor
The Waldheim
White Lake Hotel
White Lake Lodge
White Lake Maples — A. Resnick & M. J. Maurer

WHITE SULPHUR SPRINGS
Barsalee Country Club
Beck's Villa
Happiness House
Leona Hotel
Lesser Lodge — Joseph Lesser
Pinehurst Manor
Tel Aviv Hotel
White Sulphur Springs Hotel

WOODBOURNE
Aladdin   *Komito family*
Armstrong Hotel
Belvedere (later Haywire Ranch)
Chester's Zumbarg (now Chalet Vim)
                          Herman & Anne Chester
Friedman's Lake Hotel
Highview Hotel
Maple Crest
Maple Hill Hotel
Maple Lawn Hotel   *Effros family*
Royal Inn
Salhara Hotel   *Sally & Harry Friedman*
Sky House   *Archie Schwartz*
South Wind   *Horowitz family*
Zukor's Lodge

WOODRIDGE
Alamac Country Club   *Max Shapiro*
Allentoff Hotel
Apollo Hotel
Berger's Hotel
Biltmore Hotel and Country Club
Blinder's Village View House
Claremont House
Claremore   *Nachatovitch family*
Friedman House
Glory Hotel
Gerson's
Golub's
Gorelikoff's Welcome Inn
Hotel Israel   *Kleinberg family*
Hotel Lindy   *B. Rabinowitz*
Hotel Weingerson
Kantrowitz' Hotel
Kleinberg's Hotel   *F. Kleinberg*
Lake House   *Abe Schwartz*
                 (formerly Jacob Ezersky family)

Panoramic Health Farm
Pine Tree Country Club
Rosemond Hotel
Roseville Hotel
Shein's Hotel   *Nathan & MollyShein*
Slater House   *Tillie Slater*
Stratton Farm House   *Mrs. Elmer Stratton*
Sunny Acres Dude Ranch   *Novick Brothers*
Sunny Oaks   *Miles Levinson, Cynthia*
                                      & Ted Aronson
Vegetarian Hotel   *F. Shaffer & Konviser*
Village View House   *M. Blinder*
Waldorf Hotel & C. C.

WURTSBORO
Bill's Vegetarian Manor
Blue Paradise
Dorrance House
Gumaer House

YOUNGSVILLE
Clair Hotel
Crystal Springs Hotel
Frey's
Greene's
Kaiser's
Kramer's' Union House
Kraussman's
Miller's
Muller's Breezy Hill Cottage
Pammer House
Rasmussen's
Ritterhausen's
Spring Lake Hotel
Youngsville Inn

YULAN
Highland Hotel and Cottages

OTHER JEWISH-INTEREST BOOKS
PUBLISHED BY PURPLE MOUNTAIN PRESS

Herbert M. Engel:

SHTETL IN THE ADIRONDACKS
The Story of Gloversville and Its Jews

Shtetl in the Adirondacks recounts the story of a unique Jewish community in upstate New York from the 1880s to the 1940s when everyone's livelihood in the small city of Gloversville depended on the manufacture and marketing of fine leather gloves. The reader meets well-to-do German-Jewish factory owners and their hard working craftsmen, mostly Jewish leather cutters from Eastern Europe. The author explores the interaction of these two local Jewish groups that found themselves divided by social and economic class and one or two generations of American acculturation.

Baila R. Shargel and Harold W. Drimmer:

THE JEWS OF WESTCHESTER
A Social History

The Jewish settlement in many American cities and small towns has been well chronicled, but suburban communities have been overlooked. This book relates the story of the Jews of America's first suburb, Westchester County, New York. The few hardy souls who ventured into the undeveloped county in colonial times struggled for legal equality, largely achieved, and economic security, never fully accomplished. After new commuter railroads transformed rural hamlets into suburbs, the mostly immigrant Jewish population of peddlers, petty shopkeepers, and a few farmers remained financially insecure and not well received by their neighbors. Only in the latter half of the twentieth century did Jews rise from a position of marginality to assume leadership roles in business, the professions, education and the arts in the county. They fought for their rights, established a political presence and built robust religious, secular and educational institutions.

John Conway:

RETROSPECT
An Anecdotal History
of Sullivan County, New York

Three railroads, a canal, dozens of industries, and hundreds of hotels have come and gone since Sullivan County was formed in 1809. Famous stars of sport and screen have worked and played here; infamous and despicable gangsters have lived and died here. Sullivan's history is rich and colorful, and *Retrospect* is a look back at that history, with reflection, with scrutiny, and, occasionally, with longing.

John Conway writes columns of historical interest for the *Times-Herald-Record* and serves as County Historian in Sullivan County.

Stephen Crane:

SULLIVAN COUNTY
TALES AND SKETCHES
Edited and with an Introduction by R. W. Stallman
Preface by John Conway

This collection will hold a special attraction for those interested in Sullivan County as the wellspring for Stephen Crane's development as a writer. Here, in his earliest published pieces, there is clear evidence of Crane's painterly and impressionistic style and his addiction to color adjectives, metaphor, and symbol. Also seen are the seeds of themes which were soon to appear in *Maggie: A Girl of the Streets* and *The Red Badge of Courage*.

R. W. Stallman is the author of Stephen Crane: A Biography and has edited several volumes of Crane's work.

ESTERITA BLUMBERG grew up at Green Acres Hotel in Sullivan County, New York, and eventually, with her late husband, Larry, owned and operated that hotel. She graduated from Syracuse University and attended Columbia, majoring in English Education. Ms. Blumberg is the vice president of the board of Associated Mutual Insurance Company, writes a monthly column for the *Catskill/Hudson Jewish Star*, and lectures throughout the country bringing the Catskill experience to life for diverse audiences. "Cissie" is the mother of two children, Paul Blumberg and Amy Goldbas, and grandmother of four, Matt, Jamie, Jessie and Jake. She resides in Liberty, New York.

PURPLE MOUNTAIN PRESS is a publishing company committed to producing the best original books of New York State interest as well as bringing back into print significant older works. For a free catalog, write: P.O. Box E3, Fleischmanns, NY 12430 or call: 914-254-4062.

$\mathcal{I}ndex$